Visual Guide to

Elliott Wave Trading

Visual Guide to

Elliott Wave Trading

Jeffrey Kennedy
Wayne Gorman

Foreword by Robert R. Prechter

Visual Guide to Elliott Wave Trading

The content in this book was previously published by John Wiley & Sons, Inc., Hoboken, New Jersey.

Printed in the United States of America

ISBN: 978-1-61604-129-8

Publisher: New Classics Library
Gainesville, Georgia USA

Elliott Wave International
www.elliottwave.com

Address for comments: customercare@elliottwave.com

Cover design: C. Wallace. Cover images: Waves by Peter Firus/iStockphoto, charts courtesy Jeffrey Kennedy and Wayne Gorman.

Contents

How to Use This Book

The *Visual Guide to Elliott Wave Trading* is designed to be a comprehensive and easy-to-follow guide to learning to trade using Elliott waves. All charts are in full color and presented in a large format to make them easy to read and use. We've also included the following elements to reinforce key information and processes:

- **Definitions:** Terminology and technical concepts that arise in the discussion
- **Key Points:** Critical ideas and takeaways from the full text
- **Tips:** Things to think about as you apply the concepts

Go Beyond Print

The authors have created video tutorials to supplement the text and help you see the concepts in action. Be sure to view these videos by visiting www.elliottwave.com/wave/ReaderResources.

To learn how to apply the concepts in this book in real time with real opportunities from Jeffrey Kennedy, check out *Trader's Classroom*. Book readers, like you, get an extra premium. www.elliottwave.com/wave/VGB-TCSpecialOffer.

Welcome to the rewarding world of Elliott wave trading.

Foreword

For many years, I have wanted to have my company produce a trading book based on the Elliott wave model. As with markets, sometimes you have to wait patiently for the time to be right. The time is finally right, as two highly qualified Elliott-wave traders have partnered to write a book on the subject.

Jeffrey Kennedy traded for a living and handles *Trader's Classroom*, EWI's 3-times-a-week educational and trade-identifying service. He also teaches our trading seminars. Wayne Gorman ran a trading desk at Citibank and Westpac Banking Corporation and became the primary provider of Educational Resources at Elliott Wave International. Both guys write well, too.

This is not a book about how some market method sets up perfect paper trades. Jeff and Wayne walk you step by step through their thinking process during a number of trades they took in real life. They also present hypothetical setups that you might encounter in your own market experience and show you how to handle them. They aren't easy layups but real conundrums that require thoughtful analysis and careful action. Unlike many experts, Jeff and Wayne aren't shy about relating some of their mistakes and what they learned from them. When you read their discussions, you will know they have walked the hard road of experience.

You will also realize how much work it takes to do things right. Even if this book leads you to decide that successful trading takes too much effort, it will have proved useful. Books that make trading look easy actually cost you a lot of money in the end.

Frankly, most people are not cut out for trading. No book can cure impulsiveness, timidity, laziness, or a self-destructive personality. But this book does show you, very carefully, how two traders repeatedly negotiate the minefield of the market and come out alive and happy on the other side.

If you want to trade your own money for a living, if you want to be employable as a trader, if you just want to trade the occasional ideal setup, or even if your goal is simply to stop losing money in the markets, you are in the right place.

Successful trading takes work, discipline, and smarts. With those three things, you're mostly there. The final thing you need is knowledge—that's what this book provides.

Robert R. Prechter
Elliott Wave International

Acknowledgments

We want to thank our colleagues for their valuable assistance in producing this volume: Sally Webb, Paula Roberson, Susan Walker, Cari Dobbins, Dave Allman, Debbie Hodgkins, Bob Prechter, Will Rettiger, Michael McNeilly, Pam Greenwood, Angela Hall, Shannon Clark, John Watson and Katrena Peck.

Introduction

Welcome! *Visual Guide to Elliott Wave Trading* is a must-have book on how to use the Elliott Wave Principle—how to use it to find trades, assess trades, enter trades, manage trades throughout by raising or lowering protective stops, and exit trades.

Visual Guide to Elliott Wave Trading assumes a basic familiarity with the Wave Principle and its application. Much like a strategy book for chess assumes a basic knowledge of how the pieces move around the board, this book assumes a basic knowledge of the various patterns of the Wave Principle and how they fit together.

If you are already an experienced Elliott wave practitioner and simply need a refresher, the Appendix reviews these basic building blocks and their structures.

If you are a complete newcomer or you want a more in-depth review, we suggest you consult the free resources and access your free copy of the Wall Street classic *Elliott Wave Principle* by Frost and Prechter at your exclusive Reader Resources site: www.elliottwave.com/wave/ReaderResources.

Both of us have traded for a living at one time or another. Each of us during those times used the Elliott Wave Principle as our primary discipline. *Visual Guide to Elliott Wave Trading* walks you through a highly personal journey of our thought processes throughout each trade: what we looked at, what we ignored, what we did right, and what we did wrong.

We do not present perfect-world examples that will leave you convinced that you can trade your way to wealth in 30 minutes while golfing the rest of the day. Rather, we have tried to produce a realistic trading book, warts and all, recognizing that while there may be no one perfect way to trade, there are various ways to trade successfully using the Wave Principle as your primary discipline.

We hope you enjoy *Visual Guide to Elliott Wave Trading*. Let's get started.

Jeffrey Kennedy and Wayne Gorman

Disclaimer

The trading examples throughout this book are solely for the purpose of demonstrating the mechanics of applying the Wave Principle. The profit or loss outcomes are not meant in any way to represent or imply a particular rate of success or return on capital.

Visual Guide to

Elliott Wave Trading

PART I

Trade Setups

CHAPTER 1

The Anatomy of Elliott Wave Trading

When teaching the Wave Principle, I begin each class by stating that analysis and trading represent two different skill sets. Although you may be a talented analyst, that does not mean you will be a successful trader and vice versa. I learned the hard way over many years that skilled analysis is a mastery of observation, while successful trading is a mastery of self.

When it comes to trading, there is no right way or wrong way—only your way. One trader's tolerance for risk will be starkly different from another's, just as time frame, portfolio size, and markets traded will also be different. Thus, the guidelines offered within this chapter on how to trade specific Elliott wave patterns are just that—guidelines, but ones that have served me well for many years.

My best advice to you as you look for a trading opportunity is to start your search by asking the question, "Do I see a wave pattern I recognize?" You should look for one of the five core Elliott wave patterns: impulse wave, ending diagonal, zigzag, flat, or triangle. These forms will become the basis of all your trade setups once you learn to identify them quickly and with confidence.

An even simpler question to ask is, "Do I see either a motive wave or a corrective wave?" Motive waves define the direction of the trend. There are two kinds of motive waves: impulse waves and ending diagonals. Corrective waves travel against the larger trend. The three kinds of corrective waves are zigzags, flats, and triangles. If all you do is identify a motive wave versus a corrective wave correctly, you can still identify some useful trade setups.

In this chapter, we will examine how to use key components of analysis and trading to help you become a better Elliottician and a consistently

KEY POINT

Analysis is a mastery of observation, while successful trading is a mastery of self.

successful trader. Specifically, we will examine how the Wave Principle improves trading, which waves are the best to trade, which guidelines to use for trading specific Elliott wave patterns, and why the psychology of trading and risk management—what I call the neglected essentials—are important.

How the Wave Principle Improves Trading

Every trader, every analyst, and every technician has favorite techniques to use when trading. Let's go over why the Wave Principle is mine.

How the Wave Principle Improves Upon Traditional Technical Studies

There are three categories of technical studies: trend-following indicators, oscillators, and sentiment indicators. Trend-following indicators include moving averages, Moving Average Convergence-Divergence (MACD), and Directional Movement Index (ADX). A few of the more popular oscillators many traders use today are stochastics, rate-of-change, and the Commodity Channel Index (CCI). Sentiment indicators include put-call ratios and Commitment of Traders report data.

Technical studies like these do a good job of illuminating the way for traders, yet they each fall short for one major reason: They limit the scope of a trader's understanding of current price action and how it relates to the overall picture of a market. For example, let's say the MACD reading in XYZ stock is positive, indicating the trend is up. That's useful information, but wouldn't it be more useful if it could also help to answer these questions: Is this a new trend or an old trend? If the trend is up, how far will it go?

Most technical studies simply don't reveal pertinent information such as the maturity of a trend and a definable price target—but the Wave Principle does.

Five Ways the Wave Principle Improves Trading

Here are five ways the Wave Principle can benefit you and improve your trading:

1. The Wave Principle identifies the trend.
2. It identifies countertrend price moves within the larger trend.
3. It determines the maturity of the trend.
4. It provides high-confidence price targets.
5. It provides specific points of invalidation.

1. Identifying the Trend

". . . action in the same direction as the one larger trend develops in five waves. . . ."

—*Elliott Wave Principle* by Frost and Prechter

The Wave Principle identifies the direction of the dominant trend. A five-wave advance identifies the overall trend as up. Conversely, a five-wave decline determines that the larger trend is down. Why is this information important? Because it is easier to trade in the direction of the dominant trend, since it is the path of least resistance and undoubtedly explains the saying, "The trend is your friend." I find trading in the direction of the trend much easier than attempting to pick tops and bottoms within a trend, which is a difficult endeavor and one that is virtually impossible to do consistently.

2. Identifying the Countertrend

". . . reaction against the one larger trend develops in three waves. . . ."

—*Elliott Wave Principle* by Frost and Prechter

The Wave Principle also identifies countertrend moves. The three-wave pattern is a corrective response to the preceding impulse wave. Knowing that a recent move in price is merely a correction within a larger trending market is especially important for traders because corrections give traders opportunities to position themselves in the direction of the larger trend of a market.

Being aware of the three basic Elliott wave corrective patterns—zigzags, flats, and triangles—enables you to buy pullbacks in an uptrend and to sell bounces in a downtrend, which is a proven and consistently successful trading strategy. Know what countertrend price moves look like, and you can find opportunities to rejoin the trend.

3. Determining the Maturity of a Trend

As R. N. Elliott observed, wave patterns form larger and smaller versions of themselves. This repetition in form means that price activity is a fractal, as illustrated in Figure 1.1. Wave (1) subdivides into five small waves yet is part of a larger five-wave pattern. How is this information useful? It helps traders recognize the maturity of a trend. If, for example, prices are advancing in wave 5 of a five-wave advance and wave 5 has already completed three or four smaller waves, a trader knows that this may not be the best time to add long positions. Instead, it may be time to take profits or at least to raise protective stops.

Since the Wave Principle identifies trend, countertrend, and the maturity of a trend, it's no surprise that the Wave Principle also signals the return of the dominant trend. Once a countertrend

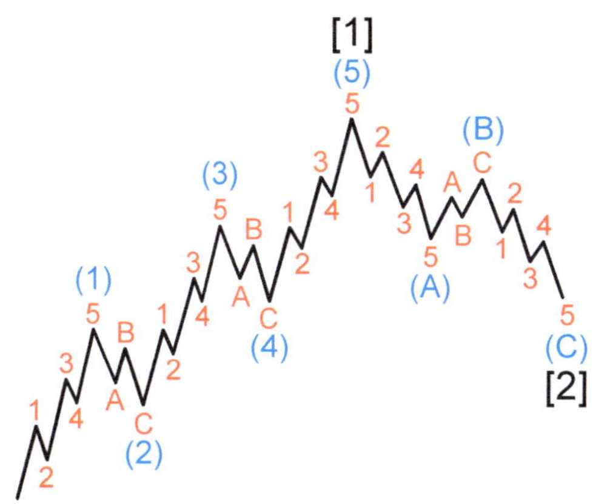

Figure 1.1

Source: Elliott Wave Principle.

move unfolds in three waves (A-B-C), this structure can signal the point where the dominant trend has resumed, namely, once price action exceeds the extreme of wave B. Knowing precisely when a trend has resumed brings an added benefit: It increases the likelihood of a successful trade, which is further enhanced when accompanied by traditional technical studies.

4. Providing Price Targets

What traditional technical studies simply don't offer—high-confidence price targets—the Wave Principle again provides. When R. N. Elliott wrote about the Wave Principle in *Nature's Law*, he stated that the Fibonacci sequence was the mathematical basis for the Wave Principle. Elliott waves, both impulsive and corrective, adhere to specific Fibonacci proportions. For example, all three motive waves tend to be related by Fibonacci mathematics, whether by equality, 1.618, or 2.618 (whose inverses are .618 and .382). See Figures 1.2, 1.3, and 1.4.

Also, corrections often retrace a Fibonacci percentage of the preceding wave. These Fibonacci-derived regions allow traders to set profit-taking objectives and identify areas where the next turn in prices will likely occur (see Figures 1.5 and 1.6).

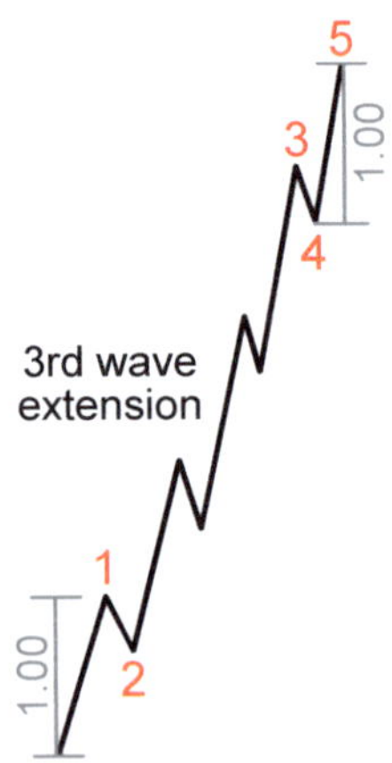

Figure 1.2
Source: Elliott Wave Principle.

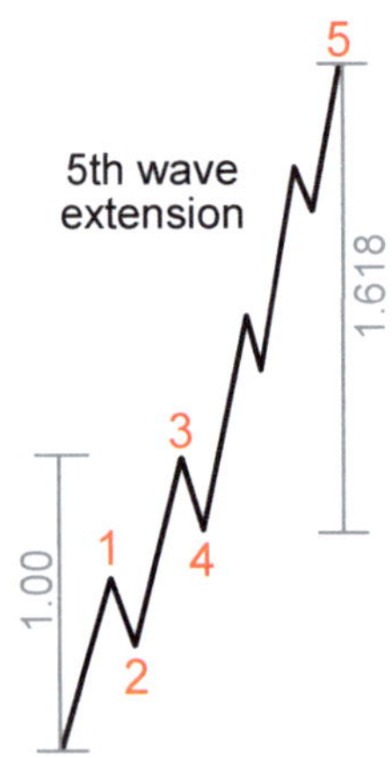

Figure 1.3
Source: Elliott Wave Principle.

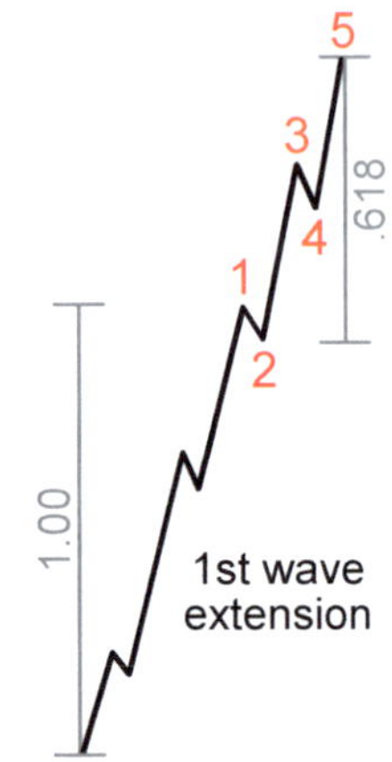

Figure 1.4
Source: Elliott Wave Principle.

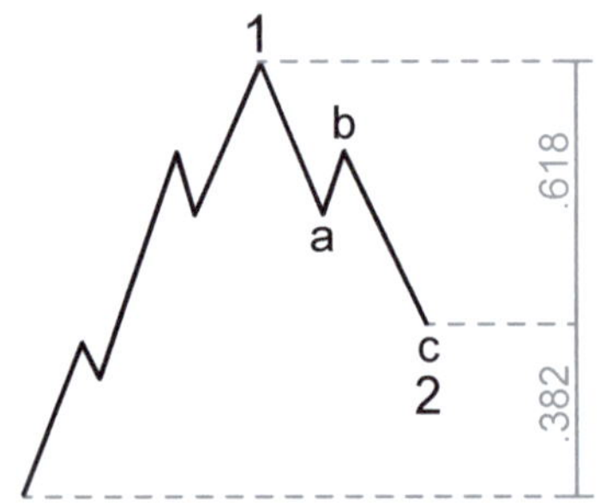

Figure 1.5
Source: Elliott Wave Principle.

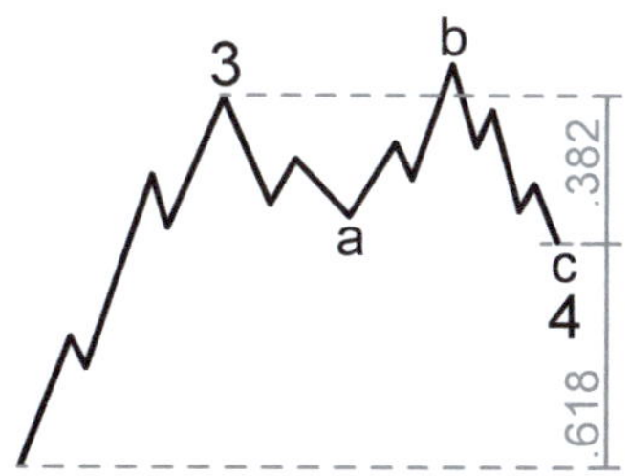

Figure 1.6
Source: Elliott Wave Principle.

5. Providing Specific Points of Invalidation

Wave analysis provides a specific point of invalidation, which is the level at which an interpretation is no longer viable. Knowing when you are wrong is perhaps a trader's most important piece of information.

At what point does a trade fail? Many traders use money management rules to determine the answer to this question, because technical studies simply don't offer the answer. Yet the Wave Principle does—in the form of these three Elliott wave rules for impulse waves:

Rule 1: Wave 2 can never retrace more than 100 percent of wave 1.

Rule 2: Wave 4 may never end in the price territory of wave 1.

Rule 3: Out of the three impulse waves (waves 1, 3, and 5), wave 3 can never be the shortest.

A violation of any of these rules implies that the operative wave count is incorrect. How can traders use this information? If a technical study warns of an up-turn in prices, and the wave pattern is a second-wave pullback, the trader knows specifically at what point the trade will fail: a move beyond the origin of wave 1. That kind of guidance is difficult to come by without a framework such as the Wave Principle.

The Four Best Waves to Trade

Here's where the rubber meets the road. Waves 3, 5, A, and C are the most advantageous to trade, because they are oriented in the direction of the one larger trend. Odds favor traders who are long in bull markets (and short in bear markets) versus short sellers in bull markets (and buyers in bear markets). Overall, trading in the direction of the trend is the path of least resistance.

The Wave Principle helps to identify these high-confidence trades in place of lesser-confidence set-ups that traders should ignore. Remember, five-wave moves determine the direction of the larger trend, while three-wave moves offer traders an opportunity to join the trend. So in Figure 1.7, waves (2), (4), (5), and (B) are actually setups for high-confidence trades exploiting waves (3), (5), (A), and (C).

For example, a wave (2) pullback provides traders an opportunity to position themselves in the direction of wave (3), just as a wave (5) rally offers them a shorting opportunity for wave (A). By combining the Wave Principle with traditional technical analysis, traders can improve their trading by increasing the likelihood of a successful trade.

Technical studies can pick out many trading opportunities, but the Wave Principle helps traders discern which ones are more likely to be successful.

KEY POINT

Knowing when you're wrong on a trade is as important as knowing when you're right.

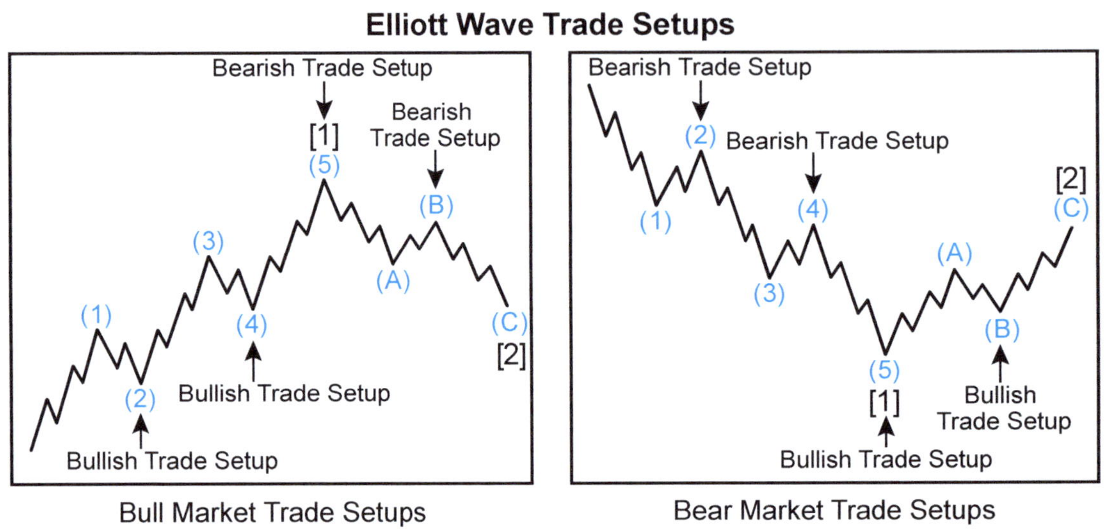

Figure 1.7

This is because the Wave Principle is the framework that provides history and context, current information, and a peek at the future.

Elliott Wave Trade Setups

This next chart (see Figure 1.7) shows bullish and bearish versions of trade setups. In each, waves (2), (4), (5), and (B) are trade setups that introduce the four primary Elliott-based trading opportunities. These corrective waves offer the trader an opportunity to rejoin the larger trend. In such trend trading, a trader buys pullbacks in uptrends and sells bounces in downtrends.

When to Trade Corrections

Corrective waves offer less desirable trading opportunities because of their potential complexity. Impulse waves are trend-defining price moves in which prices typically travel far. Conversely, corrective wave patterns fluctuate more and can unfold slowly while taking a variety of shapes, such as a zigzag, flat, expanded flat, triangle, double zigzag, or combination. Corrections generally move sideways and are often erratic, time-consuming, and deceptive. Thus, it is emotionally exhausting to trade corrections, and the odds of executing a successful trade during this type of price action are low.

Even though I view corrective waves and patterns as providing low-confidence trade setups, there are times when I would consider trading them—but it depends on the potential duration of the correction. If I count five waves up, for example, on a 15-minute price chart of Crude Oil, I do not consider waves 2 or 4 to be viable trading opportunities. I prefer, instead, to wait for waves 2 and 4 to terminate before entering a position. Let's say, though, that we have a market that has also formed an impulse wave, but it has taken weeks or months to do so. In this instance, waves 2 and 4 would form over many weeks and might offer traders many short-term trading opportunities.

Guidelines for Trading Specific Elliott Wave Patterns

Before we review guidelines for trading specific Elliott wave patterns, here is my most important analytical and trading rule: Let the market commit to you before you commit to the market . In other words, look for *confirming price action* . Just as it is unwise to pull out in front of an oncoming car on the basis of its turn signal alone, it is equally unwise to take a trade without confirmation of a trend change.

The following guidelines incorporate this idea and benefit the trader in two ways. First, waiting for confirming price action tends to decrease the number of trades executed. One of the biggest mistakes traders make is overtrading. Second, it focuses attention on higher-confidence trade setups. If a trader believes that a particular market is topping—and appropriate price action does indeed corroborate this belief—then the trader is more likely to execute a successful trade.

Smart Investor Tip

Let the market commit to you before you commit to the market.

Impulse Waves

Whenever an impulse wave is complete, the Elliott wave guideline regarding the depth of corrective waves applies: "[C]orrections, especially when they themselves are fourth waves, tend to register their maximum retracement within the span of travel of the previous fourth wave of one lesser degree, most commonly near the level of its terminus."

— *Elliott Wave Principle* by Frost and Prechter

Smart Investor Tip

Waiting for confirming price action allows traders to use an evidence-based approach and to focus their attention on higher-confidence trade setups.

Although that guideline may sound complicated, it's easy to follow in real trading. The trading technique is to enter on a break below the extreme of wave (iv) of 5 (see Figure 1.8). Doing so prevents top picking and requires the market to take out a prior swing low to act as initial evidence that the impulse wave is indeed finished. Set the initial protective stop at the extreme of the price move.

Ending Diagonal

The guidelines for entry and initial protective stops for ending diagonals are similar to those for impulse waves: Wait for a break of the extreme of wave 4 before taking a position, and place the initial protective stop at the extreme of the price move (see Figure 1.9).

Remember, these entry techniques demonstrate a conservative approach that I think of as "ready, aim,

Impulse Wave

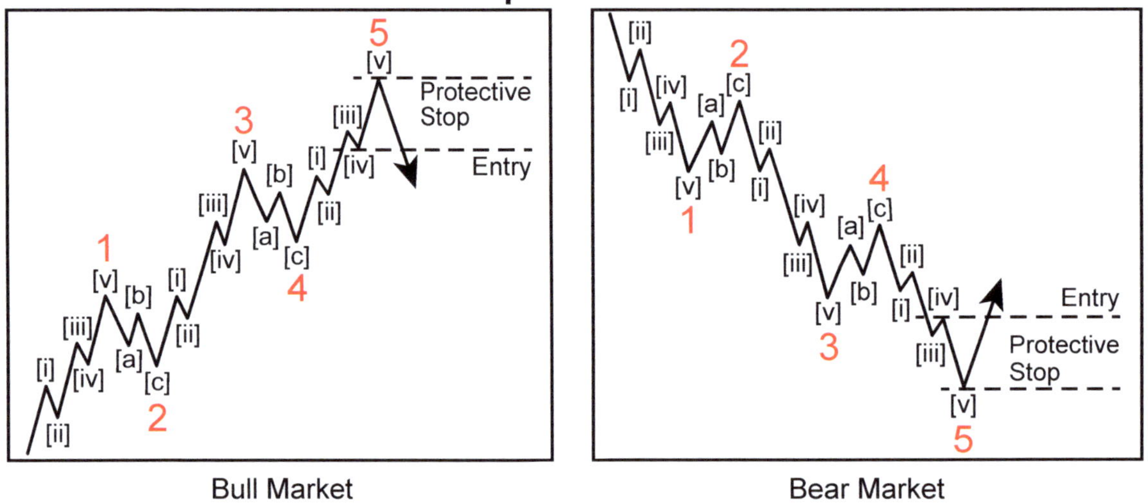

Figure 1.8

Ending Diagonal

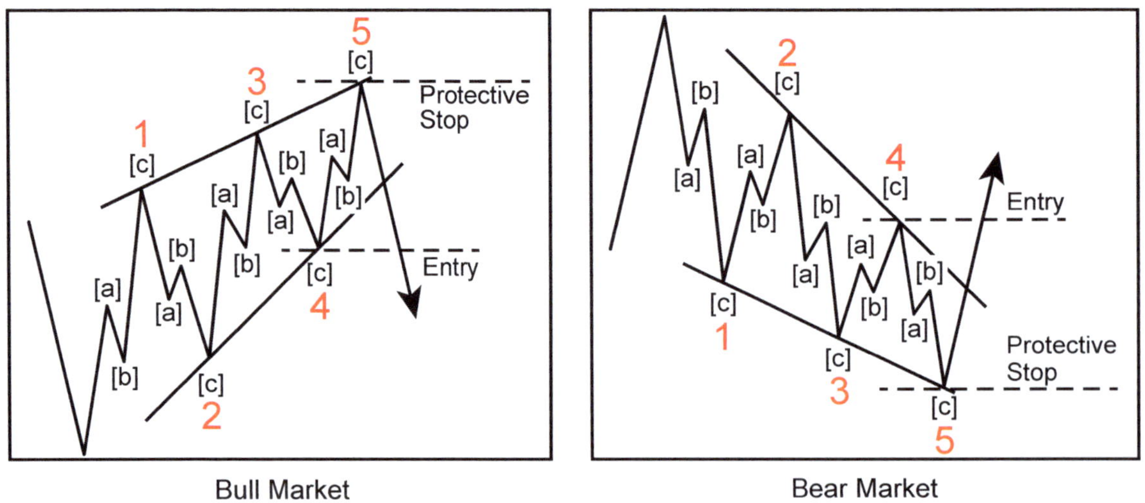

Figure 1.9

aim, aim . . . fire" trading. But if you are a more aggressive trader, how do you enter an ending diagonal trade setup? One approach is to enter on a decisive close beyond the trendline that connects the extreme of waves 2 and 4. In this instance, the initial protective stop placement is the same, the extreme of the pattern (see Figure 1.10).

If you define yourself as an out-and-out aggressive trader, here's an entry technique for you. More often than not, wave 3 of an ending diagonal is shorter than wave 1. When this is the case, the rules state that wave 5 cannot be longer than wave 3, since even within an ending diagonal, wave 3 may never be the shortest wave among waves 1, 3, and 5. Thus, you can begin acquiring positions or scale into a position as wave 5 is forming. The protective stop under this aggressive entry technique would be the point at which wave 5 becomes longer than wave 3, since the Wave Principle identifies that as a specific point of invalidation.

Zigzag

The first of two guidelines for entering a trade during a zigzag is on a break of the extreme of wave [iv] of C, provided this level is beyond the termination of wave A (see Figure 1.11).

A second entry guideline is to wait for the extreme of wave B to give way before taking action (see Figure 1.12). The initial protective stop is then the extreme of wave C. This conservative

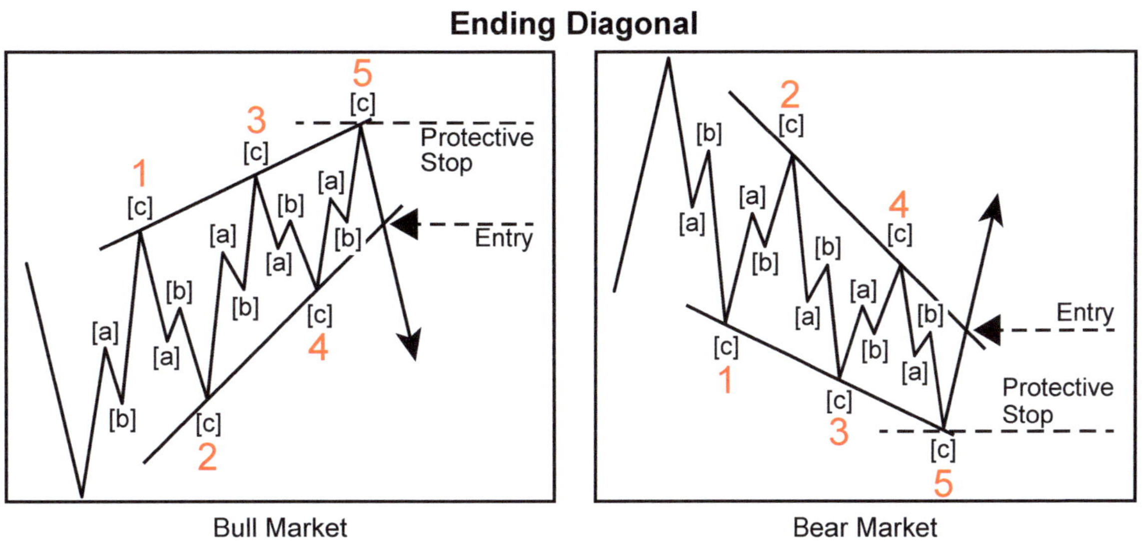

Figure 1.10

Zigzag

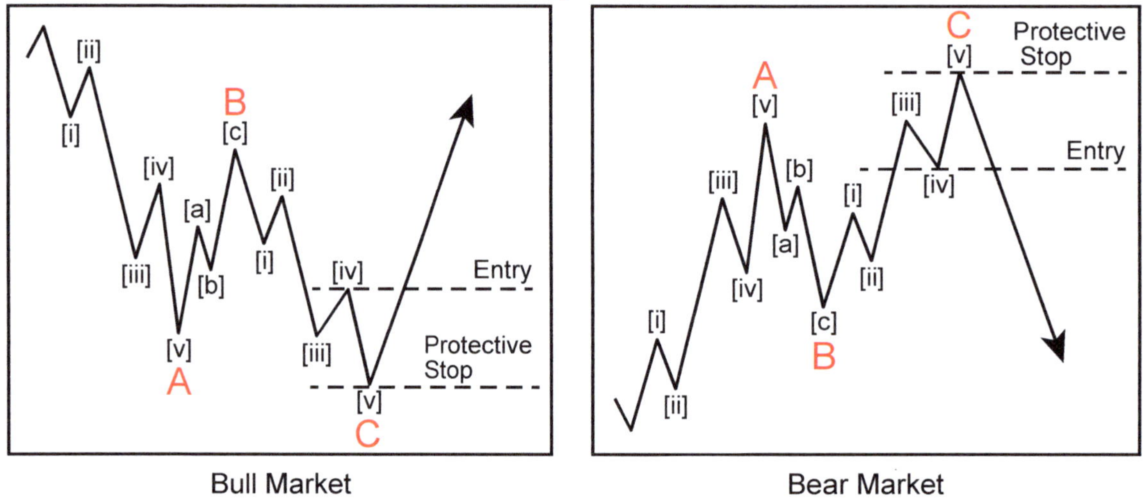

Figure 1.11

Zigzag

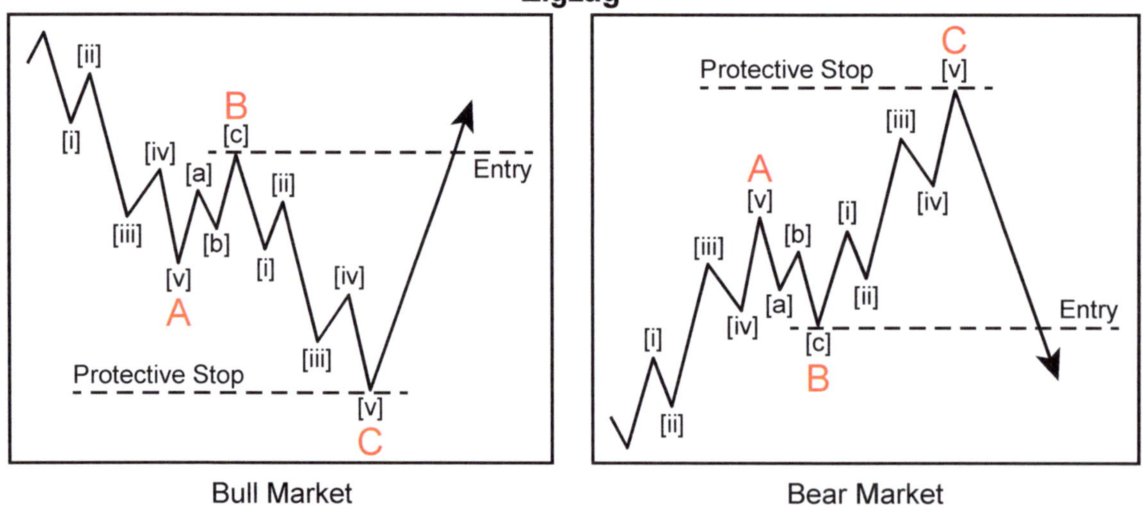

Figure 1.12

approach prevents picking tops or bottoms without sufficient evidence.

Ideally, traders will take these guidelines and adapt them to their own specific trading style. In fact, using a zigzag as an example, an even more conservative trader could wait a bit longer before entering and demand a five-wave move through the extreme of wave B followed by a corrective wave pattern.

Flat

Since the final wave of a flat correction subdivides into five waves, the recommended entry technique is similar to that of an impulse wave: Wait until prices exceed the extreme of wave (iv) of C to enter a trade (see Figure 1.13). This approach is not used with zigzags—where wave C also subdivides into five waves—because in a bullish zigzag, for instance, wave (iv) of a C terminates *below* the extreme of wave A, whereas in a bullish flat, it tends to form *above* the extreme of wave A.

Triangle

The final guideline applies to triangles (see Figure 1.14). A triangle is a sideways price move—typically bounded by converging trendlines—that subdivides into waves A, B, C, D, and E. The entry guideline is to wait for prices to break the extreme of wave D and place an initial protective

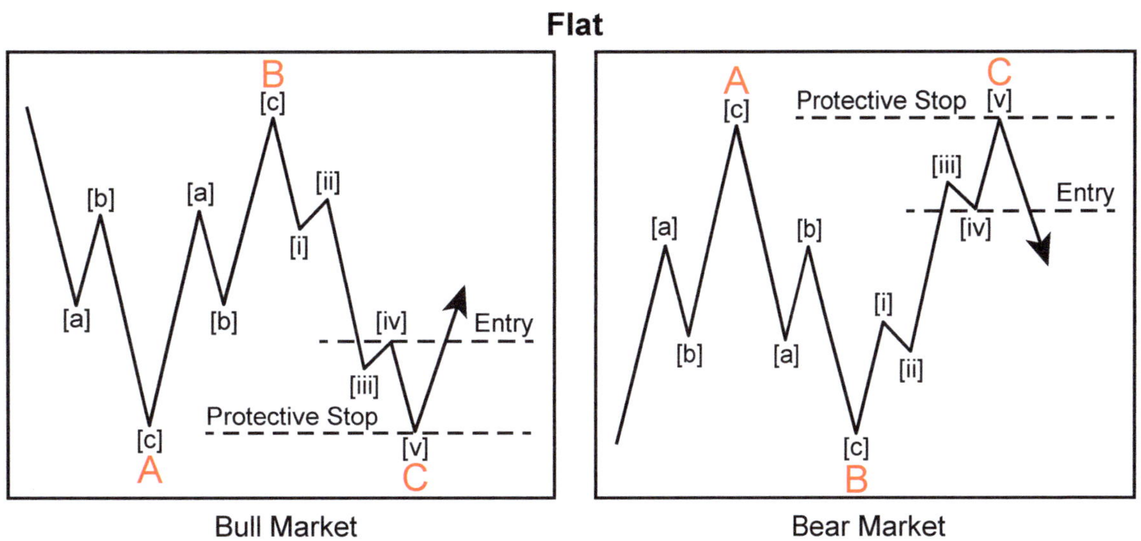

Figure 1.13

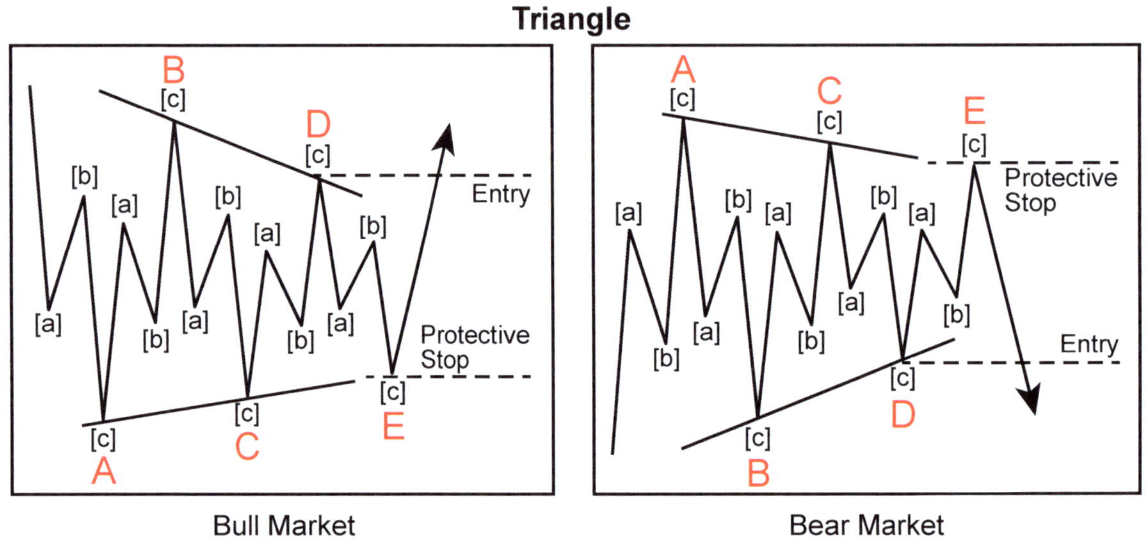

Figure 1.14

stop where wave E terminates. I do not endorse a more aggressive entry technique because triangles are sometimes deceptive: Since they can form in the wave 4, B, or X wave positions, what may appear to be a bullish fourth-wave triangle could actually be a bearish triangle B wave.

A trader with a more aggressive trading style will most likely enter a position well before prices penetrate the termination point of wave D. If so, I recommend using the extreme of wave A as an initial protective stop rather than the end of wave C. It is not uncommon in equities or thinly traded markets for intraday price action to exceed the extreme of wave C and reverse.

Smart Investor Tip

The psychology of the individual is the key to becoming a consistently successful trader.

DEFINITION:

Risk to reward

Risk-Reward Ratio is a ratio used to compare expected returns against the amount of risk taken. In line with market convention, risk-reward ratios are expressed in terms of total reward per one unit of risk.

The Neglected Essentials—Risk Management and the Psychology of Trading

When discussing how to become a consistently successful trader, two subjects you don't hear enough about are risk management and the psychology of trading.

Because the topic of risk management is critically important to the success and longevity of a trader, let's briefly discuss risk-reward ratios and trade size.

Risk-Reward Ratio

Risk to reward is a ratio that quantifies the risk versus the reward of a trade. If you buy XYZ stock at $50.00 with the expectation that it will appreciate to $51.00, your expected reward is $1.00. If the protective stop on this position is $49.00, the risk-reward ratio for this trade is 1:1—you're risking $1.00 to make $1.00. If the protective stop is $49.90, then the risk-reward ratio is 10:1.

Note: Even though it's called a risk-reward ratio, the ratio is conventionally stated with the reward figure first. So, in this example, even though risk is 1 and the reward 10, the ratio is stated as 10:1, rather than 1:10. This explains why a 3:1 risk-reward ratio is desirable. It's actually a reward-risk ratio.

A high risk-reward ratio is desirable as a function of probabilities. Let's say that you're right about the market 70 percent of the time, and the risk-reward ratio on each of your trades is 1:1. Thus, out of 10 trades, seven trades were closed with a $1.00 profit, while three were exited with a $1.00 loss. The bottom line is that you walked away with $4.00. What do you think will happen if we increase the risk-reward ratio from 1:1 to 3:1 and decrease the probability of being right from 70 percent to 40 percent? With this 3:1 ratio, for the same $1.00 profit, four winning trades would net $12.00. If we then subtract $6.00 in losing trades, we walk away with a $6.00 profit.

This difference shows how important the risk-reward ratio is—by decreasing the probability of winning trades from 70 percent to almost half (i.e., 40 percent) while increasing the risk-reward ratio, you increase profitability by 50 percent. A misconception about trading is that a trader need be right only on the direction of the market to make money. This is not entirely correct. As you've just seen, a trader can be right as little as 40 percent of the time and still succeed, provided he or she keeps an eye on the risk-reward ratio.

Trade Size

How large a position should a trader take? The risk on a single trade should never exceed 1 to 3 percent of the total portfolio size. Retail traders tend to balk at these small percentages, while professional traders embrace them. Thus, at 1 percent, for every $5,000 a trader has in a trading account, he or she should risk only $50 on each position. For example, a trader with $10,000 in his account can take either two trades where the risk is $50 apiece or one trade in which the risk is $100. Many traders fail at trading because they simply don't have sufficient capital in their trading accounts to take the positions they want to take.

If you do have a small trading account, though, you can overcome this challenge by trading small. You can trade fewer contracts, trade e-mini contracts, or even penny stocks. Bottom line, on your way to becoming a consistently successful trader, you must realize that *longevity* is key. If your risk on any given position is small relative to your total capital, then you can weather a losing streak. Conversely, if you risk 25 percent of your portfolio on each trade, after four consecutive losers, you're out of business.

Smart Investor Tip

Trades that offer less than a 3:1 risk-reward ratio should be avoided.

Smart Investor Tip

Successful trading requires a methodology and the discipline to follow the methodology.

The Psychology of Trading

While I consider risk management to be an essential component of successful trading, the true key is psychology—that is, your individual psychology. Let's review a number of psychological factors that prevent traders from becoming consistently successful: lack of methodology, lack of discipline, unrealistic expectations, and lack of patience.

Whether you are a seasoned professional or just thinking about opening your first trading account, it is critically important to your success that you understand how your personal psychology affects your trading results.

Lack of Methodology

If you aim to be a consistently successful trader, then you must have a defined trading methodology—a simple, clear, and concise way of looking at markets. In fact, having a method is so important that EWI founder Robert Prechter put it at the top of his list in his essay, "What a Trader Really Needs to Be Successful." Guessing or going by gut instinct won't work over the long run. If you don't have a defined trading methodology, then you don't have a way to know what constitutes a buy or sell signal.

How do you overcome this problem? The answer to this question is to write down your methodology. Define in writing what your analytical tools are and, more important, how you use them. It doesn't matter whether you use the Wave Principle, point and figure charts, stochastics, RSI, or a combination of all of these. What *does* matter is that you actually make the effort to define what constitutes a buy, a sell, your trailing stop, and instructions on exiting a position. The best hint I can give you about defining your trading methodology is this: If you can't fit it on a 3" × 5" card, it's probably too complicated.

Lack of Discipline

Once you have clearly outlined and identified your trading methodology, you *must* have the discipline to follow the system. A lack of discipline while trading is the second common downfall of many aspiring traders. If the way you view a price chart or evaluate a potential trade setup today is different from how you did it a month ago, then you either have not identified your methodology or you lack the discipline to follow the methodology you have identified. The formula for success is to consistently apply a proven methodology.

Unrealistic Expectations

Nothing makes me angrier than those commercials that say something like, "$5,000 properly positioned in Natural Gas can give you returns of over $40,000." Advertisements like this are a disservice to the financial industry as a whole and end up costing uneducated investors a lot more than $5,000. In addition, they help to create the psychologically sabotaging mind-set of having unrealistic expectations.

Yes, it is possible to experience above-average returns trading your own account. However, it's difficult to do it without taking on above-average risk. So, what is a realistic return to shoot for in your first year as a trader—50 percent, 100 percent, 200 percent? Whoa, let's rein in those unrealistic expectations. In my opinion, the goal for every trader the first year out should be *not to lose money* . In other words, shoot for a 0 percent return your first year. If you can manage that, then in year two, try to beat the Dow or the S&P. These goals may not be flashy, but they are realistic.

Lack of Patience

The fourth psychological pitfall that even experienced traders encounter is a lack of patience. According to Edwards and Magee in their seminal book, *Technical Analysis of Stock Trends*, markets trend only about 30 percent of the time. This means that the other 70 percent of the time, financial markets are not trending.

This small percentage may explain why I believe that, for any given time frame, there are only two or three really good trading opportunities. For example, if you're a long-term trader, typically only two or three compelling tradable moves in a market present themselves during any given year. Similarly, if you are a short-term trader, only two or three high-quality trade setups present themselves in a given week.

All too often, because trading is inherently exciting (and anything involving money usually is exciting), it's easy to feel that you're missing something if you're not in a trade. As a result, you start taking trade setups of lesser and lesser quality and begin overtrading.

How do you overcome this lack of patience? Remind yourself that every week there will be another "trade of the year." In other words, don't worry about missing an opportunity today, because there will be another one tomorrow, next week and next month ... I promise.

Video:

To watch a video on the importance of patience and persistence in your trading, go to: www.elliottwave.com/wave/ReaderResources

For More Information

Learn more at your exclusive Reader Resources site. You will find a free online edition of *Elliott Wave Principle* by Frost and Prechter, plus lessons on Elliott wave analysis, how to trade specific patterns, and how to use Fibonacci and other technical indicators to increase your confidence as you apply the Wave Principle in real time. Go to: www.elliottwave.com/wave/ReaderResources.

Smart Investor Tip

Stick with realistic expectations. For instance, the goal for every trader the first year should be *not to lose money* . In other words, shoot for a 0 percent return during your first year.

Test Yourself

Answer the following True/False questions:

1. Analysis and trading employ the same skill set.
2. Wave analysis identifies the direction of the trend, based on the direction of the impulse wave.
3. The Wave Principle offers traders points of invalidation where they can re-evaluate where their analysis may have gone wrong.
4. Wave 2 can sometimes retrace more than 100 percent of wave 1.
5. A complete Elliott wave cycle consists of nine waves.
6. From origin to termination, waves 2 and 4 offer high-confidence trading opportunities.
7. An aggressive approach to trading an ending diagonal is to wait for the extreme of wave 4 to give way.
8. If you look for confirming price action, then you are letting the market commit to you before you commit to the market.
9. The entry guideline for trading a zigzag is to wait for the extreme of wave B to give way.
10. A risk to reward ratio of 1:1 is ideal.

Answers: 1. False 2. True 3. True 4. False 5. False 6. False 7. False 8. True 9. True 10. False

PART II

Trading Examples

CHAPTER 2

How Zigzags and Flats Set Up a Trade for the Next Impulse Wave

The three essential parts of a trade are analyzing price charts, formulating a trading plan, and managing the trade.

Trading a Zigzag in Caterpillar (CAT)

In Caterpillar (CAT), we'll examine each component to better understand why CAT offered a high-confidence trade setup.

1. Analyzing the Price Charts

When it comes to trade setups, it doesn't get much easier than the price chart of CAT from April and May 2011. As you can see in Figure 2.1, prices fell in five waves from 116.55 to 108.39. This wave pattern was significant because impulse waves identify the direction of the larger trend. Thus, this five-wave decline in CAT implied further selling to come that would take prices below 108.39 in either wave (C) or wave (3).

The subsequent rally in CAT that developed in three waves supported this analysis. Countertrend price action typically consists of three waves, so I knew to expect another move down in CAT. Moreover, the three-wave advance in CAT traveled to 112.47 to retrace 50 percent of the previous sell-off . That 50 percent is a common retracement for corrective waves. Also nearby was 112.84, the price level at which wave C equaled a .618 multiple of wave A, which is a common Fibonacci relationship between waves C and A of corrective wave patterns.

The only question at this point was whether the move up from 108.39 should be labeled as wave (B) or wave (2). From a short-term trading perspective, this question was academic because,

KEY POINT

Impulse waves identify the direction of the larger trend.

KEY POINT

Countertrend price action typically consists of three waves.

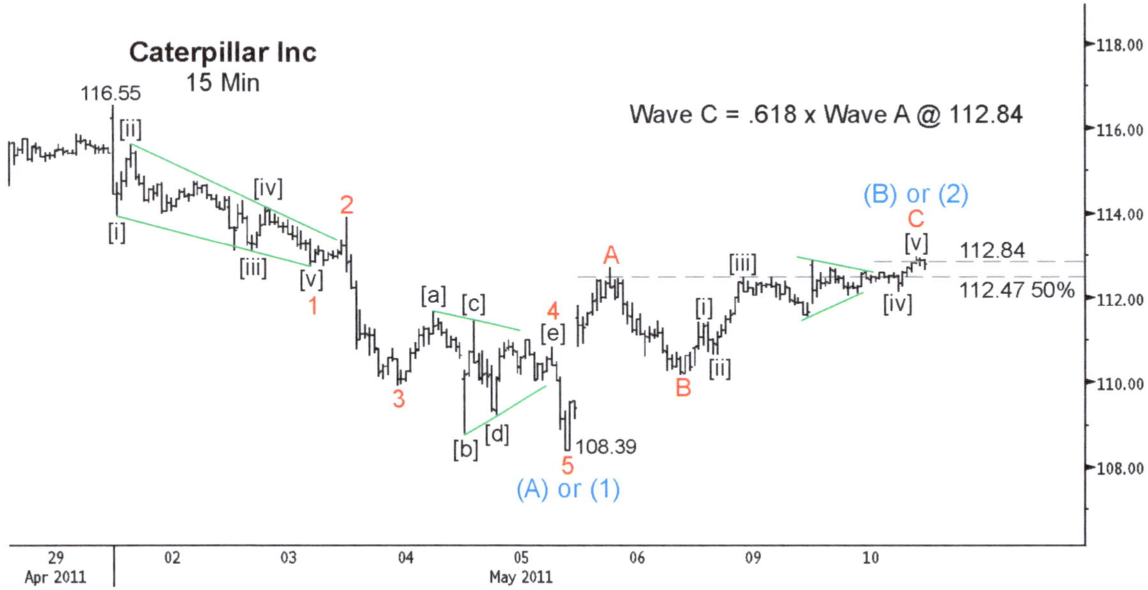

Figure 2.1

Chart reprinted with permission from Bloomberg. Copyright 2013 Bloomberg L.P. All rights reserved.

DEFINITION:
zigzags

A zigzag is a simple three-wave correction that subdivides into wave A (five waves), wave B (three waves), and wave C (five waves).

either way, the trade objective was a price move just under 108.39. A final observation about the corrective rally: The slope of wave C in this case was shallower than the slope of wave A. A shallow wave C slope, which demonstrates a decrease in momentum, is a harbinger that the larger trend is resuming. These shallower slopes within zigzags are so common that they are almost a qualifying characteristic of the pattern.

By applying the most basic Elliott wave analysis to the price chart of CAT, I could see five waves down and three waves up into Fibonacci and structural resistance at 112.47–112.84. That meant that odds strongly favored a sell-off below 108.39 from near current levels. So, the question at that point was how best to capitalize on this information.

2. Formulating a Trading Plan

In Figure 2.2, I chose to trade this setup using options, specifically, by purchasing 110 puts on May 10, 2011, at 86 cents apiece. These options

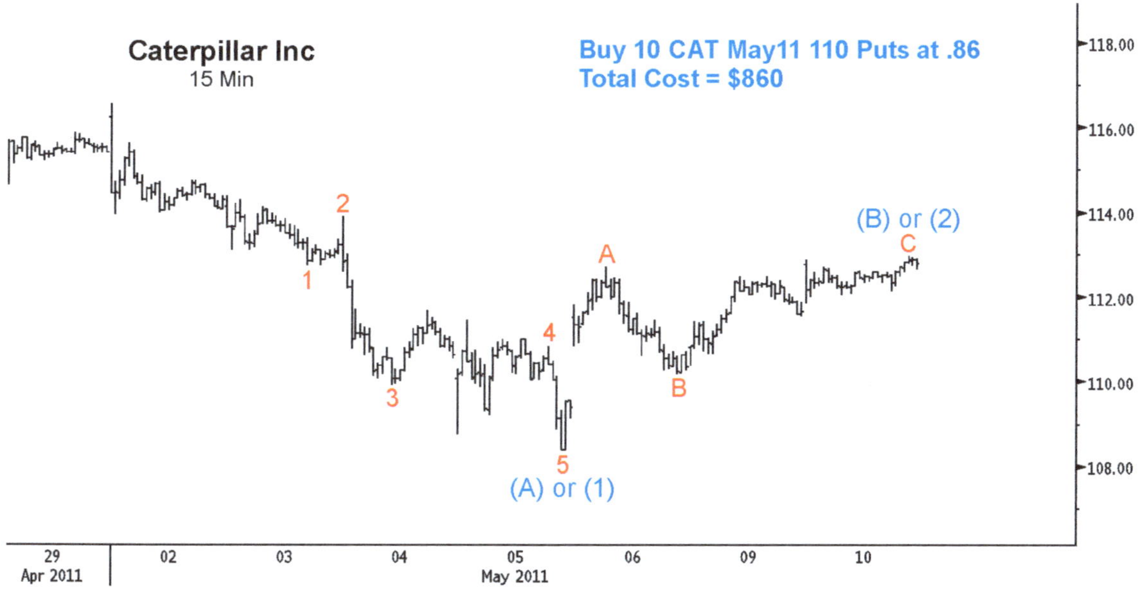

Figure 2.2

Chart reprinted with permission from Bloomberg. Copyright 2013 Bloomberg L.P. All rights reserved.

were scheduled to expire on May 20, 2011, so there were only eight trading days left on these puts. Considering that these options were to expire in just a matter of days, this kind of trade is *extremely risky*, and only the most seasoned and risk-aware trader should consider doing it.

Since the initial sell-off in CAT from 116.55 to 108.39 transpired in four days, here was my thinking at the time: If the next wave down proved to be wave (3), then I would see prices fall farther in a shorter period of time; if the upcoming decline proved to be a (C) wave, then the upcoming sell-off would most likely be shallower and take more time. Even if CAT were to unfold in wave (C) and take twice as long as the initial decline, it would still trade roughly at $104.81, the level at which waves (C) and (A) would be equal by options expiration.

Again, it is important to understand that due to waning premium, an options trade should *not* be taken with the idea of holding the trade over a long period of time for a sizable move down.

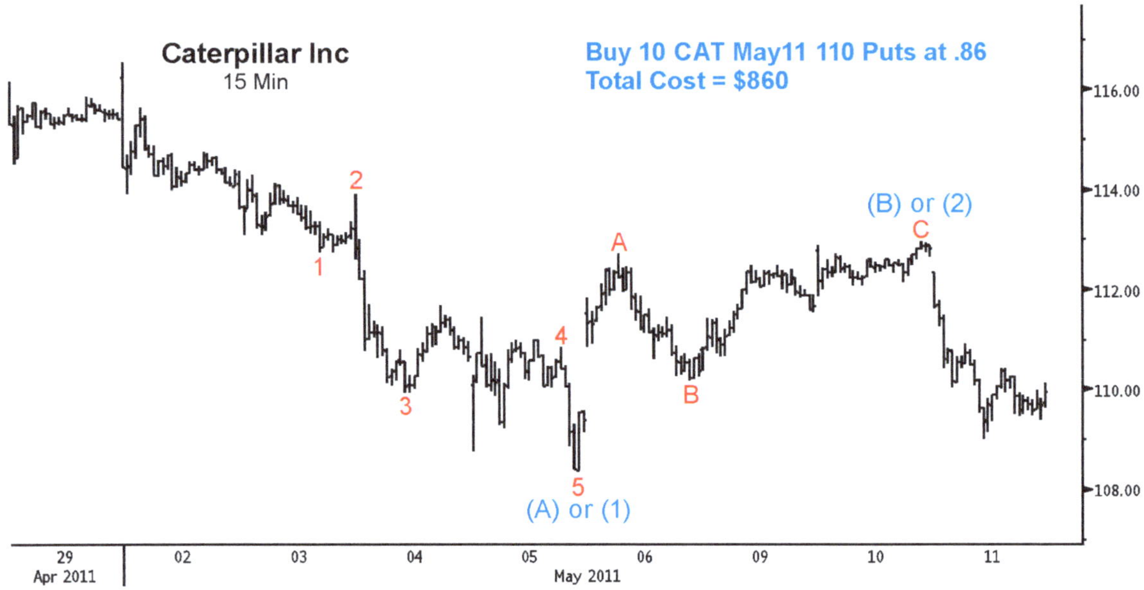

Figure 2.3

Chart reprinted with permission from Bloomberg. Copyright 2013 Bloomberg L.P. All rights reserved.

The idea was simply to catch a short-term move below the May 2011 low of 108.39 over three to five trading days.

3. Managing the Trade

The day following our analysis and entry, CAT fell sharply (see Figure 2.3). As a result, the value of the position increased substantially. In retrospect, it would have been prudent to exit the trade entirely or at least partially the day after the swift decline. However, since the original analysis called for a move below 108.39, I decided to hold the position.

During the next few days, CAT continued lower. On Friday, May 13, 2011, I exited the position for a 336.05 percent return (see Figure 2.4), selling the options that were originally purchased at 86 cents for $3.75 apiece.

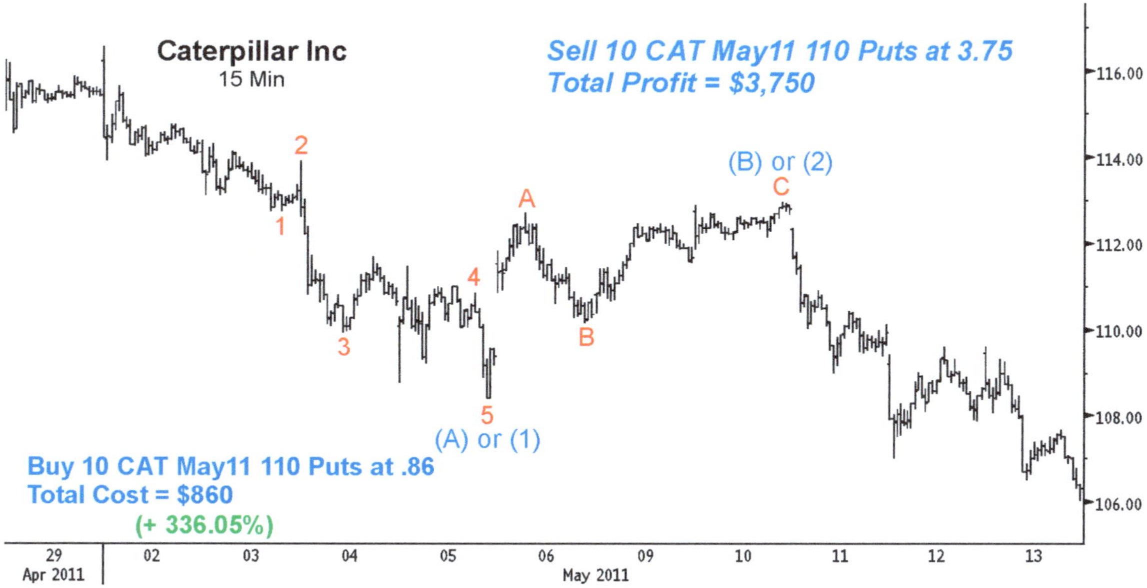

Figure 2.4

Chart reprinted with permission from Bloomberg. Copyright 2013 Bloomberg L.P. All rights reserved.

Yes, the percent return in this trading example is exciting. What is even more exciting, though, was its genesis. This trade began by simply recognizing an impulse wave and a zigzag. It did, however, take some knowledge of Fibonacci ratios and multiples to identify a high-probability reversal zone for CAT's corrective advance. The final step in this successful trading equation was to use the knowledge derived from the analysis to determine a good way to leverage the information. In this case, we set up an options trade.

I discuss zigzags and flats often in my *Trader's Classroom* lessons. If you aren't already a member of *Trader's Classroom*, you can get a Visual Guide special offer here: www.elliottwave.com/wave/VGB-TCSpecialOffer.

Video:
To watch a video on how to identify high-confidence trade setups by looking for three-wave moves within parallel lines, go to:
www.elliottwave.com/wave/ReaderResources

KEY POINT

Always ask first, "Do I see a wave pattern I recognize?"

Trading an Expanded Flat in Techne Corp. (TECH)

When looking for a trading opportunity, I always begin by asking myself one simple question: Do I see a wave pattern I recognize? If the answer is yes, then it's time to delve a bit deeper into the price chart. If the answer is no, then it's time to quickly move on to a different chart.

1. Analyzing the Price Charts

In March 2012, I recognized a possible pattern that could turn out to be an expanded flat on a price chart (see Figure 2.5) of Techne Corp. (TECH). Specifically, what caught my eye was the three-wave advance from 68.84 to 71.00, followed by the three-wave decline to 67.69.

This up-down sequence was significant because there are only two Elliott wave formations that would apply—either an expanded flat or a

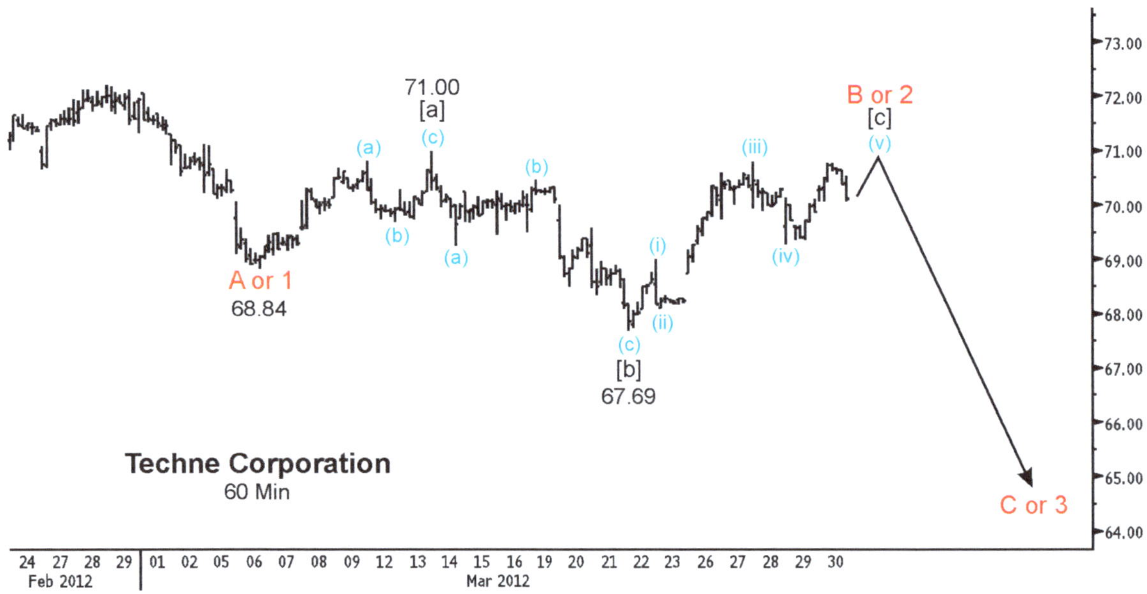

Figure 2.5

Chart reprinted with permission from Bloomberg. Copyright 2013 Bloomberg L.P. All rights reserved.

running triangle. Considering that the subsequent advance already had four of the required five waves to complete an impulse wave, odds strongly favored an **expanded flat** as the operative wave pattern in TECH.

2. Formulating a Trading Plan

Working with the hypothesis that an expanded flat was forming in TECH, I put together my trading plan, which was to sell 100 shares of TECH on a move below the extreme of wave (iv) at 69.28 (see Figure 2.6). As mentioned in Chapter 1, the guideline for entering a trade when the operative pattern is a flat is to enter when prices move through the extreme of wave four of C. This conservative approach should help prevent you from trying to pick tops or bottoms.

DEFINITION:

expanded flat

An expanded flat is a simple three-wave correction that subdivides into wave A (three waves), wave B (three waves), and wave C (five waves), with wave B ending beyond the starting point of wave A.

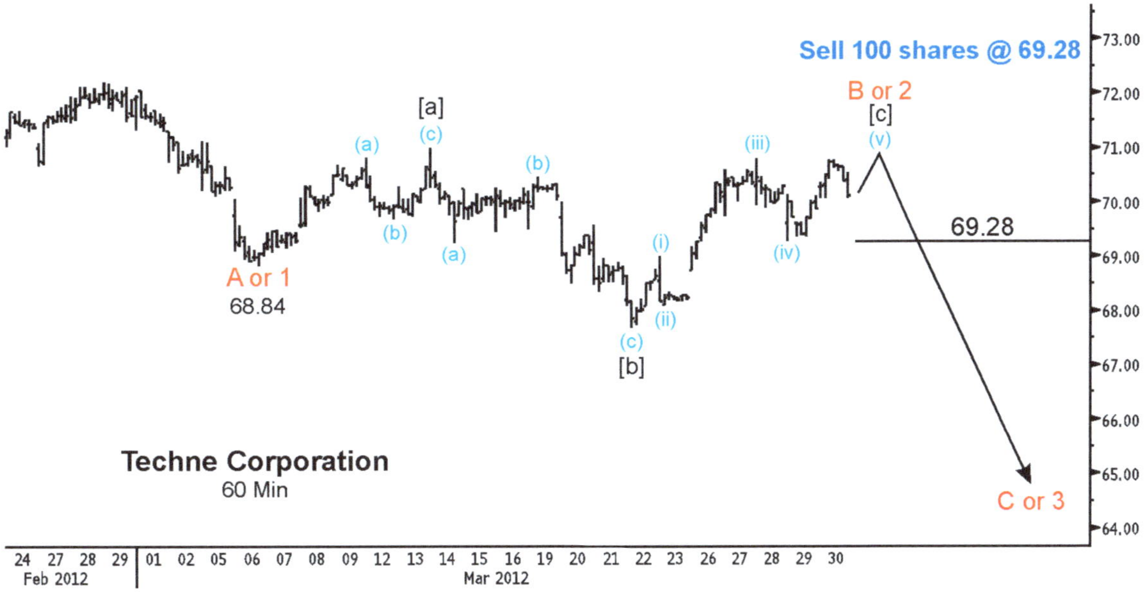

Figure 2.6

Chart reprinted with permission from Bloomberg. Copyright 2013 Bloomberg L.P. All rights reserved.

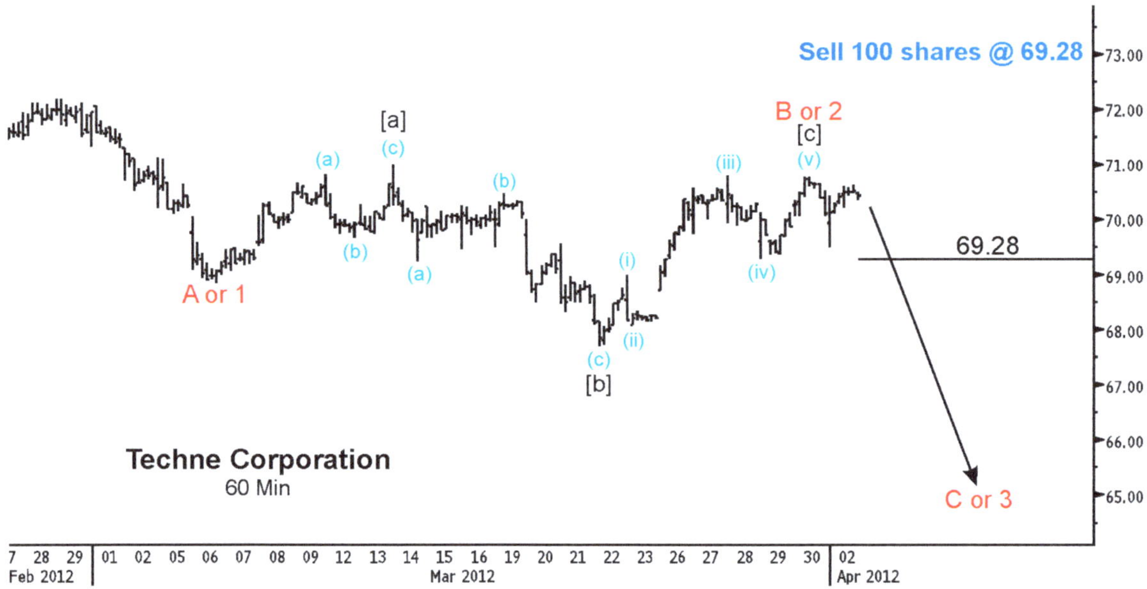

Figure 2.7
Chart reprinted with permission from Bloomberg. Copyright 2013 Bloomberg L.P. All rights reserved.

In the days that followed the original analysis, TECH rallied to 70.78 (see Figure 2.7). The prior extreme, wave (iii), was 70.80, which made wave (v) a small truncation. When waves that normally make new price extremes fail to do so, it's called a truncation in Elliott wave analysis. For example, wave five normally terminates beyond the extreme of wave three. When a wave truncates, it suggests that there is hidden or underlying pressure to either buy or sell. Even though the wave pattern ended on a truncation, the order remained the same: Sell 100 shares at 69.28.

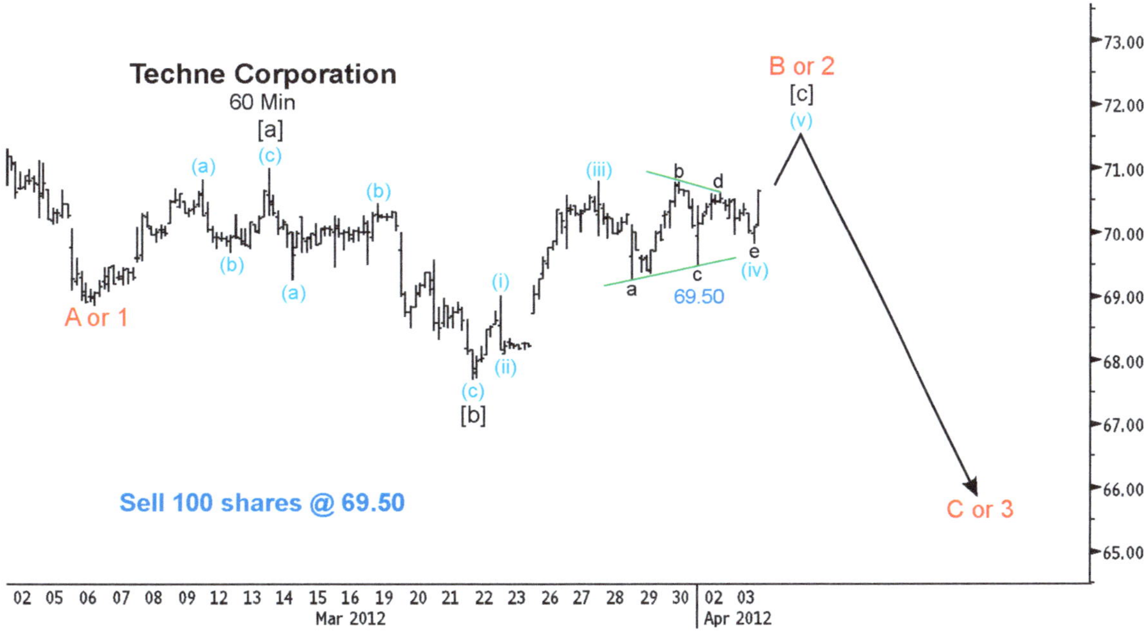

Figure 2.8

Chart reprinted with permission from Bloomberg. Copyright 2013 Bloomberg L.P. All rights reserved.

Following the 70.78 peak in TECH, prices moved sideways (see Figure 2.8). This type of price action argued against a fifth-wave truncation and supported the notion that a triangle was taking shape in the fourth wave. Triangles may form independently only in waves four, B, or X, which means that they always precede the final wave of a sequence. Thus, since I believed that the waves would develop into an expanded flat, identifying short-term price action as a triangle made sense at this juncture. So, it was time to raise the sell order from 69.28 to 69.50, the extreme of wave c of (iv).

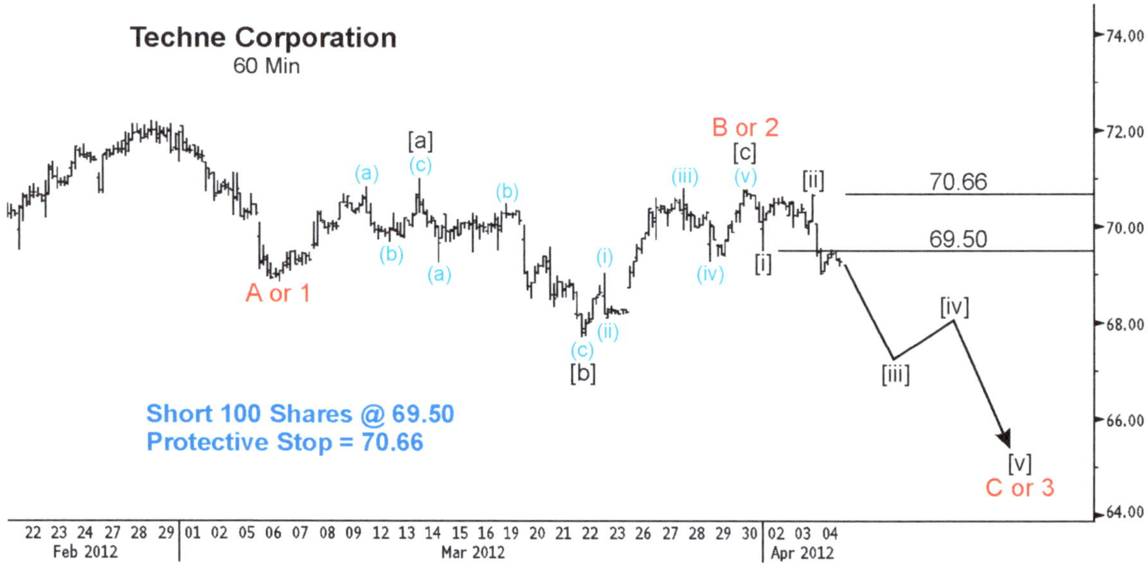

Figure 2.9
Chart reprinted with permission from Bloomberg. Copyright 2013 Bloomberg L.P. All rights reserved.

As you can see in Figure 2.9, subsequent price action in TECH did not unfold according to plan. It no longer looked like a triangle. In fact, the labeling that identified the 70.78 peak as a truncated fifth wave seemed to have been correct all along. The open order at 69.50 was triggered on April 4, 2012, with an initial protective stop placed at 70.66. Why there? Because it represented the extreme of wave [ii]. One of the three cardinal rules of impulse waves is that wave two may never retrace more than 100 percent of wave one. Thus, my logic was that if another second wave were to develop in wave [iii], it would hold below the previous second wave at 70.66.

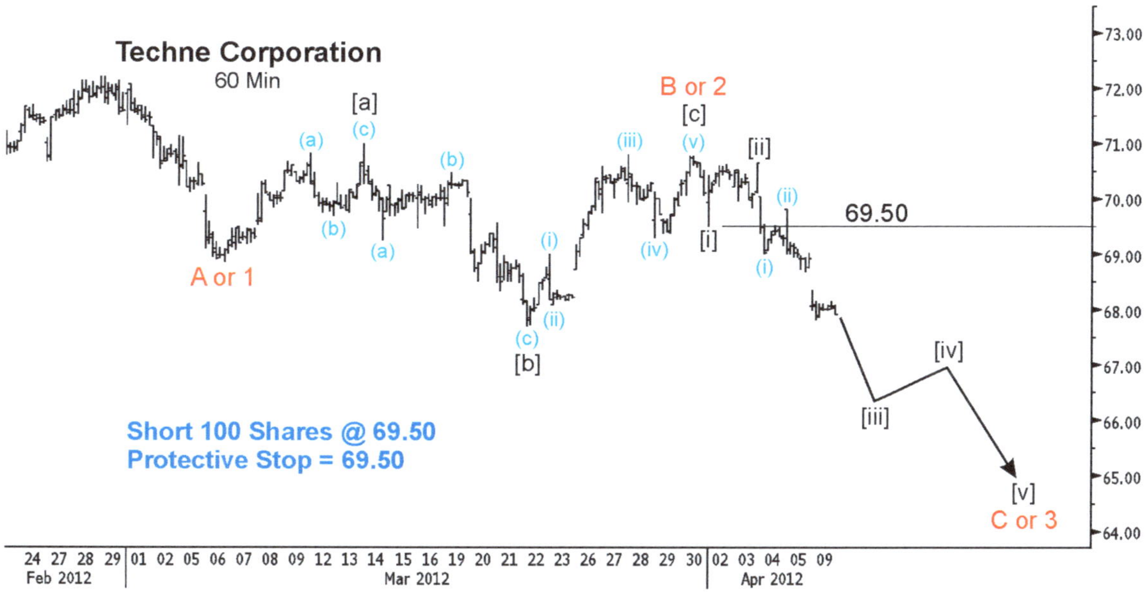

Figure 2.10
Chart reprinted with permission from Bloomberg. Copyright 2013 Bloomberg L.P. All rights reserved.

And, indeed, following our entry in this trading example, TECH pushed steadily lower (see Figure 2.10). Furthermore, price action in TECH included a gap down on April 9. A price gap occurs when the current bar's range does not include the previous bar's range. From an Elliott wave perspective, price gaps form most often in the wave three position—especially in wave three of wave three—because that's when prices are traveling far in a short period of time. Traditional technical analysts refer to this type of price gap as an acceleration gap.

3. Managing the Trade

Since prices were trading below the entry price of 69.50 on April 10, it was a good time to lower the

Smart Investor Tip

Remember the three phases of risk management during a trade: (1) lessen risk, (2) eliminate risk, and (3) protect open profits.

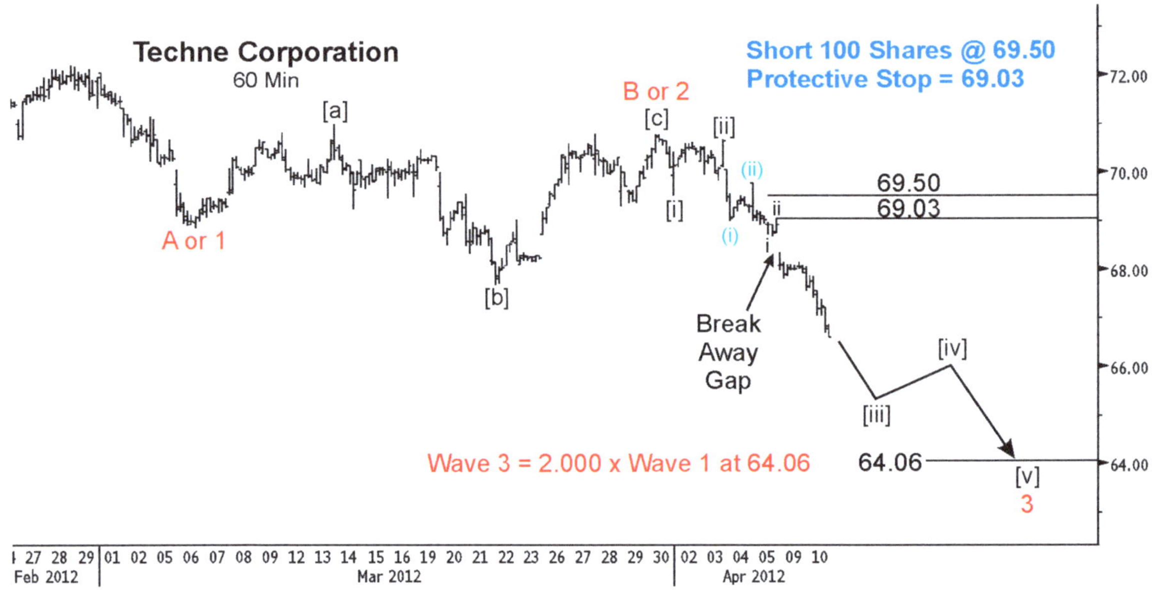

Figure 2.11

Chart reprinted with permission from Bloomberg. Copyright 2013 Bloomberg L.P. All rights reserved.

protective stop to break even at 69.50. It is important for traders to focus not only on the trade but also on risk management, the three phases of which are: lessen risk, eliminate risk, and protect open profits.

Figure 2.11 shows that TECH pressed lower. Also, the depth of subsequent selling allowed us to redefine the price gap that occurred on April 9 as a breakaway gap rather than an acceleration gap. Traditionally, technicians define price gaps as break-away, acceleration, and exhaustion. From an Elliott wave perspective, you might experience a breakaway gap in wave three of wave one, an acceleration gap in wave three of wave three and an exhaustion gap in wave three of wave five.

We could now lower our protective stop to 69.03. This price level represented a small second-wave extreme that allowed us to lock

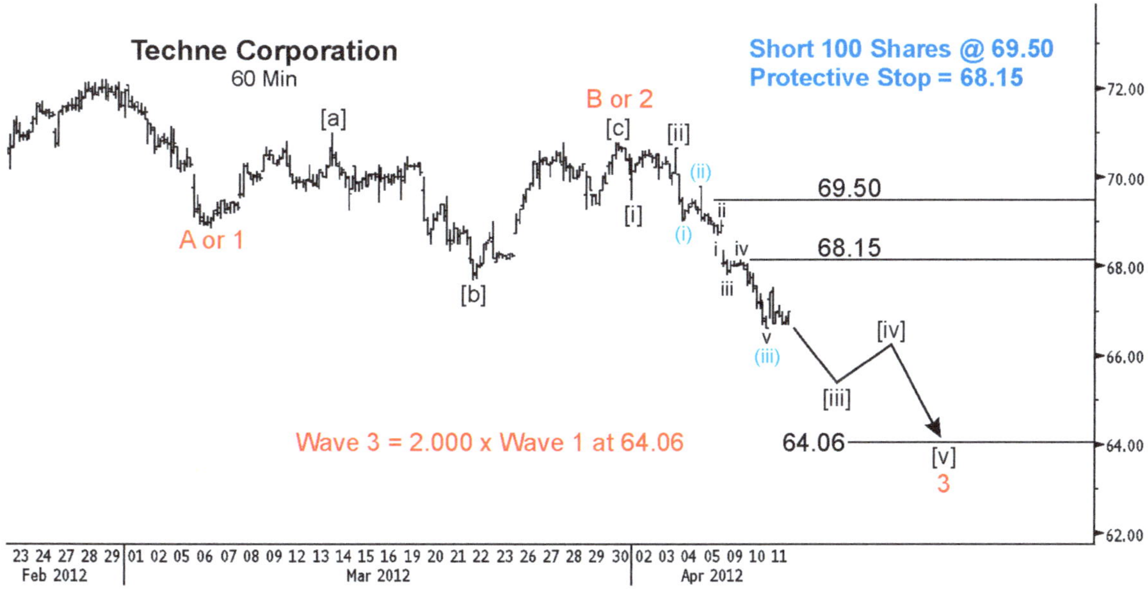

Figure 2.12

Chart reprinted with permission from Bloomberg. Copyright 2013 Bloomberg L.P. All rights reserved.

in a small profit. Moreover, the protective stop was far enough away from current trading that the odds of being stopped out prematurely on a rogue spike were low.

Brief review of risk management: Throughout this trading example, we have followed the principles of lessening risk, eliminating risk, and protecting open profits. When the position was initially triggered, our protective stop was 70.66. As prices pushed lower, we lowered it to breakeven. Following an additional decline in prices, we continued to incrementally lower the stop from our breakeven point of 69.50 to 69.03, then 68.15 (see Figure 2.12).

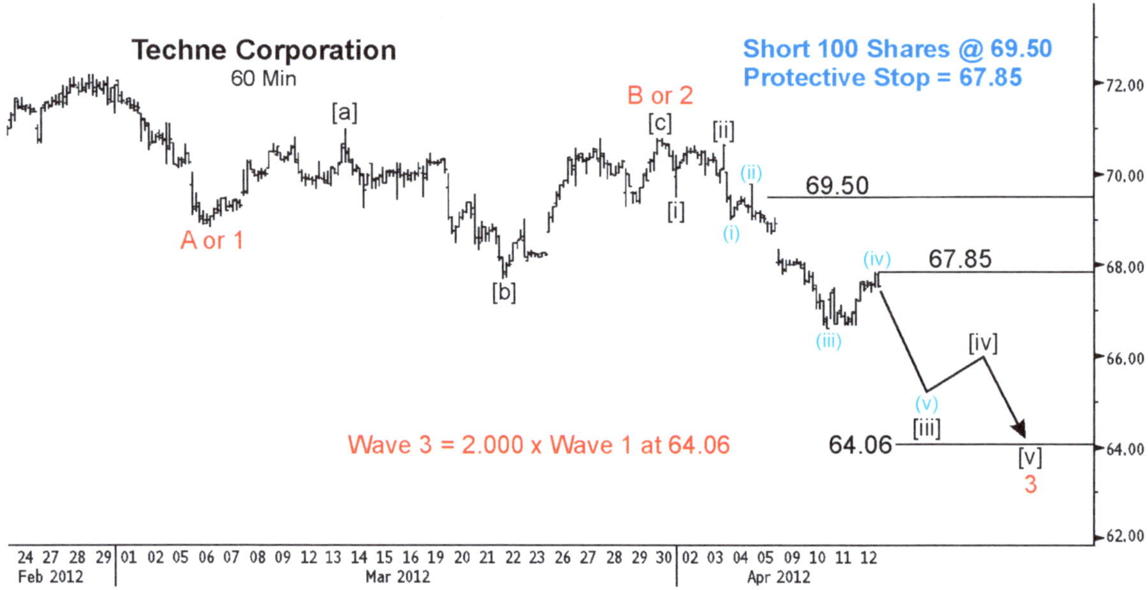

Figure 2.13

Chart reprinted with permission from Bloomberg. Copyright 2013 Bloomberg L.P. All rights reserved.

Smart Investor Tip

While an impulsive decline is unfolding, prior swing highs make suitable protective stops. From an Elliott wave perspective, these extremes tend to be second or fourth waves.

Here's a tip on how to set your protective stops: While an impulsive decline is unfolding, as seen in TECH, prior swing highs make suitable protective stops. From an Elliott wave perspective, these extremes tend to be second or fourth waves. At this point in the trading example, we have now lowered the protective stop to 67.85, a small fourth-wave extreme (see Figure 2.13).

The small three-wave advance from 66.60 to 67.85 was clearly a fourth wave in TECH. The only question was at what degree. As you can see, I identified the move up as wave (iv) of wave [iii]. I could have, instead, relabeled wave (iii) as a larger degree wave [iii] and then labeled the fourth wave as a larger degree wave [iv]. Either way, the message remained the same: Any

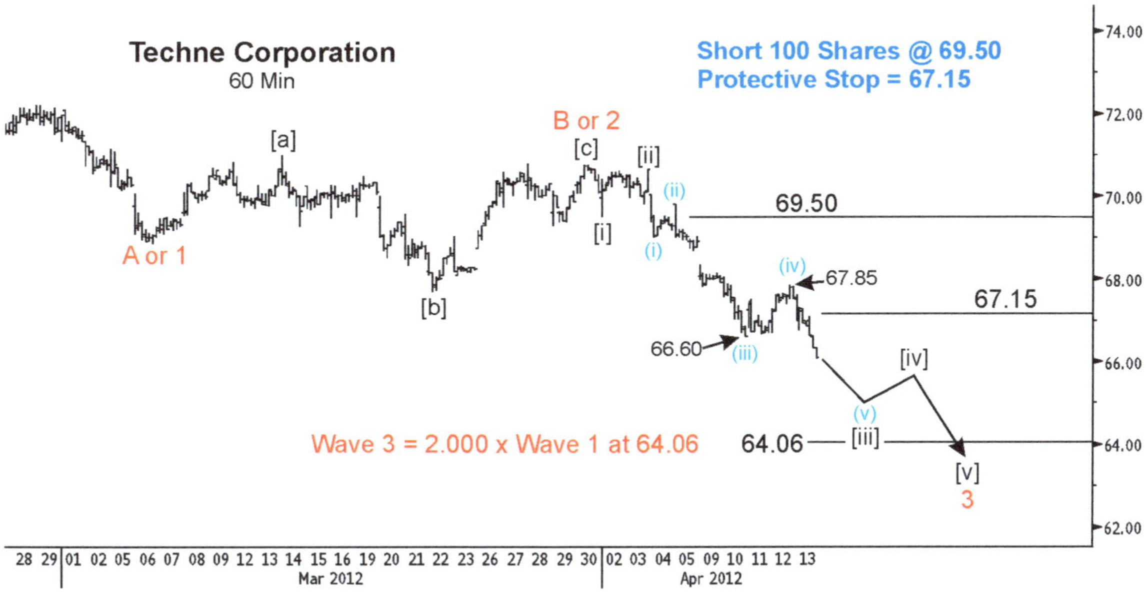

Figure 2.14

Chart reprinted with permission from Bloomberg. Copyright 2013 Bloomberg L.P. All rights reserved.

trading below 66.60 would be a fifth wave. It could have been wave (v) of [iii] or wave [v] of 3. It really didn't matter. The sell-off represented a fifth wave of one degree or another, which meant that the downside was limited and that the next significant move would be up. Thus, I lowered the protective stop on this position to 67.15, another swing high (see Figure 2.14).

In early trading on April 17, prices hit the protective stop at 67.15 (see Figure 2.15). In the days that followed, TECH continued moving lower to below 65.00 a share before it staged a sizable reversal. The profit for this real-time trading example was $235.00, or a return of 3.38 percent. Although it may not seem like it was a spectacular trade, it was profitable and it did yield a 3.38 percent return over a seven-day period.

Remember, too, that we never confidently determined whether the April 2012 sell-off in TECH was a C-wave or a third-wave decline. The position was closed before it became essential to answer the question. And yet we could still trade the chart.

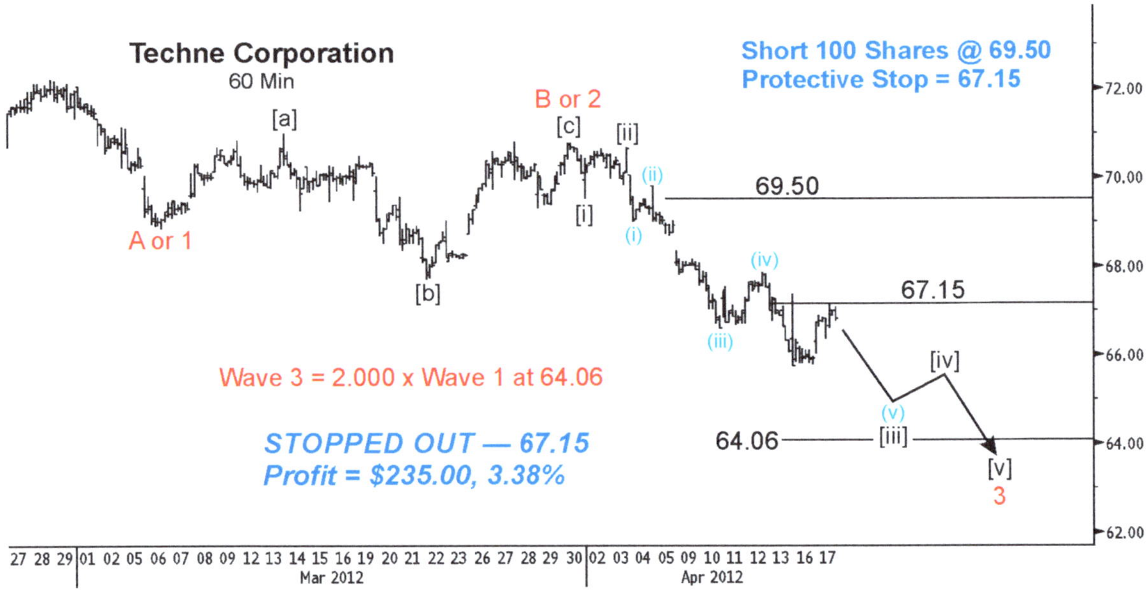

Figure 2.15
Chart reprinted with permission from Bloomberg. Copyright 2013 Bloomberg L.P. All rights reserved.

Overall, this trade shows the beauty of the Wave Principle and the incredible power of one very simple question: "Do I see a wave pattern I recognize?" Because I could answer yes to this question, I was able to formulate a trading plan that ultimately proved to be profitable.

Might I have done a better job trading this position, perhaps by getting in earlier or exiting the position when TECH fell below 65.00? Did I trail my protective stops correctly or was I too aggressive or too conservative? My simple answer remains true: There is no right or wrong way to trade—only *your* way of trading. Bottom line, this was a profitable position that was vulnerable to a loss for only two trading days before we could implement a break-even stop.

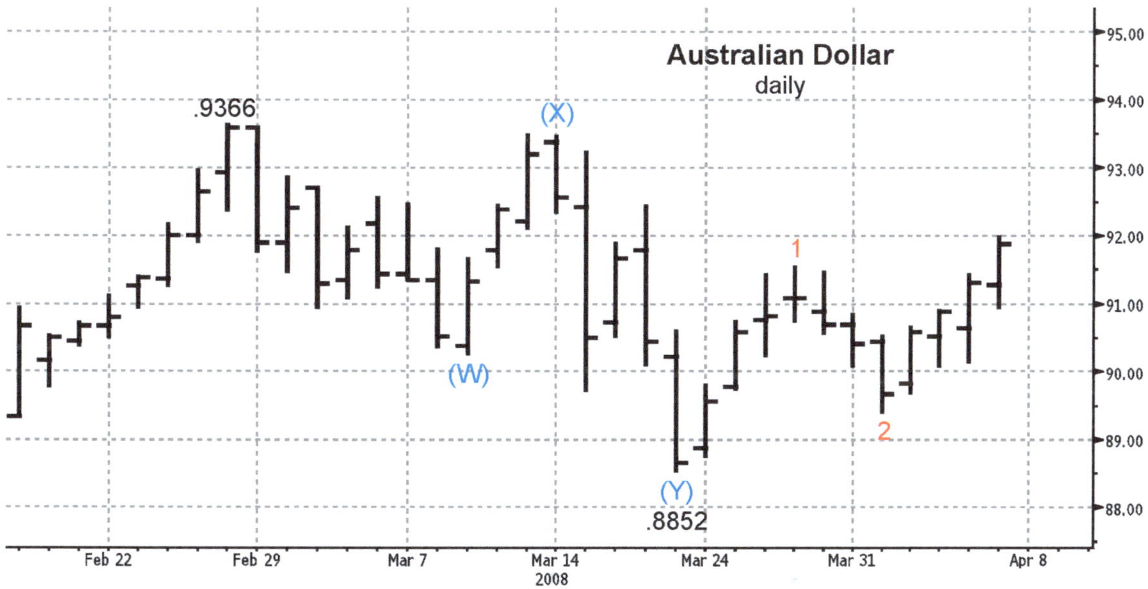

Figure 2.16

Trading a Double Zigzag in the Australian Dollar

Searching for the current dominant trend in a stock or, in this case, a foreign exchange market, is a sure way to feel more confident about riding a trade for a relatively long time. Figure 2.16 gives an example, using the price chart of the Australian dollar.

1. Analyzing the Price Charts

In early April 2008, it was clear that the decline from the February high to the March low in the Australian dollar was a three-wave move (see Figure 2.16). Upon closer examination, each individual wave within this sell-off subdivided into three smaller waves. Therefore, this structure could be identified as a double zigzag rather than

Figure 2.17

Chart reprinted with permission from Bloomberg. Copyright 2013 Bloomberg L.P. All rights reserved.

a simple zigzag, and it could be labeled (W)-(X)-(Y), where (W) and (Y) are three-wave zigzags labeled A-B-C. The countertrend wave (X) also comprises three waves.

This corrective pattern argued that the larger trend was still up in the Australian dollar and that the March advance would persist beyond the February 2008 high of .9366.

2. Formulating a Trading Plan

The trading plan, based on the double-zigzag interpretation, was to buy June 2008 Australian dollar futures at .9180 with an initial protective stop at .9080 (see Figure 2.17). Furthermore, the upside objective for the anticipated price advance was .9430, the level at which wave 3 would equal a 1.618 multiple of wave 1. This trade was immediately taken because the bulls were in control of the market on April 7, 2008, as expressed by the close of the price bar, which was at the high of the day. In fact, they had been in control for four days.

An important point: Even though I labeled the March 2008 advance as a 1–2, that does not mean that it actually was a wave 1 and a wave 2. Remember that the only thing that can confirm a wave count is price action. Until it occurs, even the best labeling, no matter how probable, may not turn out to be the correct labeling. For example, it would have been possible to label the March 2008 advance as an A–B–C of perhaps a larger flat or complex correction. However, right or wrong, at some point you have to evaluate the probabilities, assess the risk-reward ratio, follow your money management rules, and take the trade.

3. Managing the Trade

In the days that followed the opening of this position, the Australian dollar climbed as high as .9267 (see Figure 2.18). While this move up supported my bullish expectations, prices did not

Figure 2.18

Chart reprinted with permission from Bloomberg. Copyright 2013 Bloomberg L.P. All rights reserved.

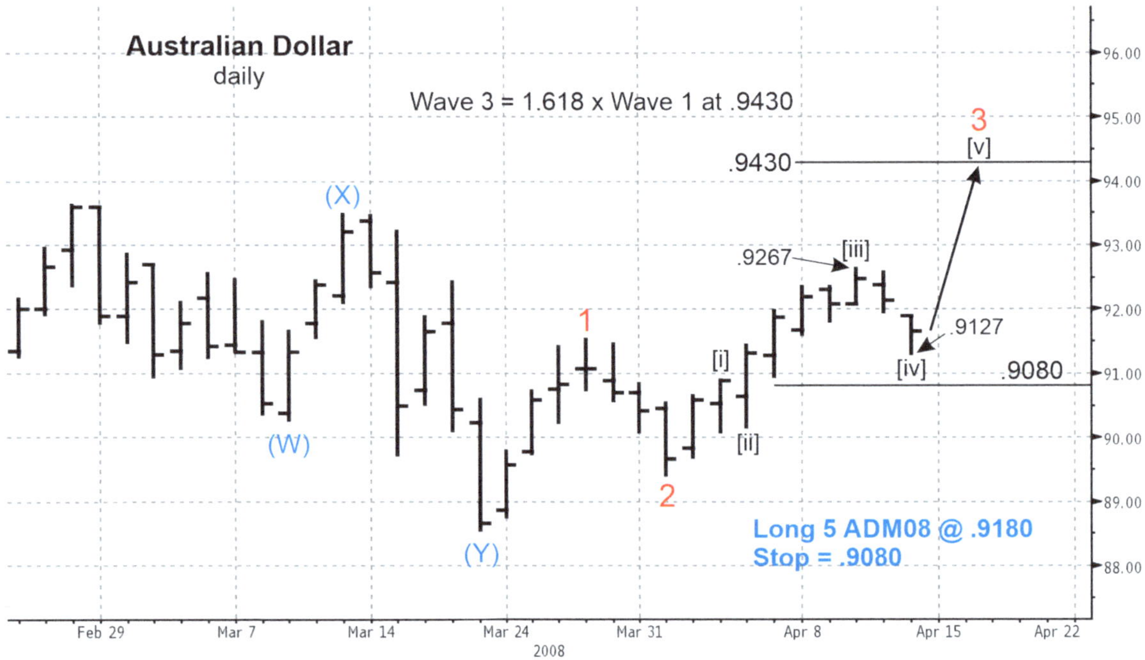

Figure 2.19

Chart reprinted with permission from Bloomberg. Copyright 2013 Bloomberg L.P. All rights reserved.

travel high enough to allow me to raise or tighten the protective stops. Thus, the initial protective stop remained at .9080.

Then price action created what appeared to be a small wave 3 peak at .9267 (see Figure 2.19). In the days that followed, the Australian dollar fell 140 pips to .9127. This decline of 1.51 percent in two days was a decent-sized move, and it initially supported my bearish interpretation of the March advance. But what prevented me from adopting a bearish assessment on April 14, following the 140 pip sell-off, was the close of the daily price bar. It was .9166, basis the June contract.

By itself, this information seemed to be unimportant. But combined with the high and low

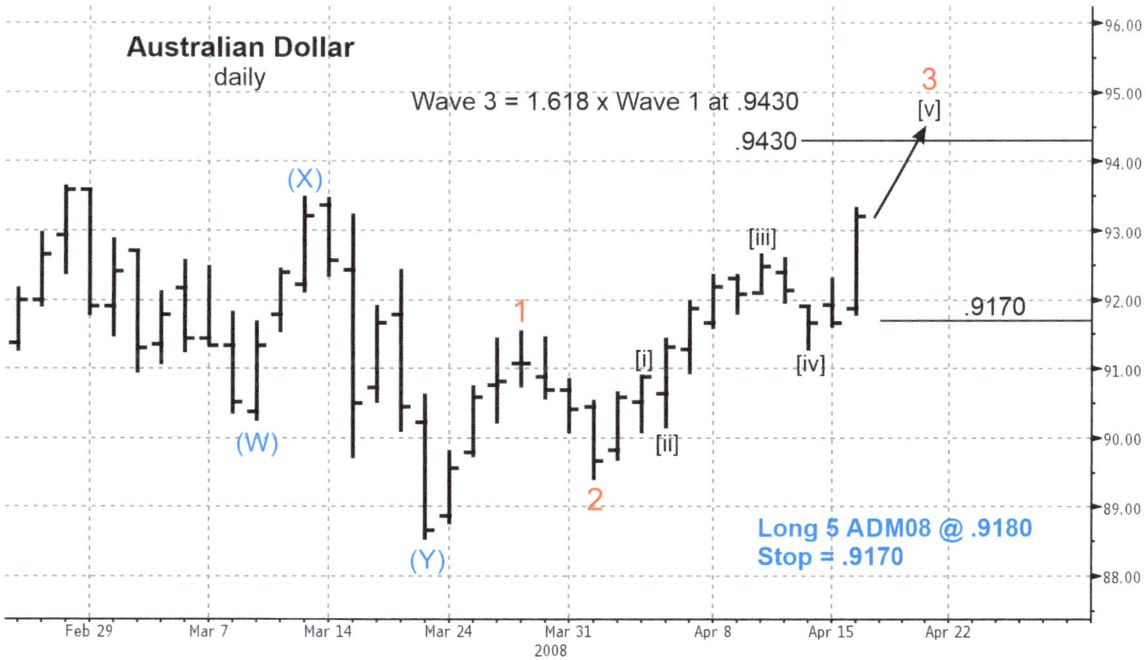

Figure 2.20

of the day, which were .9192 and .9127, I could see that the daily close was above the 50 percent retracement of the daily trading range. If the bears were indeed in control of the market on April 14, then the close of the day would most likely have been in the bottom 20 percent or even 10 percent of the daily range, not above 50 percent.

This individual price bar analysis was proved correct on April 16 when the Aussie dollar rallied to .9334. In response to this not-so-surprising advance, I raised the protective stop to .9170, making the risk on this trade 10 pips, or $100.00 per contract (see Figure 2.20).

Following the strong daily close at .9359 on April 21, I raised the protective stop again to

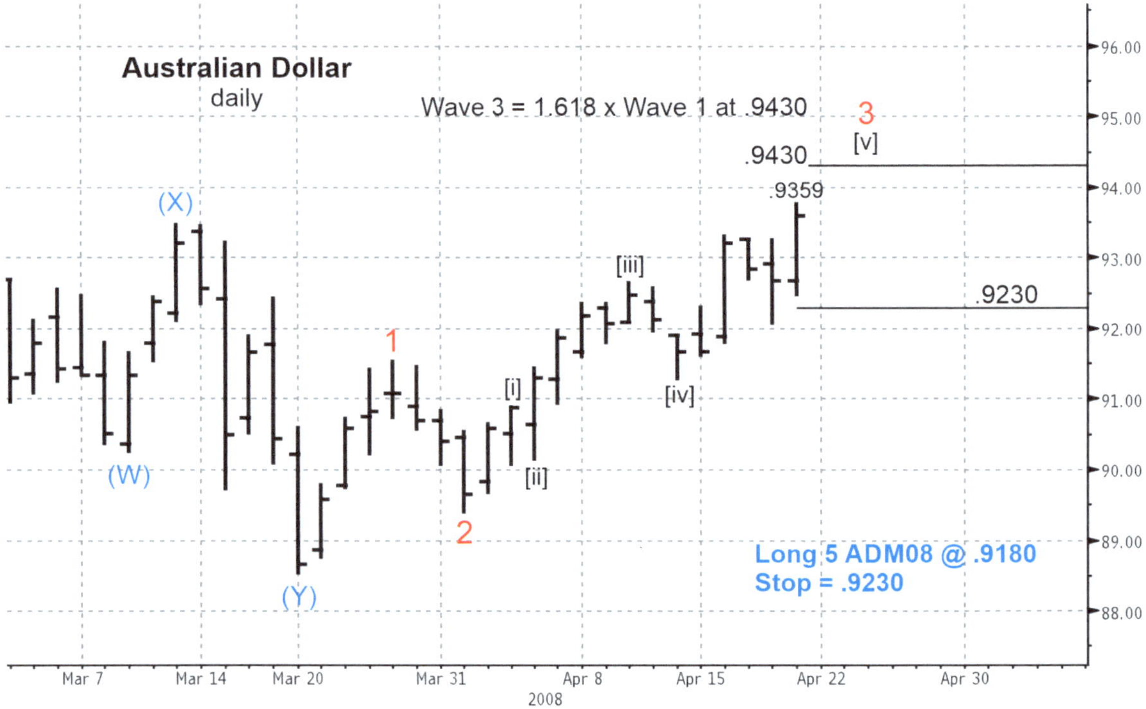

Figure 2.21
Chart reprinted with permission from Bloomberg.

.9230 and locked in a small profit on this position (see Figure 2.21).

In the days that followed, the Aussie dollar achieved the .9430 objective, and on April 24, the position was stopped out at .9354, for a profit of $1,740.00 per contract (see Figure 2.22). On the day that the Australian dollar hit the .9354 target, the close was .9432. The midpoint of that day's trading range was .9435. Again, if the Aussie dollar bulls had still had convincing control in this market, odds favored a substantially higher daily close on April 23.

Two interesting points about this example: the importance of single-bar price analysis and the absence of price charts on different time frames.

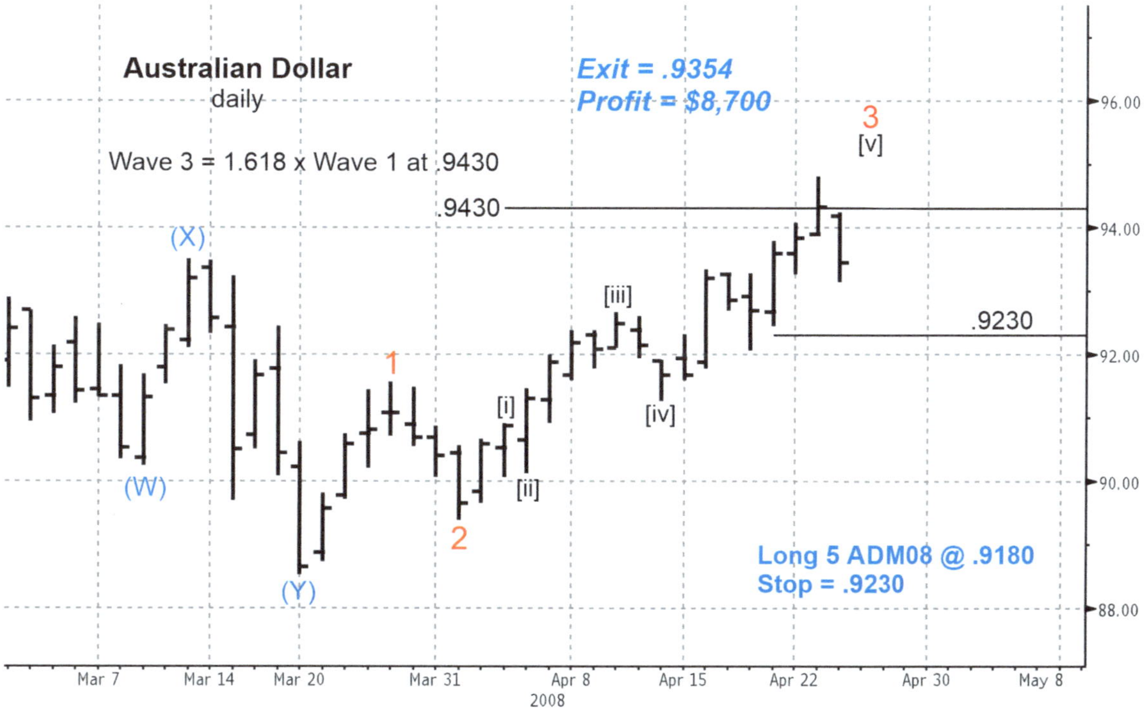

Figure 2.22

If you do not already perform single- or multi-bar price analysis, I strongly recommend that you start doing so. Understanding the relevance of the relationships among the open, high, low, and close are an integral part of technical analysis.

Also, I did not see the need to refer to intraday and longer-term price charts during this trade because the wave patterns on the daily level were so clear from start to finish. Even so, I do recommend examining multiple time frames when employing the Wave Principle. As a rule of thumb, I use weekly price charts to determine trend, daily time frames to identify wave patterns, and intraday price charts to finesse entry and exit points of trades.

Smart Investor Tip

Use weekly price charts to determine trend, daily time frames to identify wave patterns, and intra-day price charts to finesse entry and exit points of trades.

Trading a Zigzag in Silver

In this segment, I will describe some silver trades I made when I traded for a living from 1998 to 2002. I had subscribed to Elliott Wave International's publications for more than a decade, so I was comfortable doing my own Elliott wave analysis. This price chart for silver came from EWI in January 1998, and it indicated a bullish opportunity in silver (see Figure 2.23) because the developing pattern was best interpreted as an impulse wave. As you will see, I was able to use information from a zigzag pattern in silver to help me with the trade.

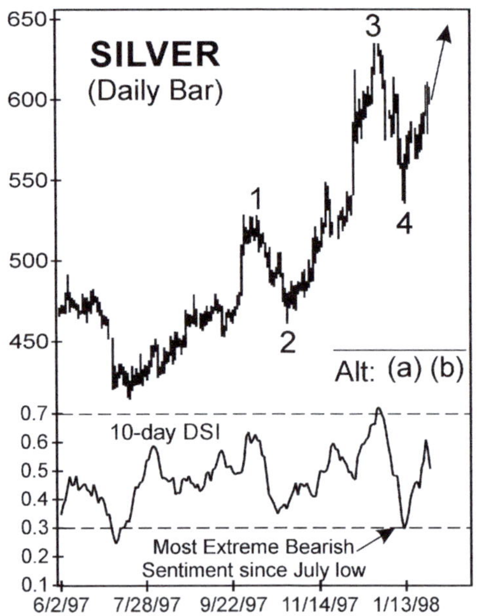

Figure 2.23
Source: The Elliott Wave Theorist, February 1998; DSI courtesy www.trade-futures.com.

KEY POINT

On these silver charts, prices are displayed in terms of total cents per ounce rather than dollars and cents per ounce. Divide any num-ber by 100 to get the dollar figure you're probably most familiar with.

1. Analyzing the Price Charts

At the close on January 29, 1998, wave 5 of an impulse wave seemed to be in progress. I was bullish on silver at the time and planning to go long for that fifth wave up, so this chart gave me some confidence to carry on with that trading plan. On the bottom of the chart, you see the 10-Day Daily Sentiment Index, an indicator I use to look for extremes in market sentiment. (We discuss using Elliott wave analysis with other indicators in Chapter 6.)

Before taking a trading position, I prefer to look at the big picture first. So, on February 2, I pulled up this monthly continuation chart in silver futures (see Figure 2.24).

I planned to trade the March 1998 silver futures contract, which closed at 625.0 on February 2. Over the longer term, silver appeared to be tracing out a double three correction, consisting of an (A)-(B)-(C) zigzag for wave [W], an (A)-(B)-(C) flat for wave [X], and an (A)-(B)-(C) expanded flat for wave [Y].

The important information was that, within wave [Y], wave (C) was still unfolding in the form of an impulse wave (as shown in Figure 2.23), with wave 5 in its early stages. Since I was looking for some potential target points, I noticed that wave [Y] equaled wave [W] at 649.0, which was not too far from that day's close at the 625 level.

Silver was volatile at the time, so a target zone only 24 points away was not useful. Next, I checked some of the Fibonacci relationships on

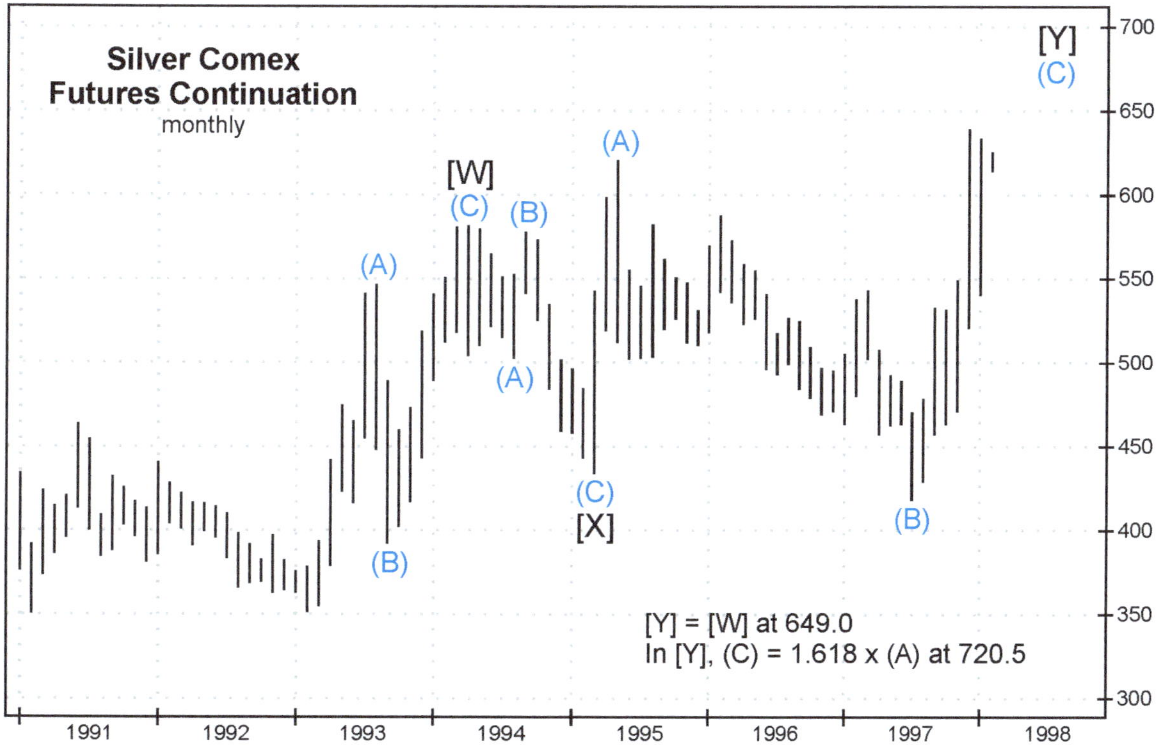

Figure 2.24
Source: Data courtesy TradeNavigator.com.

the chart. Within wave [Y], wave (C) would equal 1.618 times the length of wave (A) at 720.5. That calculation gave me 720.5 as one potential price target for the end of wave 5 of wave (C) of wave [Y].

I then looked at the wave (C) impulse on the daily continuation chart in silver futures to nail down some more price targets for the wave 5 top by doing some Elliott wave analysis. I wanted to see how much progress wave 5 had made and whether there was potential for further upside.

I drew a trend channel, first by connecting the termination points of waves 2 and 4 and then by drawing a parallel line from the termination point

KEY POINT

Within an expanded flat, it is common for wave C to equal 1.618 times the length of wave A.

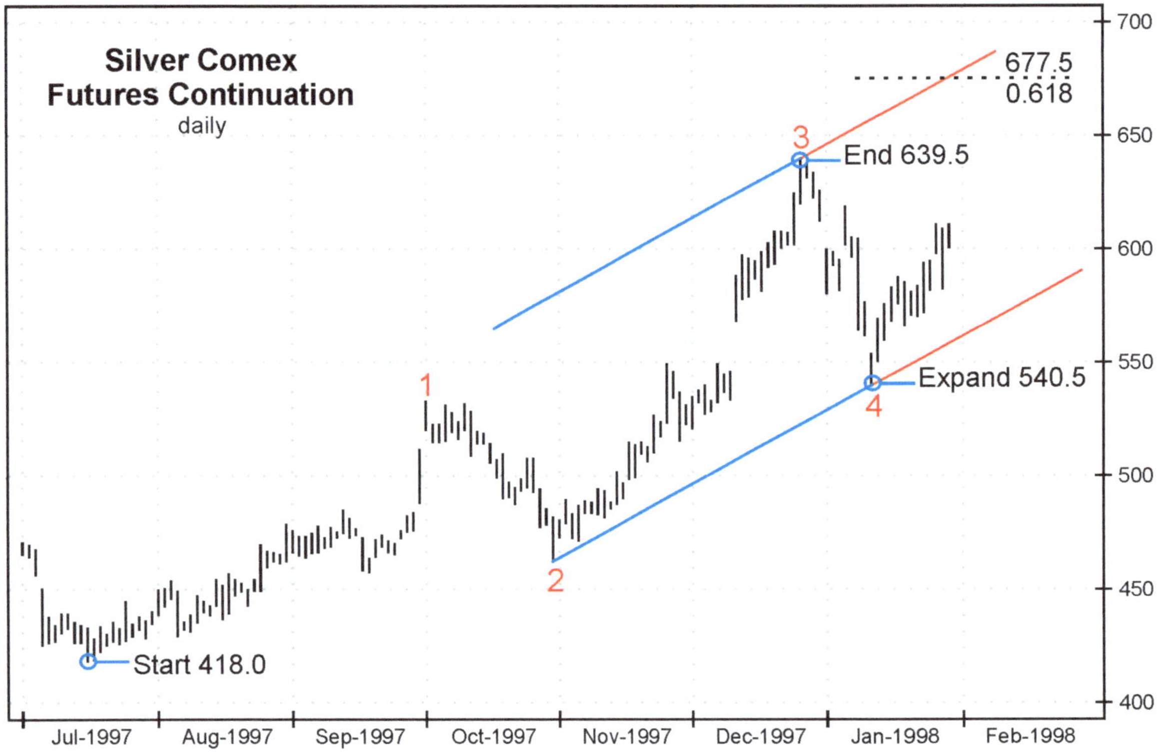

Figure 2.25
Source: Data courtesy TradeNavigator.com.

DEFINITION:
Fibonacci Expansion

A Fibonacci expansion or multiple is the relationship between the net distance traveled of waves 1 through 3 and the length of wave 5.

of wave 3 (see Figure 2.25). Using a **Fibonacci expansion** guideline, I calculated the net distance traveled of waves 1 through 3, multiplied it by .618, and added that number to the end of wave 4. That calculation resulted in a price estimate of 677.5 for the end of wave 5. If wave 5 did not rise quickly, 677.5 would fall somewhere within the middle of the trend channel. Therefore, I decided that 677.5 was a good short-term target, with 720.5 a good long-term target.

2. Formulating a Trading Plan

Next came figuring out entry and exit points. I often follow a market using a 15-minute bar chart (see Figure 2.26) to determine entry and exit

Figure 2.26
Source: Data courtesy TradeNavigator.com.

points. I had been monitoring this price action on February 3 with the idea of going long but hadn't yet taken a position in silver.

Even though I wasn't exactly sure of the internal wave count for wave 5, I did not think that it was over yet, because silver still hadn't reached the likely price targets of 677.5 or 720.5. Starting from the low at the end of the day on January 30, I identified a completed impulse wave to the upside at lower degree followed by a correction that looked much like a completed zig-zag (see Figure 2.26). It seemed that this structure was still part of wave 5. At this point, the high was 650.0, and silver was currently trading at about 635.0.

A zigzag is a corrective wave pattern and thereby merely interrupts the main trend, which in this situation was to the upside. Therefore, after completion of the zigzag, it looked like silver's next move should be another impulse wave to the upside, still within wave 5.

If there were evidence that wave (v) of the impulse wave had ended, it would be important, because the subsequent down move would have to be a correction—a zigzag that should be followed by another impulse wave to higher price levels. In other words, a trade setup.

Yes, there was evidence. The impulse wave adhered well to its trend channel, with wave (v) reaching the top of the channel. At 653.0, only three cents beyond the high, wave (v) equaled the net distance traveled of waves (i) through (iii) times a Fibonacci .618 (see Figure 2.27).

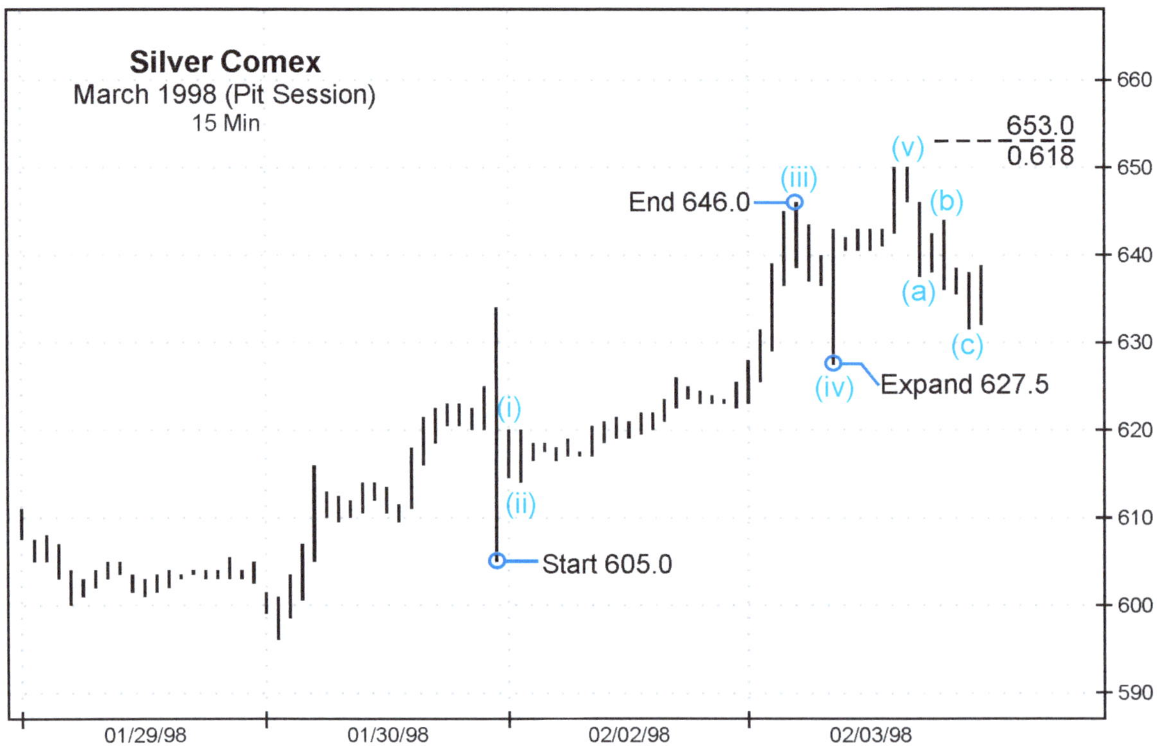

Figure 2.27
Source: Data courtesy TradeNavigator.com.

Figure 2.28
Source: Data courtesy TradeNavigator.com.

There was more supporting evidence: As shown in the next chart (see Figure 2.28), if wave (v) had ended at 650.0, then the end of wave (iv) would have divided the entire price range of the impulse wave into two equal parts, which is a Fibonacci relationship in completed impulse waves called a Fibonacci price divider. More commonly, fourth waves divide the entire price range into the **Golden Section**.

Other evidence also supported the idea that the zigzag on the 15-minute chart was complete. As

DEFINITION:
Golden Section

The beginning or end of wave 4 will often divide an impulse wave into the Golden Section (.618 and .382) or two equal parts. This relationship is called a Fibonacci price divider.

Figure 2.29
Source: Data courtesy TradeNavigator.com.

KEY POINT

The most common length relationship for wave C of a zigzag is C equals A.

shown in Figure 2.29, the zigzag adhered well to its own trend channel and achieved a nearly exact .382 retracement of the impulse wave. Also, wave (c) had almost reached the lower trendline of the channel.

In addition, Figure 2.30 shows that wave (c) equaled wave (a) at 631.5, which so far was the low for the zigzag.

Looking at the chart in Figure 2.29, silver appeared to have broken the upper trendline of the

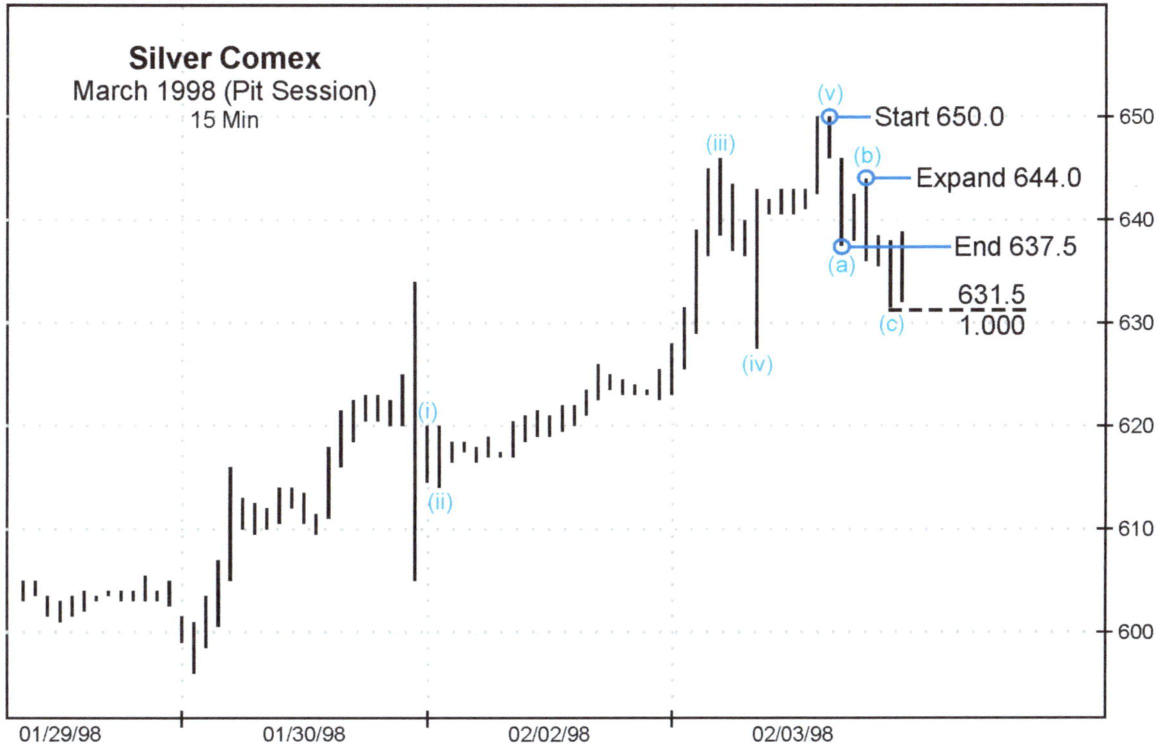

Figure 2.30
Source: Data courtesy TradeNavigator.com.

channel formed by the zigzag, although not by much. Even so, the evidence seemed clear that the zigzag was complete and that the next impulse wave to the upside had begun. It was time to go long. I called my broker to put in an order to go long silver, but before my broker picked up the line, this news suddenly came across the tape:

NEWS ALERT: "Warren Buffett, on behalf of Berkshire Hathaway, has purchased 129.7 million ounces of silver from July 1997 to January 1998."

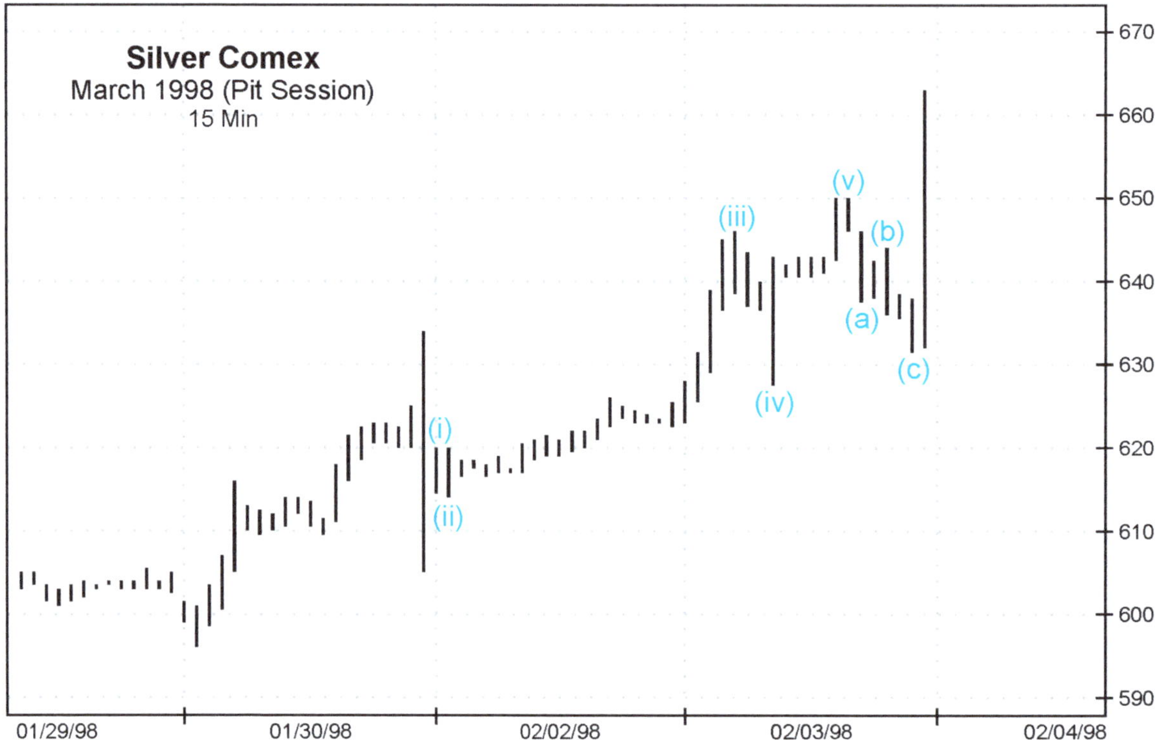

Figure 2.31
Source: Data courtesy TradeNavigator.com.

Figure 2.31 shows you the move I then witnessed.

It just blasted up like a rocket to a high of 663.0 and closed at 661.5. Usually, blow-offs like this occur near the end of a move—not the middle or the beginning. So then I thought, "Now what am I going to do? Still go long, even though everyone will pile into this market based on Buffett's purchases?"

Obviously, the Buffett purchase news threw a wrench into my whole strategy because I didn't want to follow the crowd. On the other hand, my Elliott wave analysis told me that silver should go higher, regardless of the news buyers. So here was my quandary: Should I be a contrarian and just stay out, or stick with my strategy despite the news? In any case, if I were going to go long, should I wait for a pullback, or should I just dive in?

In retrospect, once I had identified waves (a) and (b) of the zigzag, I should have drawn the trend channel, before waiting for wave (c) to finish. Before the news announcement, I should have put in an order with my broker to buy March silver "on a stop" at a price level just beyond the top of the channel. Along with that order, I could have included my protective stop. Although it was a fast-moving market, I probably would have been filled.

At the time, though, Figure 2.32 shows what the daily silver chart looked like at the end of the day on February 3.

Figure 2.32
Source: Data courtesy TradeNavigator.com.

You can see that silver was closing in on the 677.5 level, near the top of the trend channel. Remember, though, that there was the other target at the 720.5 level, where wave (C) equaled 1.618 times the length of wave (A). I concluded that although silver might be nearing the end of this bull market, it still had more upside. Maybe that news was a sign that prices were getting *close* to the top, even though they weren't necessarily *at* the top. I still planned to go long the next day. The key here was to stick with my analysis of a higher price target at 720.5 and not use the news as a contrarian indicator to get out of the market—at least, not yet.

Figure 2.33 shows what happened as the trading day opened on February 4.

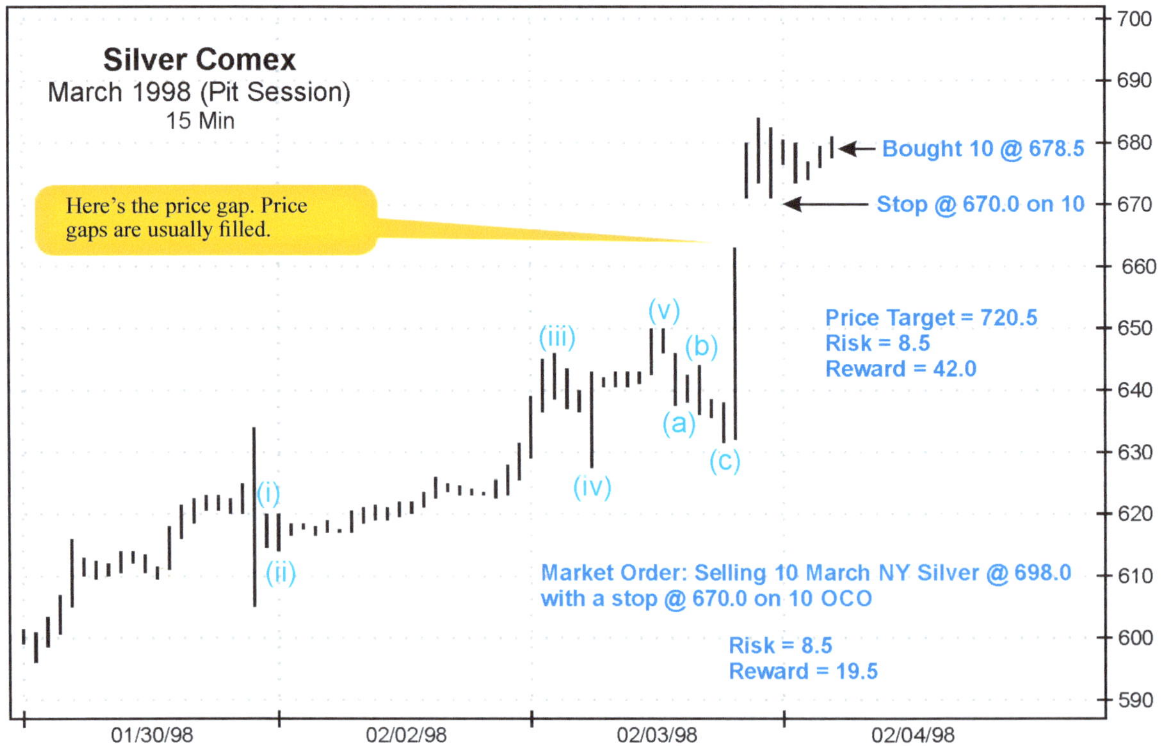

Figure 2.33
Source: Data courtesy TradeNavigator.com.

It gapped up! It hit 684.0 before it started to consolidate. I decided to wait for a pullback that might close the gap. But after an hour and a half, still there was no pullback. This sideways move began to look more like a corrective structure rather than a new trend to the downside. So I bought 10 March contracts at 678.5.

I planned to trade about 40 contracts, scaling into my position by doing smaller amounts at different price levels. My price target was 720.5, and I put my stop at 670.0, which was just below the end of the gap at 671.0. I decided that if it were to break 671.0, sellers would probably take it down to where the gap started at 663.0. That was a loss I did not want to endure.

3. Managing the Trade

Initially, my ratio of reward to risk was about 5:1, or 42 cents reward versus 8.5 cents risk. But I changed that risk-reward profile by selling 10 March silver contracts at 698.0, with a stop at 670.0 on 10 contracts, OCO (One Cancels the Other). I often use this strategy of putting a protective stop and profit-taking order at the same time, especially if I don't feel comfortable holding a position over-night. Why did I pick 698.0 to take a profit? Well, at that time, although I was totally converted to Elliott wave analysis, I still suffered from a few market myths that I had yet to purge from my trader's psyche. One of those myths was that whenever the market reaches a new, big round figure—or "handle," as they're sometimes called—there's usually resistance, and prices bounce off that level. (If it's a downtrend, support would appear at a new, big figure.) As we'll see later, that myth cost me some additional profits. In this case, we were going from the $6 per ounce range up to $7 per ounce. Although one of my price targets was $7.20, I did not expect silver to go through $7 level so soon—at least not on this particular day. In the meantime, I did want to add to my position, especially if we got a pullback.

As shown in Figure 2.34, silver moved higher.

When silver got as high as 687.0, I decided that it wasn't pulling back, because it had had plenty of time to fill the gap, but it hadn't filled it. So, I bought 2 March contracts at 682.5. I was long 12 contracts at an average price of 679.17. As the market moved higher, I raised my stop.

Talk about a bull market; silver shot right through 700.0. So much for resistance at new big figures!

It reached a high of 708.0. I had certainly underestimated the strength of the market, at least for the remaining hour of that day. In any case, my market order was filled at 698.0, resulting in a profit of $11,300 (see Figure 2.35).

This last chart in Figure 2.36 shows the aftermath of the impulse wave in silver. Wave 5 achieved a throw-over and peaked at 740.0 in the March contract on February 5, about 20 cents above my target of 720.5.

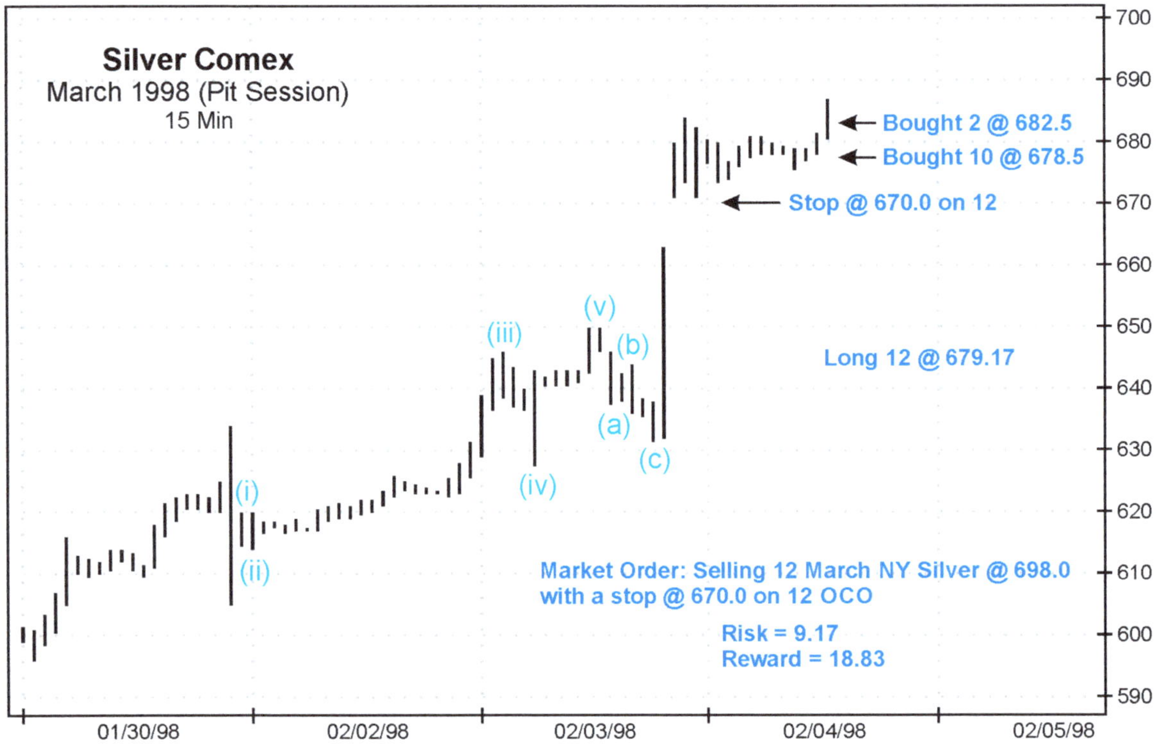

Figure 2.34
Source: Data courtesy TradeNavigator.com.

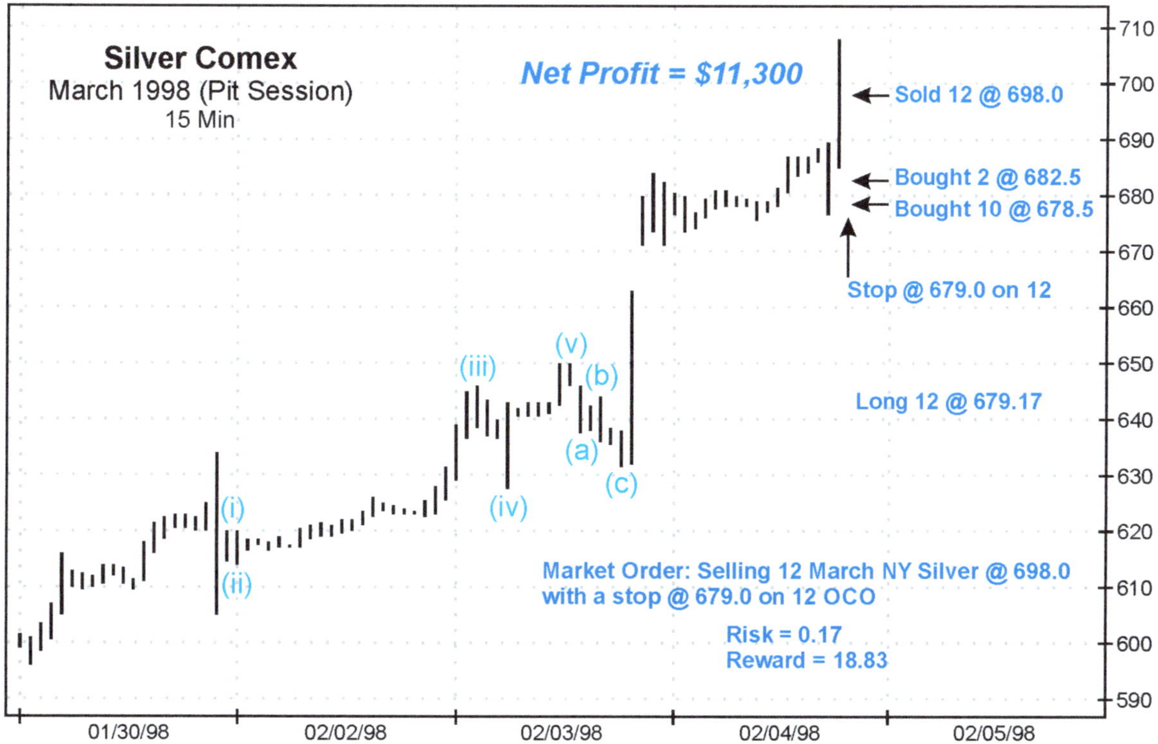

Figure 2.35

Source: Data courtesy TradeNavigator.com

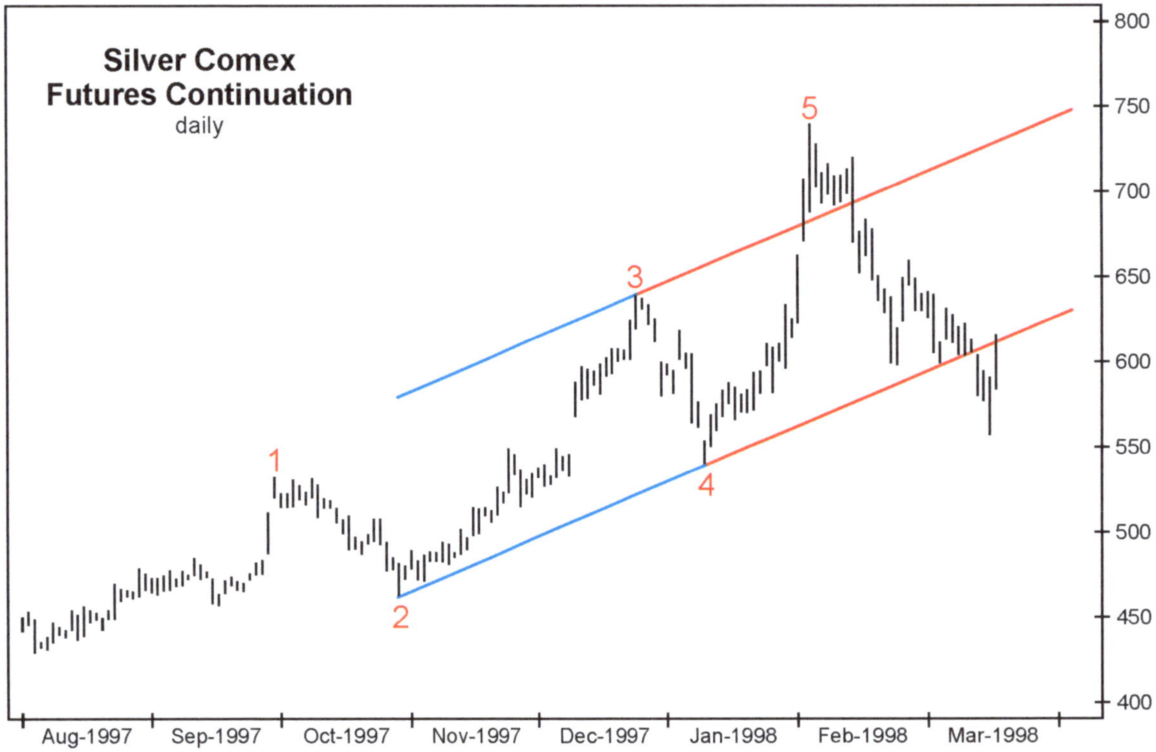

Figure 2.36
Source: Data courtesy TradeNavigator.com

Then silver reversed and fell back through the bottom of the channel. Silver continued to decline all the way to 401.5 in 2001.

Trading lesson learned: Most traders react to news, but they would be better off working with the wave pattern and completely ignoring the news. That's because newsworthy events normally lag market trends as opposed to leading them. The Warren Buffett buying news was not an indication of a new bull market in silver but rather a sign that the recent bull market in silver was approaching its end. The best source of information about the future path for silver was the Elliott Wave Principle, because of the way it depicts mass psychology, the true driver of financial trends. Crowd behavior results in *patterned* price movements. If you understand the pattern, you can predict the market.

As for the zigzag setup: The setup was there, but I was a tad late in taking advantage of it. Because of the news, that short delay cost me a much larger profit. I blame myself for poor execution rather than blaming Warren Buffett. After all, if it hadn't been for the conviction behind the herding mentality following that news, I might not have made money on those silver trades.

Elliott wave analysis provided me with an effective road map for the path of silver. Rather than getting caught up in the buying frenzy that followed the Warren Buffett news, I had already used wave analysis to estimate how far silver would go before making a major reversal. In other words, Elliott analysis helped me project the extent of the fifth wave's emotional euphoria. Many other traders at that time stayed long silver well past the peak and bailed out at lower prices, no doubt on bad news.

Trading a Combination in Robusta Coffee

As you may know from reading *Elliott Wave Principle* by A. J. Frost and Robert Prechter, corrections can occur in three forms, and these patterns and their variations can make entering a trade challenging. So far in this chapter, we've shown how Elliott wave analysis can help set up trades using some of the simpler corrective patterns. But what happens if the corrective pattern is more complicated? We call these kinds of patterns combinations, and they can turn a trader's dream situation into a nightmare. In this section, we will use a monthly chart from 1998 to 2006 of robusta coffee, based on the nearest futures contract (see Figure 2.37), to show how to cope with this type of pattern and how to take advantage of it.

1. Analyzing the Price Charts

Robusta coffee is traded on the Euronext exchange, and the minimum tick movement is $1.00 per ton. The unit trading size, or contract size, is five tons, so the minimum tick value is $5.00. I chose this monthly chart to show hypothetically how a trader could go about

KEY POINT

It's beneficial to start with the big picture and then work down to lower degrees for evidence to support your wave count before taking a position.

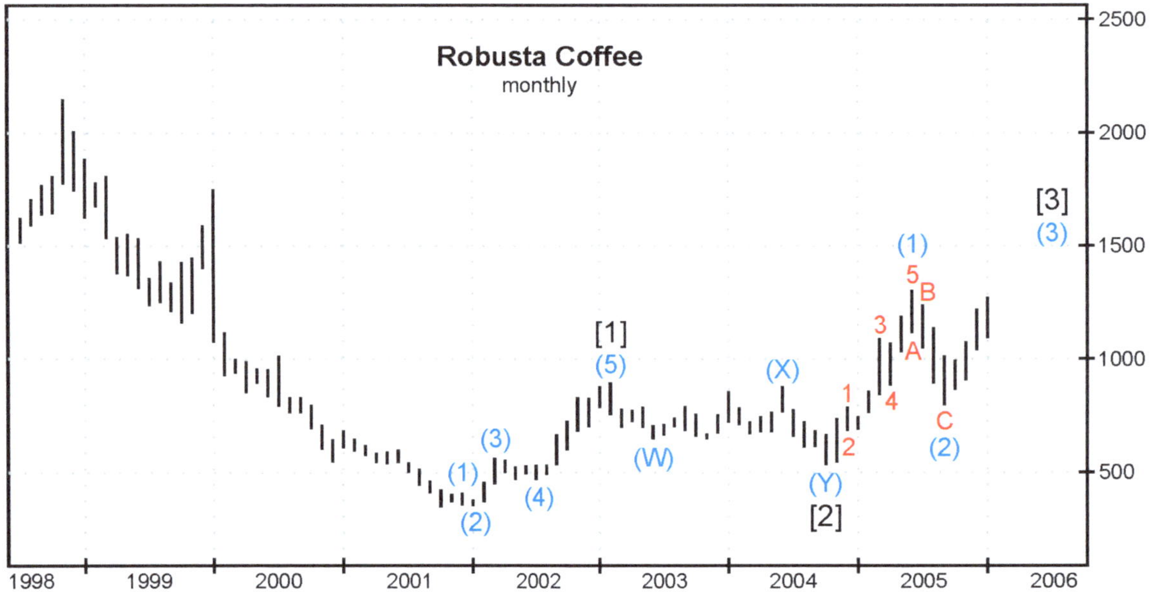

Figure 2.37

Source: Data courtesy TradeNavigator.com.

trading a combination. We're going to start trading on the current bar, January 2006. On the daily chart it is January 19. First, though, we will look at the big picture and then work down to lower degrees to find evidence that supports the wave count before we take a position.

It's best to start looking for a recognizable wave pattern at a major low or a major high. On this chart, we can start counting from the major bottom in late 2001 at 345. There's a completed Primary wave [1] impulse wave followed by a completed Primary wave [2] double zigzag. Now, prices are in Primary wave [3]. Within Primary wave [3], robusta coffee has completed Intermediate waves (1) and (2), and is now into Intermediate wave (3), or so it appears at this juncture. (As an alternate count, we can label this move as Primary waves [A], [B], and [C].)

Figure 2.38

Chart reprinted with permission from Bloomberg. Copyright 2013 Bloomberg L.P. All rights reserved.

Let's look at the weekly chart (see Figure 2.38). Wave (2) is an A-B-C zigzag, and prices have moved into Intermediate wave (3) of Primary wave [3]. I've been able to label Minor waves 1 and 2. We see five waves up for Minor wave 1, followed by an expanded flat for Minor wave 2. Now it looks like Minor wave 3 of Intermediate wave (3) has begun.

What does all this mean? If the wave labeling is correct, the next move after the zigzag correction should be a third of a third of a third wave. It will be a powerful move, and robusta coffee should really blast off from this level, additionally because expanded flats often precede strong moves. We would want to go long in anticipation of a huge move to the upside. But before going

Figure 2.39

Chart reprinted with permission from Bloomberg.

long, let's investigate more by blowing up the area of Intermediate waves (2) and (3) to make sure that our wave counts are correct.

This close-up view of Intermediate wave (2) in Figure 2.39 shows that this is indeed an A-B-C zigzag. Look at the subdivisions. Wave A is an impulse wave, wave B is a contracting triangle, and wave C is an impulse wave. Now, let's take a look at Minor wave 1 of Intermediate wave (3) to make sure it's an impulse wave (see Figure 2.40).

For Minor wave 1, we see a clear five waves up that form an impulse wave. I've labeled Min-

Figure 2.40

Chart reprinted with permission from Bloomberg. Copyright 2013 Bloomberg L.P. All rights reserved.

ute waves [i], [ii], [iii], [iv], and [v]. I was even able to discern the subdivisions of Minute wave [iii] and a nice triangle for wave [iv]. We can see an expanded flat [a]-[b]-[c] for Minor wave 2. It's a bit of a stretch, but possibly there's also a Minute wave [i], which starts Minor wave 3, and maybe a running flat for Minute wave [ii]. Since I don't have enough price action to be sure about it, I put a question mark there on the chart. In any case, this chart looks like an Elliottician's dream—a third of a third of a third of a third, dead ahead!

2. Formulating a Trading Plan

So, if we were trading this chart, we would go long on the most recent bar, which is January 19. The range of that bar is 1,247 to 1,210. Ideally, we would get long in the middle of that range at 1,229. For our protective stop, the .618 retracement of Minute wave [1] of Minor wave 3 should work. This wave went from 1,090 up to 1,233, and .618 of that distance results in an approximate price level of 1,145, so I would set the stop one tick below at 1,144. A move just beyond that point would not invalidate our wave count, but it would cast doubt on our chances of success.

The best practice is to set a stop just beyond the point where the wave count becomes invalid. At the lower degree, that point would be 1,090, which is the beginning of Minute wave [i]. However, setting stops using Elliott wave analysis is a function of both wave structure and personal risk tolerance. Setting a stop below 1,090 may be too large a loss for some people to incur. In that case, traders have to pick a level that they're more comfortable with.

Smart Investor Tip

The best practice is to set a stop just beyond the point where the wave count becomes invalid.

To establish a price target for Minor wave 3, we would take the length of Minor wave 1 and multiply that by 1.618. We could set a longer term price target based on the third wave at the next higher degree, but since there will be a number of corrections along the way, we would like to exit our position before the pullbacks occur and then get back in at a better level to optimize our gain. The net advance of a bull market (or net decline of a bear market) is never as large as the sum of the individual advances (or sum of the individual declines).

Smart Investor Tip

When analyzing their risk-reward ratio, most traders prefer that the possibility for reward outweighs the risk by a ratio of 3:1 or greater.

Minor wave 1 went from a low of 795 to a high of 1,220. The difference of 425 multiplied by 1.618 equals 688 points. We add 688 to the end of wave [c] of 2 at 1,090 (the beginning of Minor wave 3) to get a target of 1,778.

It is often difficult to estimate the end of wave 3 in the early stages of price action, and we could apply several different multiples. For impulse waves, the strongest Fibonacci projections pertain to the manner in which wave 4 (beginning or ending) divides an impulse wave, when either wave 1 or wave 3 is not extended. For example, wave 5 is often in Fibonacci proportion to the net distance traveled of waves 1 through 3, and the end of wave 4 will often divide the entire impulse wave into the Golden Section (.618 and .382). Therefore, the key is to monitor the subwaves within a third wave and apply these Fibonacci relationships. Our potential risk is 85 points and our potential reward is 549 points, which is a risk-reward ratio of about 6:1.

Figure 2.41 shows what happened up until March 15.

3. Managing the Trade

Rather than moving up, the market went down to 1,088, stopping out the trade at 1,144 for a loss of 85 points. This trade definitely did not go the

Figure 2.41

Chart reprinted with permission from Bloomberg. Copyright 2013 Bloomberg L.P. All rights reserved.

way we planned. It first looked like a sure thing, a "no-brainer." Apparently, it wasn't. The wave count could still be (1)- (2), 1-2, where Minor wave 2 is strung out over time as an expanded flat, but our original wave count called for an immediate acceleration upward in an extended wave. In the alternate scenario, a more strung-out Minor wave 2 expanded flat would represent wave A of wave 2, followed by wave B to a new high, followed by wave C down to 1,088. However, within a flat, wave A is normally not a flat.

Were there any warning signs that January 19 was not the best time to go long in this market? Let's go back and look at Figure 2.38 . Yes, there were signs that wave (2) was not yet over. The slope of wave (2) was steeper than that of wave (1).

Smart Investor Tip

Many times the direction of a trade is correct but not the timing. This requires patience and perseverance. Sometimes I have to trade a scenario two to three times before I time it right.

Figure 2.42
Chart reprinted with permission from Bloomberg. Copyright 2013 Bloomberg L.P. All rights reserved.

Normally, second waves are less steep than first waves. Our wave count of multiple overlapping 1-2s implied an extended Intermediate wave (3) and Primary wave [3]. An extension's actionary waves are usually longer than the non-extended actionary waves at the next higher degree. But Minor wave 1 of Intermediate wave (3) was shorter than Intermediate wave (1).

In any case, what's important now is to reassess the best wave count, given the most recent price action.

Let's look again at the weekly chart in Figure 2.42.

Figure 2.43

From the 1,306 high, prices moved in three waves down to 795, followed by three waves up to 1,308. Both three-wave structures appear to be zigzags, based on the internal wave counts shown in the previous charts. After 1,308, we see a move to the downside that breaks the previous uptrend. Figure 2.43 displays a better wave count.

Wave (2) is possibly unfolding as a flat, which is a 3-3-5 structure. Waves A and B are zigzags. Within wave B, Minute wave [c] is

Figure 2.44

probably an ending diagonal. If that's so, it's reasonable to expect a five-wave move down to about 795 for wave C. Does this mean it's time to go short for wave C down? No, it's best to do nothing yet and just wait, because there are other possible wave counts. We have to watch the price action to see if this pattern could be a double three combination (W-X-Y) as shown in Figure 2.44.

If waves W and X are zigzags, then wave Y could unfold as a flat or a triangle. Wave Y could not be a zigzag, though, because in a double zig-

Figure 2.45
Chart reprinted with permission from Bloomberg. Copyright 2013 Bloomberg L.P. All rights reserved.

zag, wave X cannot go beyond the start of wave W. Let's move forward a few days to see what happens in the market.

It is now June 2, and this market doesn't seem to be going anywhere. It's meandering sideways (see Figure 2.45).

Here's a question: From the 1,306 high, could this still be a flat for wave (2) per Figure 2.43? That's doubtful, because from the 1,308 high, there's no clear five-wave move down yet for wave C; only three waves down. More important, in a flat, wave C usually has a steeper

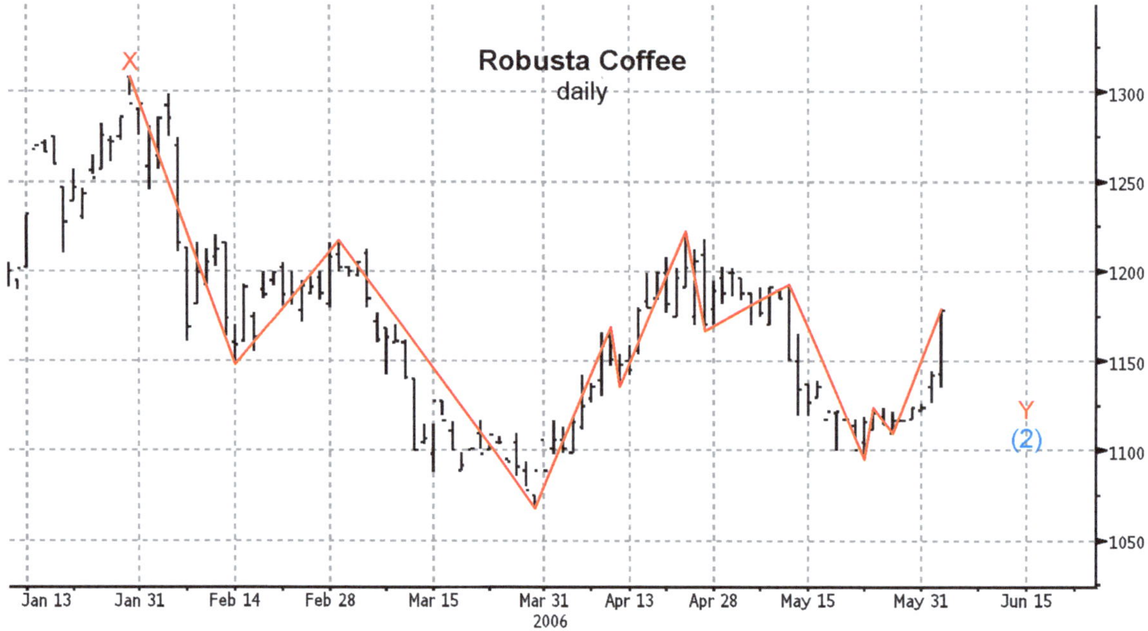

Figure 2.46

Chart reprinted with permission from Bloomberg. Copyright 2013 Bloomberg L.P. All rights reserved.

slope than wave A. At this rate, if wave C were in force, it would be less steep than wave A. Most likely, wave (2) is a double three combination, where wave Y would be a flat (3-3-5) or a triangle (3-3-3-3-3). If it turns out to be a flat, then prices would have to go all the way back up to around the 1,308 level—and maybe even higher—and then go down in a five-wave structure.

Another possibility would be that wave Y is forming a triangle. Figure 2.46 shows a close-up view on the daily bar chart.

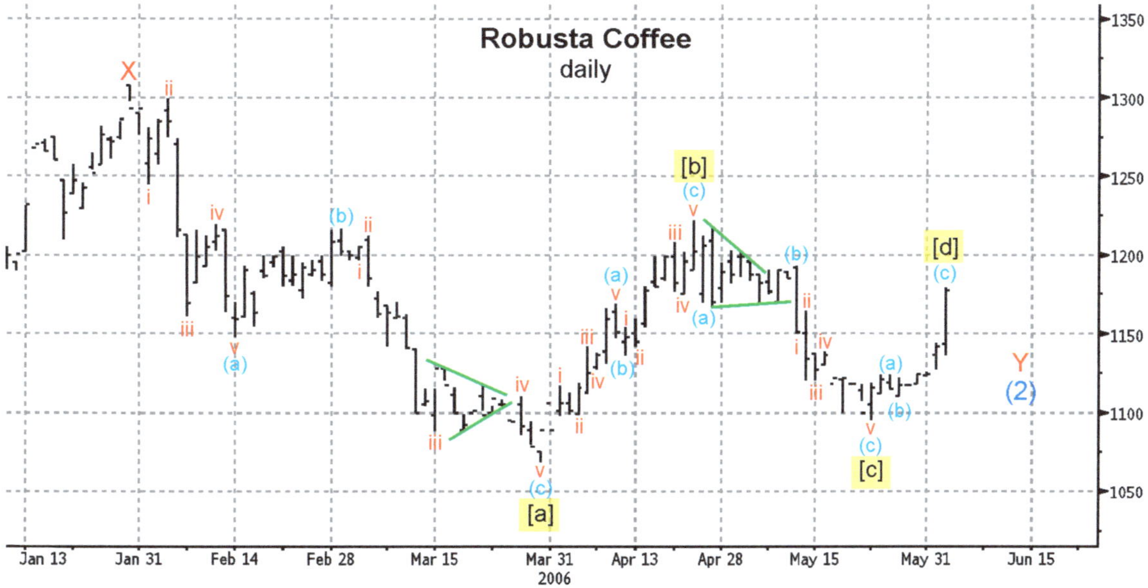

Figure 2.47

Chart reprinted with permission from Bloomberg. Copyright 2013 Bloomberg L.P. All rights reserved.

We can see a series of three-wave structures that might form waves [a], [b], [c], and [d] of the triangle. Figure 2.47 shows a detailed labeling of a triangle scenario.

Still not trading, we would wait a few days to see what unfolds. We know that in a contracting triangle, wave E cannot go beyond the end of wave C. We would have a big potential here

Figure 2.48

with just a small risk: We can wait for wave [e] to unfold and then go long and set our stop one tick below the low of wave [c] at 1,095. The idea for this trade plan would be to anticipate a thrust out of the triangle for the start of Intermediate wave (3). That would give us a small potential risk with a large potential reward.

In Figure 2.48, prices have moved ahead to June 7.

This most recent down move could be wave [e], the last leg of the triangle. If so, the next major move should be to the upside. What if wave Y is unfolding as a flat instead of a triangle? In that case, prices should still go up in wave B of the flat to the high of wave X, which is at 1,308.

Therefore, we would go long in the price range of the current bar—1,136 to 1,113. We assume that we would get filled in the middle of that range at 1,125. We would set our stop one tick below the low of wave [c] at 1,094. For our price target, we would set it one tick above the high of wave X at 1,309. Under either scenario, a wave Y flat or a thrust out of the triangle for wave (3), we should get to that level. That gives us a potential risk of 31 points and a potential reward of 184 points. That's a risk-reward ratio of about 6 to 1.

Smart Investor Tip

The most advantageous situations occur when both the preferred wave count and the alternate wave count call for a move in the same direction.

Figure 2.49

Another viable and less aggressive strategy would be to go long after a move beyond the [b]-[d] trendline. Given the potential swiftness of thrusting out of the triangle, it would be best to leave an order with the broker (or electronic trading platform) to buy "on a stop" a few ticks beyond the [b]-[d] trendline.

Let's fast-forward to June 28 to see how the trade went (see Figure 2.49).

Prices have broken through the [b]-[d] trendline, indicating the end of the triangle and the resumption of the uptrend in wave (3). But there's more to do. We still need to identify the end of wave [e] in order to raise the stop to one tick below the end of wave [e]. If the triangle is finished, prices should not go below wave [e]. Identifying the end point of wave [e] would also help us to accurately count the first impulse wave within wave (3).

Therefore, we should set our stop one tick below 1,123 and use it as the starting point for the next impulse wave to the upside. A more conservative stop would be just below the [b]-[d] trendline. *Note*: You don't have to wait for the break of the [b]-[d] trendline to trade. It all depends on your own personal risk tolerance.

Figure 2.50

Chart reprinted with permission from Bloomberg. Copyright 2013 Bloomberg L.P. All rights reserved.

Let's go forward to July 7 and see what would have transpired (see Figure 2.50).

The price has gapped up and created a beautiful thrust out of the triangle. The pattern now has a count of Minute waves [i], [ii], [iii], [iv], and [v] of Minor wave 1 of Intermediate wave (3). The high is 1,327. It could still go farther, but considering how far prices have gone beyond the target and considering that there are now five waves up, it would be a good time to close this position within the price range of 1,327 to 1,250. The middle of that range is 1,289, which would produce a profit of 164 points.

Next should come a pullback for Minor wave 2, which would give us the opportunity to go long again at a price below 1,289.

Figure 2.51

Chart reprinted with permission from Bloomberg. Copyright 2013 Bloomberg L.P. All rights reserved.

Figure 2.51 shows the big picture as of September 8.

The wave Y triangle was followed by an impulse wave to complete Intermediate wave (3). Within wave (3), Minor wave 2 made a substantial pullback to 1,149.

In summary, once we had identified multiple three-wave structures, we realized that we could label the entire correction as a combination. This helped us narrow down the possibilities for trades. It kept us on watch for the major move that we were anticipating. By labeling this move as a combination, we were able to determine effective stop levels, entry points, and targets.

For More Information

Learn more at your exclusive Reader Resources site. You will find a free online edition of *Elliott Wave Principle* by Frost and Prechter, plus lessons on Elliott wave analysis, how to trade specific patterns, and how to use Fibonacci and other technical indicators to increase your confidence as you apply the Wave Principle in real time. Go to: www.elliottwave.com/wave/ReaderResources.

Test Yourself

1. Which of the following best represents a single A-B-C structure?
   (A) W-X-Y structure
   (B) W-X-Y-X-Z structure
   (C) An X wave
   (D) A zigzag
2. Which of the following is accurate about triangles within combinations?
   (A) We see them in wave Y or wave Z of a triple three.
   (B) We see them in wave W or wave X of a double three.
   (C) We see them in wave Y of a double three.
   (D) We see them only in wave X. 3.
3. Which of the following contains the orthodox end of Primary wave [2]?
   (A) Wave (W)
   (B) Wave A of triangle (Y)
   (C) Wave C of triangle (Y)
   (D) None of the above
4. In the silver trading example, which of the following was strong evidence that the zigzag had ended?
   (A) Zigzag retraced at least 38 percent of the previous impulse wave.
   (B) Zigzag had a sharp look.
   (C) Warren Buffett basically said so.
   (D) Silver broke the upper trendline of the zigzag's trend channel.
5. True or False: The most common length relationship for wave C of a zigzag is that wave C equals a Fibonacci .618 times the length of wave A.
6. In the Robusta coffee trading example, why did we rule out the possibility of a double zigzag for wave (2)?
   (A) In a double zigzag, wave X cannot go beyond the start of wave W.
   (B) In second waves, wave Y is always a triangle.
   (C) A double zigzag would have ended beyond the start of wave (1).
   (D) Second waves are usually sideways and not sharp.
7. True or False: The fifth wave of an impulse wave always ends beyond the trend channel.

Answers: 1. D 2. C 3. D 4. D 5. False 6. A 7. False

CHAPTER 3

How a Triangle Positions You for the Next Move

Sideways price action and converging trendlines often signal a triangle pattern.

Trading a Triangle in Gold (GCA)

Let's look at a good example of one in gold (GCA) to see how to trade a triangle (see Figure 3.1).

In late 2007, gold formed a contracting triangle, as indicated by the wave structure of the sideways price action in November and December and by the converging trendlines that connected the extremes of waves A and C, and B and D.

This chart also illustrates the entry guideline for trading a triangle, as discussed in Chapter 1, "The Anatomy of Elliott Wave Trading." The guideline suggests waiting for prices to break the extreme of wave D of the pattern (822.8 in this example) and then placing an initial protective stop at the extreme of wave E (788.1 in this example).

Yet, to ensure that prices are clearly trading above the extreme of wave D, the level for the order to buy 5 mini-gold contracts is set at 825.0 rather than 822.9. This practice of placing an order a few ticks above or below a significant level helps to prevent *entering* a position prematurely.

Figure 3.1
Chart reprinted with permission from Bloomberg. Copyright 2013 Bloomberg L.P. All rights reserved.

> **Smart Investor Tip**
>
> The practice of placing an order a few ticks above or below a significant level may prevent entering a position prematurely.

Recall that triangles may form by themselves only in the wave four, wave B, or wave X positions. So, we could label the larger price move alternatively as an A-B-C correction in which the triangle is wave B. Until further price action, this bearish labeling in Figure 3.2 is just as plausible as the bullish labeling in Figure 3.1.

If this bearish labeling were indeed the operative wave pattern in gold, then we would still employ the same entry guideline by trading against

Figure 3.2

Chart reprinted with permission from Bloomberg. Copyright 2013 Bloomberg L.P. All rights reserved.

the extremes of waves D and E. In this example, though, because the extremes of waves B and D are so close, it's best to enter the trade at a break of the 780.0 level to trigger a short position on five mini-gold contracts. If filled, the initial protective stop would be the extreme of wave E at 811.4, assuming that E was over.

At first glance, it might seem confusing or self-defeating to analyze this chart with both a bullish and a bearish outlook (see Figure 3.3). Quite

Figure 3.3

KEY POINT

Having buy-side and sell-side trades operating simultaneously prepares you to adapt to everchanging market environments, which in turn allows you to take advantage of the trading opportunities that financial markets offer.

the contrary; having both a bullish and a bearish outlook makes it possible to formulate dual trade plans. If 825.0 were to be penetrated, our bullish trade plan would be initiated and five mini-gold contracts purchased.

Conversely, were 780.0 to give way, then the trade would be a short position and five mini-gold contracts would be sold.

Louis Pasteur, inventor of the process of pasteurization, once said, "Chance favors the

Figure 3.4
Chart reprinted with permission from Bloomberg. Copyright 2013 Bloomberg L.P. All rights reserved.

prepared mind." I believe that having buy-side and sell-side trades operating simultaneously allows you to do just that—it prepares you to adapt to changing market environments, thus allowing you to take advantage of trading opportunities that financial markets offer.

Four trading days later, prices moved up, and our buy-side trade plan would have been engaged when gold rallied through 825.0 (see Figure 3.4). How simple was that? All we had to do was sit back, let the market show its hand, and then trade. This example shows precisely why I prefer a

Figure 3.5

Chart reprinted with permission from Bloomberg. Copyright 2013 Bloomberg L.P. All rights reserved.

"ready, aim, aim, aim . . . fire" approach to trading versus one that is more anticipatory. Furthermore, the price action that took place between December 20 and December 26 would have allowed us to raise our initial protective stop from 788.1 to 797.1, thereby lessening our risk. (Remember, the trader's primary responsibilities once a position is initiated are to lessen risk, eliminate risk, and finally to protect open profits.)

In the days that followed, gold rallied nicely (see Figure 3.5). Moreover, with gold already trading above the point where wave 3 equals a 1.618 multiple of wave 1 at 834.8 on strong momentum, we would have looked to the next Fibonacci multiple, 2.618. Wave 3 equals a 2.618 multiple of wave 1 at 858.1.

As the market moved up, we would have proactively managed risk by raising our protective

Figure 3.6

Chart reprinted with permission from Bloomberg. Copyright 2013 Bloomberg L.P. All rights reserved.

stops. In this instance, we would have raised the protective stop in gold to 815.0.

Prices hit the third-wave target of 858.1 on January 2 (see Figure 3.6). In response to this move, we would have raised the protective stop on the position quite dramatically from 815.0 to 845.0. Since wave 3 had already achieved a 2.618 multiple of wave 1, odds were that the upside was limited and that the next significant move would be down in wave 4. So, rather than weathering a wave 4 correction, which could have been deep or time-consuming, it would have been more desirable to set a tight stop to allow us to lock in a significant profit on the position at that point.

Based on intraday price action the following day, it appeared that wave 3 of (5) had finally

Figure 3.7

Chart reprinted with permission from Bloomberg. Copyright 2013 Bloomberg L.P. All rights reserved.

ended at 872.9. With wave 3 done, the next task would have been to establish a target for wave 4. The most common Fibonacci retracement for fourth waves is a .382 multiple of wave three, which implies that gold would have been vulnerable to a corrective sell-off to near 840.51. Thus, in order to protect open profits on this position, the protective stop would have been raised from 845.0 to 855.2 (see Figure 3.7).

Figure 3.8

Chart reprinted with permission from Bloomberg.

Yet instead of wave 4 unfolding as a zigzag or a flat and testing Fibonacci support at 843.0, it took the shape of a contracting triangle and moved sideways over the next week (see Figure 3.8).

At this juncture, it is important to remember the most critical trait of triangles: They always precede the final move of a sequence in either the wave four, B, or X positions. Thus, this small

Figure 3.9

triangle in gold implied that the upside would be limited in wave 5 and that it was time to become even more aggressive managing risk. Therefore, we would have ratcheted the protective stop even tighter to 860.0, then 875.0 (see Figure 3.9).

Figure 3.10 shows what happened next. Our position in gold would have been stopped out on January 9, when prices traded below 875.00. The result? In nine trading days, gold had rallied more than 6 percent, which would have provided a handsome profit of $1,660.00 per contract.

This trading example is my favorite to show how to use the Wave Principle in real time because, first and foremost, it illustrates the

Figure 3.10

Chart reprinted with permission from Bloomberg. Copyright 2013 Bloomberg L.P. All rights reserved.

awesome power of a simple question: *Do you see a wave pattern you recognize?* As I discussed in the trading example of Techne Corporation (TECH) in Chapter 2, I begin each trade by asking this question. As we review this gold trade, take a look at Figure 3.1 again and ask yourself, "Do I see a wave pattern I recognize?" I'm sure you will agree that the most obvious Elliott interpretation is a contracting triangle because of the side-ways price movement and the converging trendlines.

I also like this trading example because, initially, we couldn't be confident which direction

KEY POINT

Even with two equally viable wave counts—one bullish and one bearish—the Wave Principle helps to formulate dual trading plans, a benefit that other forms of technical analysis simply do not offer.

the market would take. There were two equally viable wave counts, one bullish and one bearish. Even so, the Wave Principle helped us to formulate dual trading plans that prepared us for a trade regardless of market direction. That's a benefit that most other forms of technical analysis simply do not offer.

Trading a Triangle in Dell

A triangle as wave four within an impulse wave provides a great setup for trading wave five. The challenge is to determine when the triangle has ended. Let's look at an example in Dell Inc. that occurred in early 2008 to see how we could have traded it.

Figure 3.11 shows a chart with the impulse wave in Dell unfolding to the downside.

On this daily bar chart from the morning of Wednesday, March 26, we can identify the first four waves of an impulse wave that began at 30.77. The fourth wave appears to be a completed contracting triangle. Triangles always precede the final

Figure 3.11
Chart reprinted with permission from Bloomberg. Copyright 2013 Bloomberg L.P. All rights reserved.

actionary wave in the direction of the main trend at the next higher degree. Therefore, we would expect wave (v) to thrust downward from here, if the triangle has finished. Had we been trading that morning, we would have shorted Dell to take advantage of this fifth wave to the downside. Let's run through how to estimate a price target for wave (v), using the post-triangle thrust measurement.

Extend the a-c and b-d trendlines back to the origin of wave a and draw a vertical line that connects the two trendlines at that point (see Figure 3.12). The length of the vertical line defines the width of the triangle. In this case, it equals 3.03. Next, subtract 3.03 from the end of wave e at 20.81 to get an estimate of 17.78 for the end of wave (v).

KEY POINT

The post-triangle thrust measurement serves as a minimum estimate for fifth waves. A significant move beyond this measurement normally leads to a prolonged fifth wave.

Figure 3.12

Chart reprinted with permission from Bloomberg. Copyright 2013 Bloomberg L.P. All rights reserved.

Figure 3.13

Chart reprinted with permission from Bloomberg. Copyright 2013 Bloomberg L.P. All rights reserved.

Video:
To watch a video on how to estimate the target price for the thrust out of a triangle, go to:
www.elliottwave.com/wave/ReaderResources

Another way to estimate the end of wave (v) is to use a trend channel, as shown in Figure 3.13.

To use the trend-channel method, draw a line that connects the termination points of waves (ii) and (iv) and then draw a parallel line from the termination point of wave (i). Normally, you would draw the parallel line from the termination point of wave (iii), but since wave (iii) is steep, it's better to use the end point of wave (i) to construct the opposing line of this channel. (If wave (v) were to make a significant break through the bottom of the channel, then we could draw another parallel line that includes the termination point of wave (iii) to get a new estimate.) Wave (v) ideally should end when it reaches the bottom line of the trend channel.

Next, we add the triangle thrust estimate of 17.78 to the chart to check whether it coincides with the lower channel line over the short term. If it does, it would provide a good target for wave (v). Unfortunately, 17.78 lies in the middle of the channel, so this method is neutered.

Before deciding to short Dell, we would still like to find other supporting evidence that 17.78 might be a useful end target for wave (v). Since wave (iii) appears to be extended, we can look at two different length relationships for wave (v). An extended wave is an elongated impulse wave whose subwaves, especially the actionary waves, are as long as the nonextended waves at the next larger degree. In this case, wave i of (iii) is almost as long as wave (i).

Using the **guideline of equality**, wave (v) equals wave (i) at 15.50. However, wave (v) equals wave (i) times .618 at 17.53, which is closer to 17.78.

Therefore, we would have initially looked for Dell to fall to the 17.78-17.53 level. If it were to trade significantly below this range, then we would have looked for 15.50 as a target and monitored progress toward the lower trendline of the channel.

To position for wave (v) down, we would have shorted Dell at 20.39, which represents the middle of the range of the last price bar in Figure 3.13 . Our protective stop would be set at 21.19, which is one cent above the end of wave c of the triangle.

Depending on your risk tolerance, you could set your protective stop one cent above wave a instead of wave c . In contracting and barrier triangles, a move beyond wave C invalidates wave E but not the whole triangle. That's because wave C might still be in progress. A move beyond wave A invalidates the whole case for a triangle. Our initial price target would be 17.66, which is midway between 17.78 and 17.53. Our potential risk would be 0.80, and our potential reward 2.73, providing a risk-reward ratio slightly above 3:1.

In general, depending on your risk tolerance, you could wait for a break of the B-D trendline before entering a position. In this case, however, that strategy would have resulted in an entry point that's too close to our price target.

In Figure 3.14, we've moved forward to Friday, April 4.

The market here is still moving sideways and has not yet broken out of the triangle. As a matter of fact, prices have gone slightly beyond the top of the channel, which is somewhat alarming. This could mean that wave (iv) did not end where

DEFINITION:

guideline of equality

The guideline of equality states that when one of the waves of an impulse wave is extended, the two nonextended waves may be related to each other by equality or the Fibonacci ratio of .618.

Figure 3.14

Chart reprinted with permission from Bloomberg. Copyright 2013 Bloomberg L.P. All rights reserved.

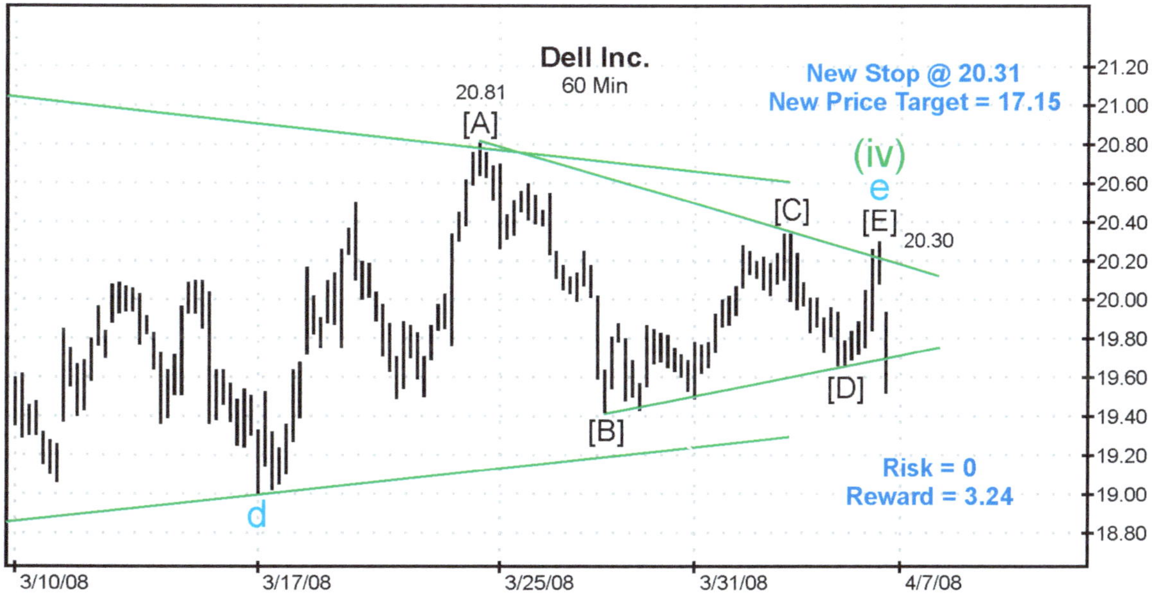

Figure 3.15

Source: Data courtesy of TradeNavigator.com.

we thought, in which case we would have to redraw our trend channel and adjust our protective stop. It could also mean that our wave count in general is incorrect.

Let's zoom in, using the hourly bar chart, to get a better look at the price action at this juncture (see Figure 3.15).

It appears that wave e did not end at 20.81, as we originally thought it would. Rather, it unfolded as a triangle within the larger triangle.

The break of the [B]-[D] trendline of triangle wave e would have strongly suggested that the wave e triangle had ended at 20.30 and that it had completed the larger wave (iv) triangle at that price. If the wave e triangle were finished, we would not want to see a move back above 20.30. Given this new price information, we could have lowered our stop to one cent above the end of wave [E] of e, which is also the end of wave (iv).

> **KEY POINT**
>
> **Within a triangle, one of the initial subwaves is usually complex and will unfold as a multiple zigzag pattern or a triangle. If one of the subwaves is a triangle, it's usually wave E.**

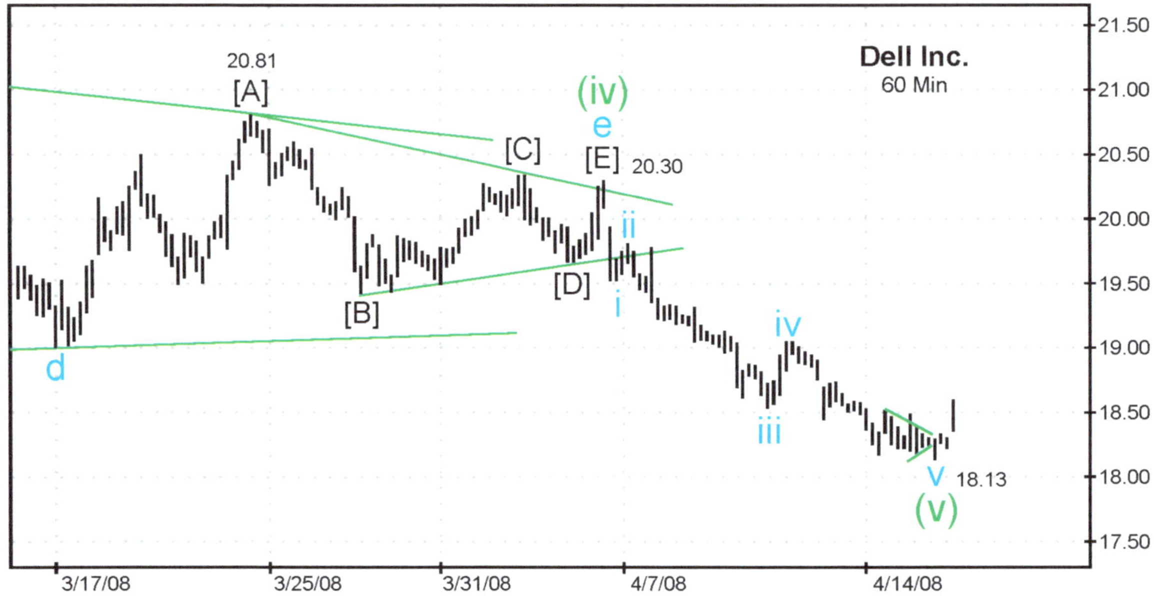

Figure 3.16
Source: Data courtesy of TradeNavigator.com.

KEY POINT

When wave E of a triangle is a triangle itself, the post-triangle thrust measurement is still based on the larger triangle.

Since wave e appeared to have ended at 20.30 instead of 20.81, we could also have adjusted our price target down by 51 cents to 17.15. Let's see what transpired over the next week.

In Figure 3.16, starting from the end of the triangle, it's possible to count five waves down to 18.13.

Within wave v of (v), there could have been a small fourth-wave triangle just prior to having

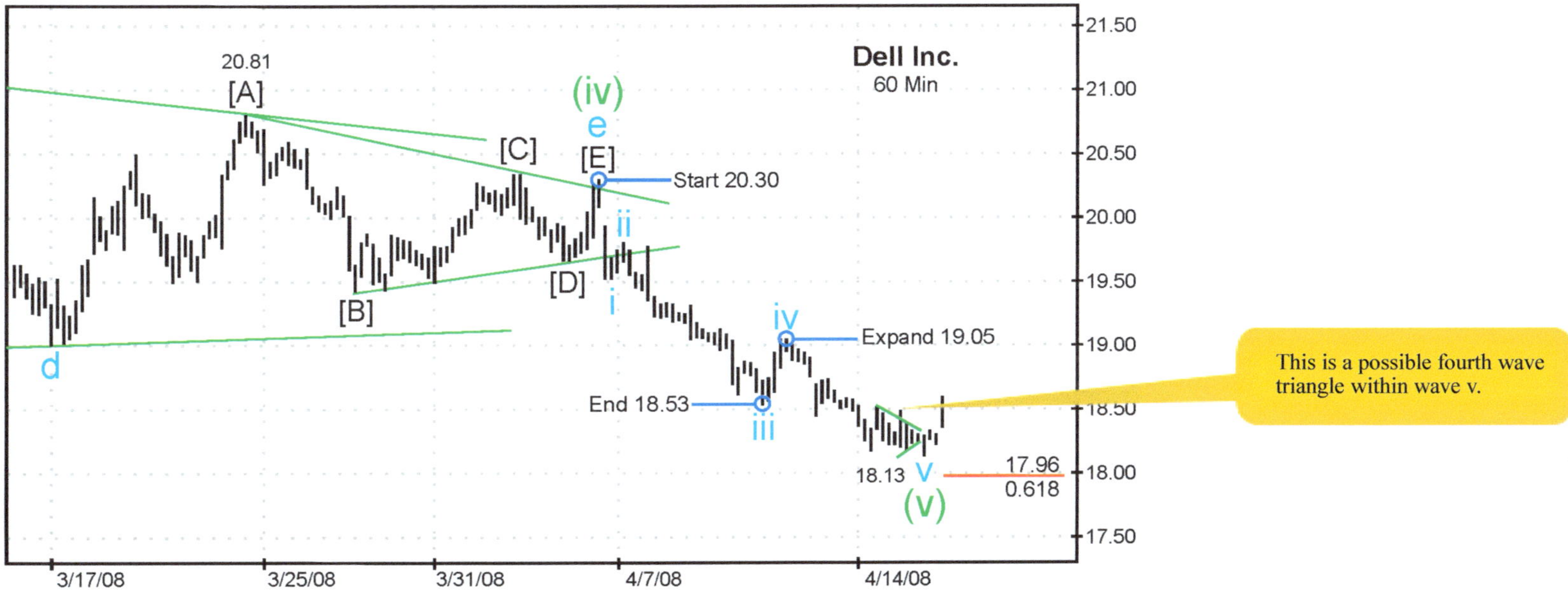

Figure 3.17
Source: Data courtesy of TradeNavigator.com.

reached 18.13, as indicated by the converging trendlines. Prices would still have been about one dollar above our price target. So, the next question would have been, is this all of wave (v), or is it just the first wave of wave (v)? It might not matter from a short-term trading point of view. What does matter is whether the impulse wave that started at 20.30 has finished. Let's look at the evidence in Figure 3.17 .

As shown in Figure 3.17, if wave v of (v) were to have ended at 17.96, it would have equaled .618 times the net distance traveled of waves i through

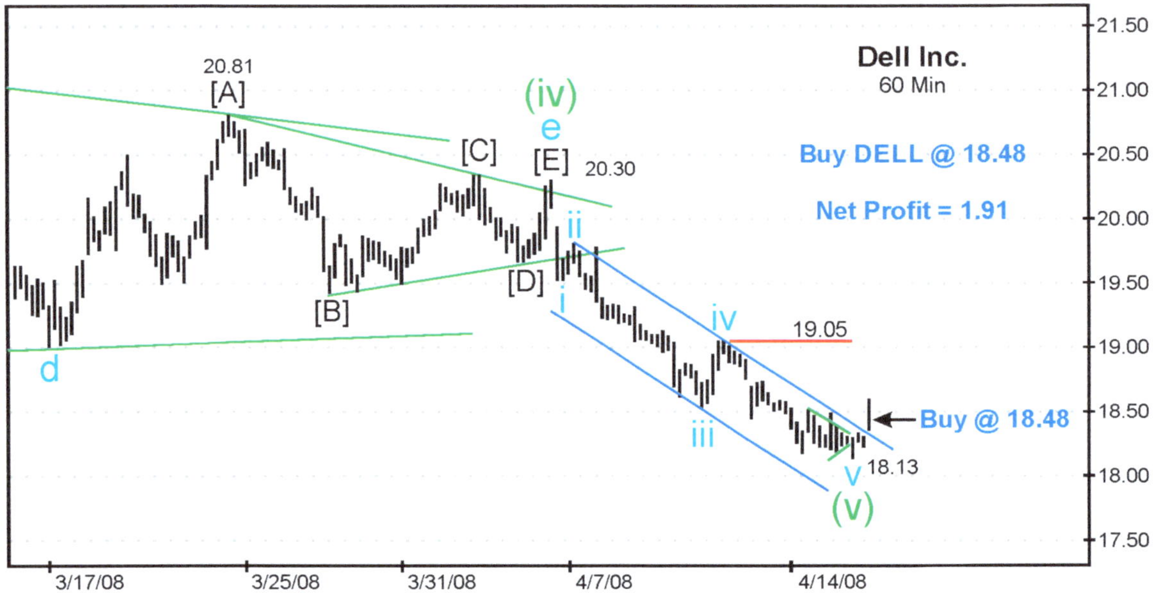

Figure 3.18
Source: Data courtesy of TradeNavigator.com.

iii, a common Fibonacci relationship. This level was close to the low of 18.13 and thereby would have supported the view that either all of wave (v) or the first wave of wave (v) had ended. In Figure 3.18, price action broke through the wave (v) trend channel to the upside.

That would have been strong evidence that the impulse wave that began at 20.30 most likely had ended at 18.13. It might have been all or part of wave (v). In either case, it seems likely that a correction would have ensued to the upside to possibly 19.05, the end of the previous fourth wave at one lesser degree. That level would have coincided with the .382 retracement, at 18.96.

Our strategy would have been to close our short position at 18.48, which is in the middle of the last hourly range bar. That would have resulted in a net profit of $1.91 per share. The next step would have been to monitor the correction in Dell for another trade setup. A move back to 20.30 would have confirmed the termination of wave (v) and the end of the entire impulse that began at 30.77.

Figure 3.19

Source: Data courtesy of TradeNavigator.com.

Let's look at the aftermath in Figure 3.19. Wave (v) did indeed end at 18.13, and a major correction followed to the upside.

In summary, identifying the fourth-wave triangle and its internal structure helped determine market direction, entry timing, a protective stop level, and a price target. Although our short trade would not have reached that price target, we would have been able to use other Elliott wave guidelines to spot an appropriate juncture to close our trading position.

For More Information

Learn more at your exclusive Reader Resources site. You will find a free online edition of *Elliott Wave Principle* by Frost and Prechter, plus lessons on Elliott wave analysis, how to trade specific patterns, and how to use Fibonacci and other technical indicators to increase your confidence as you apply the Wave Principle in real time. Go to: www.elliottwave.com/wave/ReaderResources.

Test Yourself

1. Which of the following is true about contracting and barrier triangles?
   (A) Wave E is always a triangle.
   (B) Wave E can never go beyond Wave C.
   (C) Wave E is sometimes a motive wave.
   (D) Wave E always ends at the A-C trendline
2. True or False: A triangle indicates that one more move remains in the direction of the main trend at the next higher degree.
3. In the Dell trading example, the break of the B-D trendline of triangle wave E supported which of the following conclusions:
   (A) The larger triangle had ended.
   (B) The impulse wave had ended.
   (C) The smaller triangle was still in progress.
   (D) Wave E was not a triangle.

Answers: 1. B 2. True 3. A

CHAPTER 4

Riding Wave C in a Zigzag

C waves of zigzags offer great trading opportunities, because they are five-wave structures that move in the direction of the main trend. Their setup is also clear: five waves in the direction of the main trend for wave A followed by three waves moving countertrend for wave B. These next two examples, based on trades Wayne Gorman made in 1998, demonstrate the power of trading this particular pattern.

Trading Wave C of a Zigzag in S&P 500 Futures

In this section, we will see how having alternate wave counts did not affect formulating a profitable strategy. While studying the S&P 500 stock index futures market in early January, I saw an interesting situation on the daily bar chart of the March 1998 futures contract (see Figure 4.1).

It appeared that wave (3) of an impulse had ended in early October and that several corrective structures had followed it. Knowing that it is good practice to look for alternate interpretations in case the preferred wave count does not materialize, I considered three potential counts. My top wave count had Intermediate wave (4) unfolding as a contracting triangle, based on this thinking: Wave A ended at 854.4, wave B ended at 1000.0, and wave C was unfolding as a double zigzag. Using the Elliott wave guideline that alternate legs of a triangle are related by the Fibonacci ratio of .618, I estimated that wave C should end at 908.41.

My first alternate wave count, as seen in Figure 4.2, assumed that wave (4) had already ended and that Intermediate wave (5) had begun, based on this thinking: Intermediate wave (4) ended at 854.4, wave 1 of (5) ended at 1000.0, and wave 2 was unfolding as a double zigzag. Therefore, whether the move down from the 1000.0 high was wave C of a triangle or wave 2 of an impulse wave, it was still corrective and would subdivide a-b-c-x-a-b-c or [w]-[x]-[y].

Figure 4.1

Chart reprinted with permission from Bloomberg. Copyright 2013 Bloomberg L.P. All rights reserved.

Smart Investor Tip

You should always look for alternate counts to be prepared for different scenarios and in case your preferred wave count does not materialize.

As for a price target on this alternate count: Wave 2 will often make a deep retracement equal to a Fibonacci ratio multiplied by the length of wave 1. Assuming a .618 retracement of wave 1, wave 2 should end at 910.0.

The reason this was not my top count is that wave (4) seemed too brief to be the entire correction. Also, wave 1 looked more like a corrective wave than an impulse wave, since it had no clear five-wave pattern and included many zigzags. Nonetheless, I wanted to be ready for an outcome based on this possibility.

The key point is that, under either scenario in the short term, I was looking for prices to decline to near the same level, at about 910.

Figure 4.2
Chart reprinted with permission from Bloomberg. Copyright 2013 Bloomberg L.P. All rights reserved.

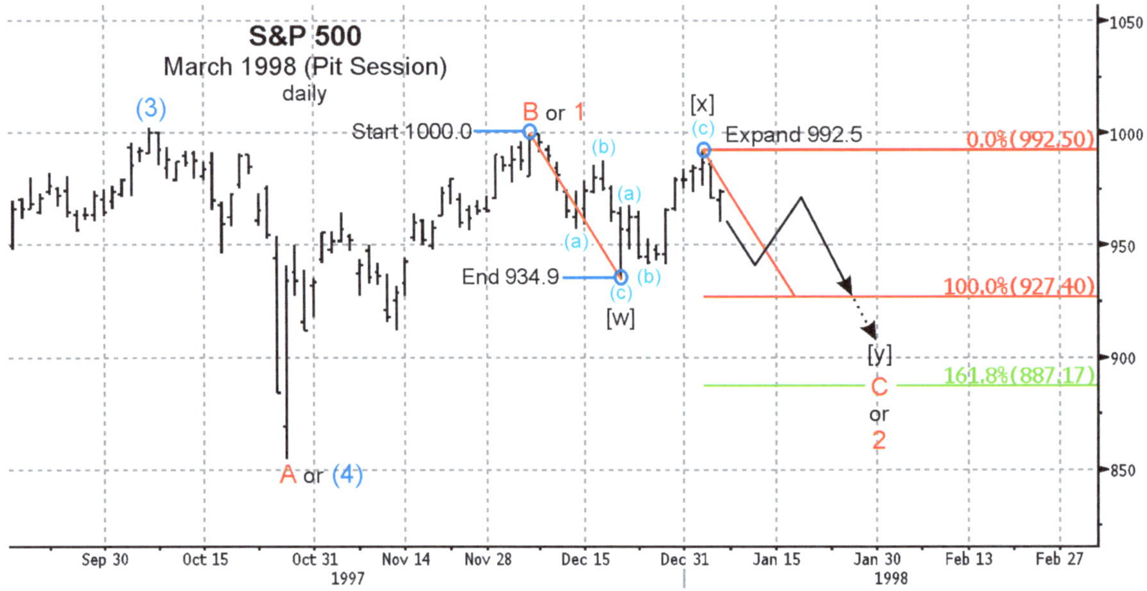

Figure 4.3

Chart reprinted with permission from Bloomberg. Copyright 2013 Bloomberg L.P. All rights reserved.

> **KEY POINT**
>
> **The Fibonacci guidelines for double zigzags are analogous to those for single zigzags. In a double zigzag, first look for wave Y to equal wave W. If it is longer, then look for wave Y to be related to wave W by the Fibonacci multiple of 1.618.**

Under each of these wave counts, I labeled the decline beginning at 1000.0 (see Figure 4.3) as a double zigzag that would end near 927.4, where wave [y] equals wave [w]. If there were further downside, I would look for 887.2, where wave [y] equals 1.618 times wave [w].

However, I also perceived another alternate wave count, although it was the least likely scenario. My second alternate count had this same decline unfolding as a single zigzag (for wave C of a triangle or wave 2 of an impulse wave), where wave [a] ended at 957.5, and wave [b]

Figure 4.4

Chart reprinted with permission from Bloomberg.

completed an expanded flat at 992.50 within the zigzag as shown in Figure 4.4.

Under this scenario, wave [c] would equal 1.618 times the length of wave [a] at 923.7. This target level was exciting because, comparing the projections using my top count and both alternate wave counts, I realized that there was a Fibonacci cluster forming in the low 900s area. That was encouraging, because it increased the odds that the market would reach a price level somewhere between 927 and 908.

On the morning of January 8, I decided to short the S&Ps and try to capture all or part of the second zigzag. To settle on entries and exits,

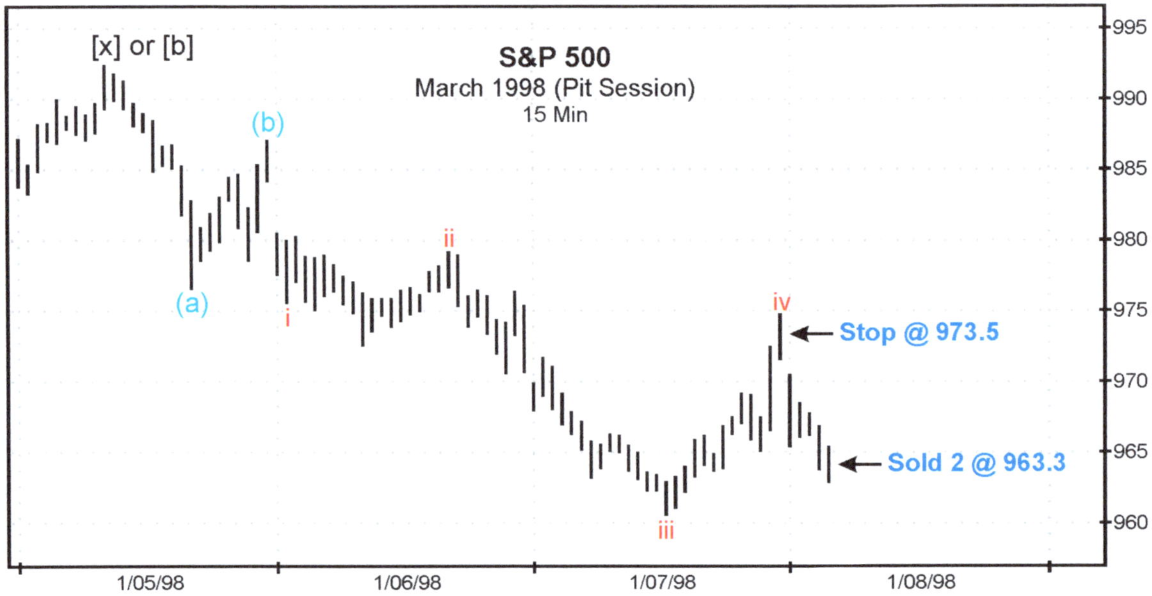

Figure 4.5
Source: Data courtesy TradeNavigator.com.

I often study a short-term chart, such as a 15- or 30-minute bar chart.

On the 15-minute chart (see Figure 4.5), it looked like the March S&P contract had already completed waves i through iv of wave (c) of the second zigzag, and it was going down in wave v. As a strong guideline for impulse waves, fourth waves should not overlap second waves, so I did not like the fact that wave iv overlapped wave ii. However, I was content that wave iv did not overlap wave i and proceeded with my trade. Normally, I would not trade the tail end of such a move in this short time frame, but the market was around 965, which was substantially above the price target range, suggesting that the fifth

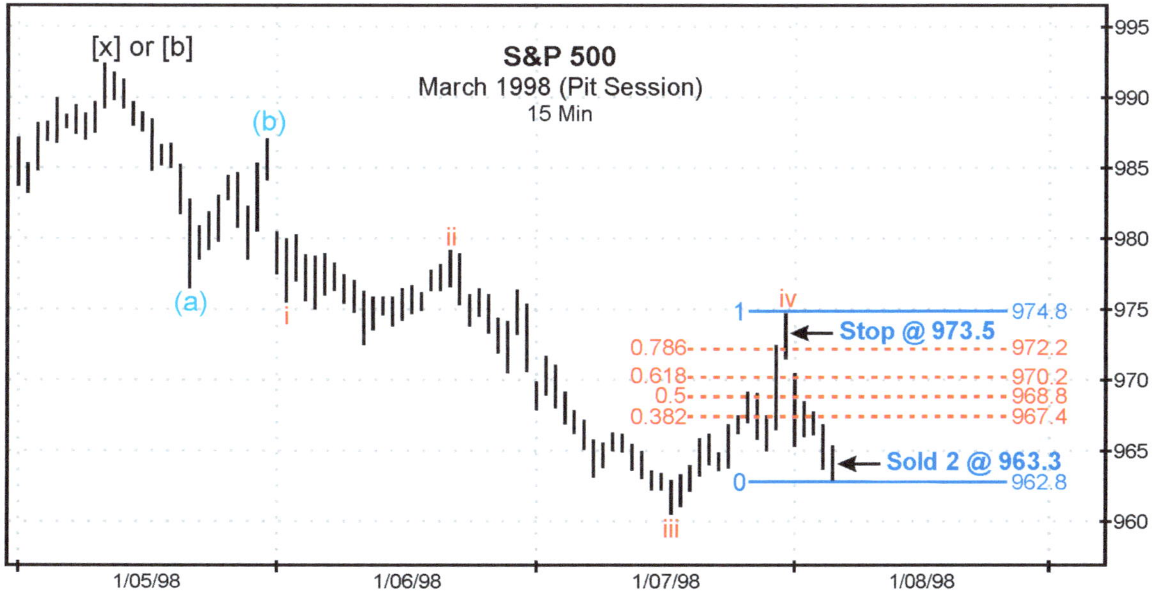

Figure 4.6
Source: Data courtesy TradeNavigator.com.

wave might extend. My trading plan was to sell a total of six contracts (big S&Ps). To scale into the position, I sold two contracts at 963.3 with a stop at 973.5. If the market rallied, I would have the opportunity and flexibility to sell more contracts at a better level.

Here is how I set the stop (see Figure 4.6): Even though the wave count from the wave iv high of 974.8 was not clear yet, I decided that greater than a .786 retracement of this initial down move to 972.2 would be highly unlikely. So, I set my stop at 973.5, which was just beyond that retracement level. To be conservative, I set my initial price target at 927.4, where wave [y] equals wave [w], keeping in mind the potential to go down to the 910 level.

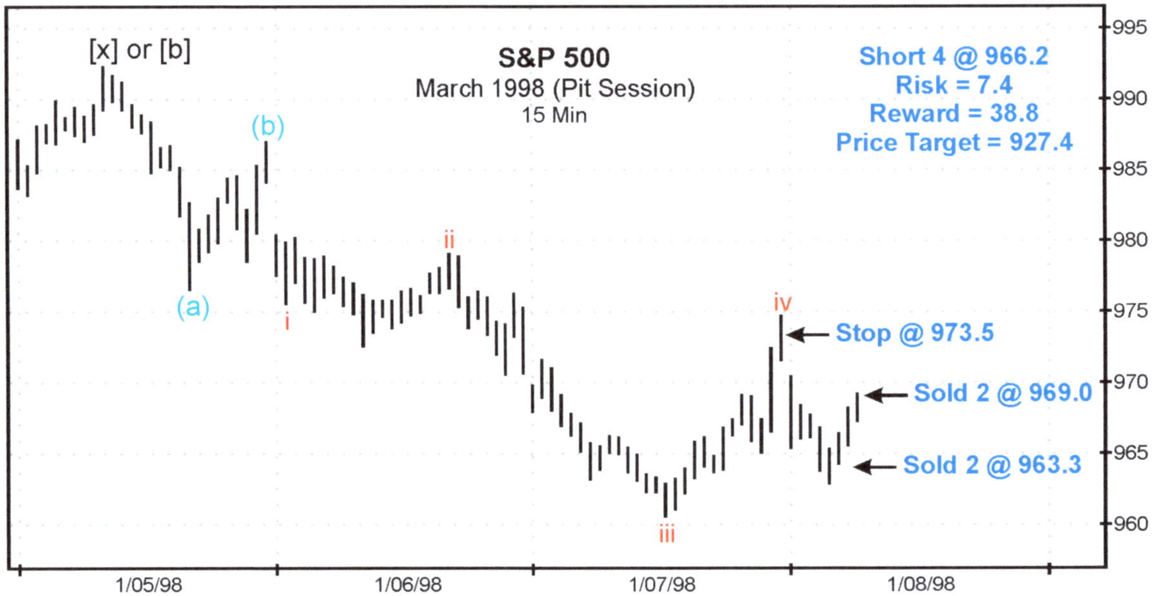

Figure 4.7
Source: Data courtesy TradeNavigator.com.

> **Smart Investor Tip**
>
> When the market is going against you, it is emotionally difficult to increase your position. However, this trading tactic, which requires confidence in your forecasting model, can enhance the overall average of your position.

Fortunately, the market did rally, and I sold another two contracts at 969.0 (see Figure 4.7).

The trade so far: four contracts at an average price of 966.2 with a great potential risk-reward ratio of 5:1. But I was not about to stop there.

After moving sideways for the rest of the day, the market declined significantly on the morning of January 9, as shown in Figure 4.8. I decided to add to my position quickly and sold one contract at 957.3 and another at 957.2, bringing the

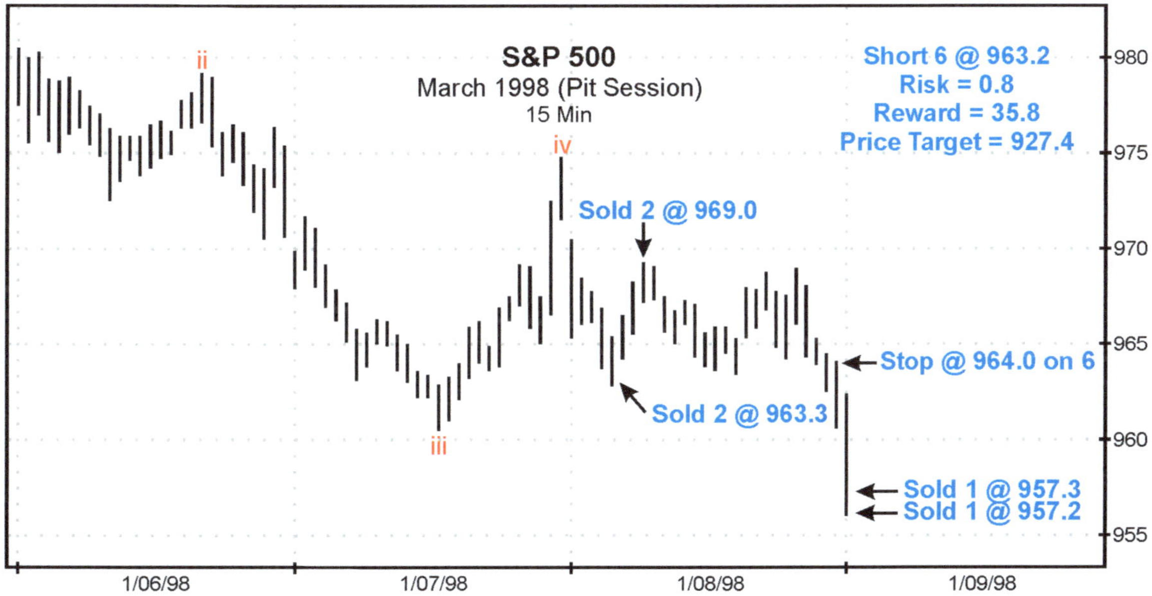

Figure 4.8

Source: Data courtesy TradeNavigator.com.

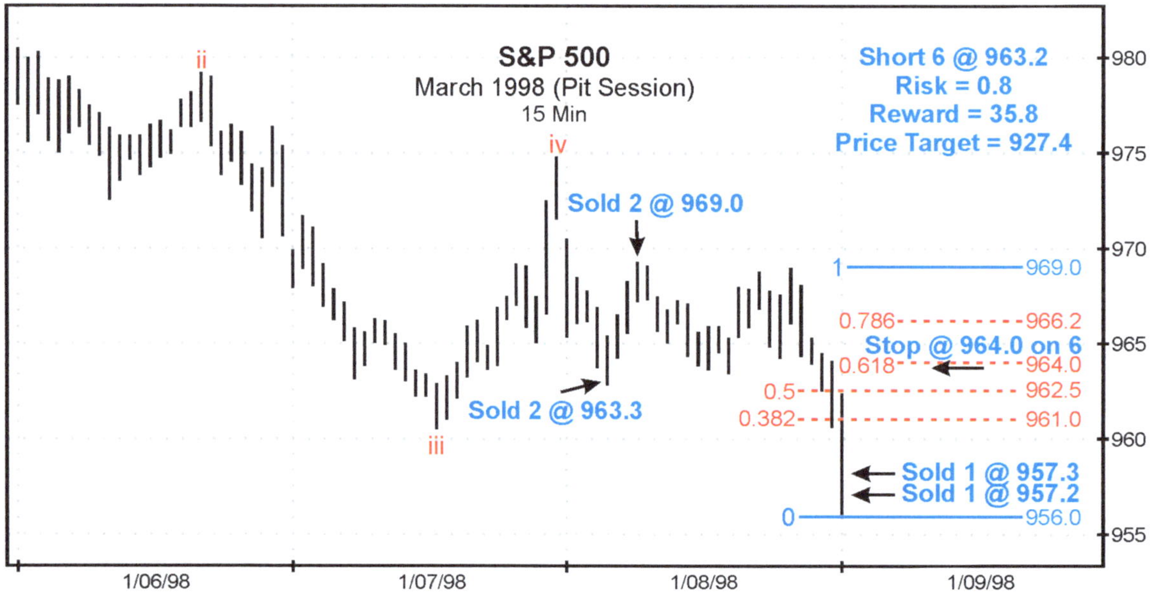

Figure 4.9
Source: Data courtesy TradeNavigator.com.

position to short six contracts at an average price of 963.2 (see Figure 4.9).

As soon as the opportunity presents itself from an Elliott wave perspective, I always try to get my stop close to or better than the average price of my position. At this time, I moved my stop down to 964.0, for two reasons. First, there was a double top at 969.0 (969.3 vs. 969.0) that seemed to form wave [2] of wave v. Second, with the low so far at 956.0, I didn't want to see a move beyond 964.0, the .618 retracement of the decline from 969.0 down to 956.0, which probably represented just part of wave [3] of wave v. (Actually, I should have set my stop one tick beyond 964.0, but fortunately I wasn't punished for this slight oversight.)

At this point, potential risk was almost zero with a potential reward of 35.8. The price target

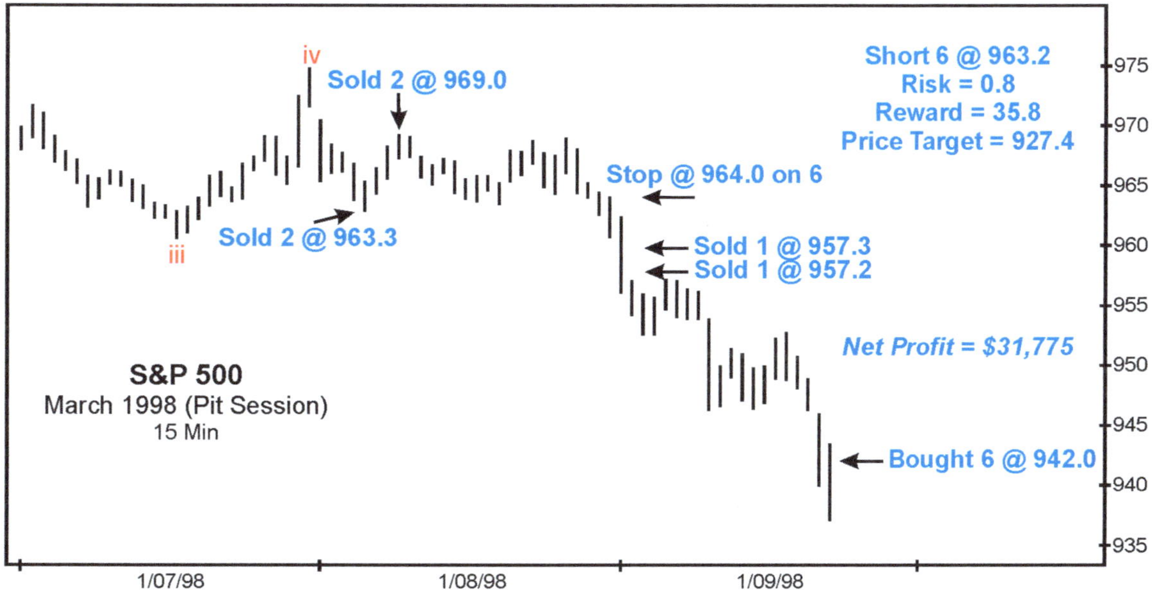

Figure 4.10

Source: Data courtesy TradeNavigator.com.

was still 927.4. The next chart (see Figure 4.10) shows how far the market declined that afternoon.

The S&Ps made a new low of 937.0 and then bounced up to 943.5. January 9 was a Friday, so the question was, "Should I hang up on the trade or let it ride over the weekend?"

Even though the market did not reach my initial target, I decided to close my entire position at 942.0 anyway. Why? First, I did not want to hold such a large position over the weekend, particularly since the net profit was $31,775 at that point. Second, looking back at Figures 4.2 and 4.3, there appeared to be important support between 935.0 and 944.0. If the market rallied, I could reopen the position at a higher level. Here is how I computed the support levels: The .382 retracement of wave 1 (or wave A) was 944.4.

Smart Investor Tip

During a market trend, the net decline (or advance) is never as large as the sum of the individual declines (or advances). To maximize gains, you can trade in and out of positions to take advantage of countertrend moves.

Figure 4.11
Source: Data courtesy TradeNavigator.com.

Wave (c) of wave [w] ended at 934.9, and wave (b) of wave [x] ended at 941.5.

Figure 4.11 shows what happened after I closed the trade at 942.0. The market continued lower that Friday, dropping below the 927.4 level to a low of 926.0. On Monday, January 12, the market opened down and made a new low at 917.7—ending up in the middle of the Fibonacci cluster. It then quickly rallied back to the 940.0 level.

How I kicked myself for having missed the rest of the move that my analysis had got right! It made me so mad that I started selling into the rally, hoping that the market would go back down to the 908-910 level again. With my emotions now firmly in the driver's seat, I rationalized that the pattern was still in wave [4] of wave v, when in fact both waves [4] and [5] had already ended. Rationality plus Elliott waves work; baseless emotional actions do not.

Figure 4.12
Chart reprinted with permission from Bloomberg. Copyright 2013 Bloomberg L.P. All rights reserved.

What was the result? I got stopped out at a loss of $17,650, cutting my profit down to $14,125. Wave C did indeed end at 917.7, and I got caught trading in the wave D rally. Figure 4.12 displays the wave (4) triangle.

Trading lesson learned: Emotion can get the best of you even when you trade with the Wave Principle. I had powerful trading information based on my wave analysis. Both my top wave count and alternate wave counts pointed not only in the same direction but also to about the same price target level. However, once wave C nearly reached its intended target without my being aboard for the last part of the drop, I let my emotions get the better of me. In trading, sometimes the biggest challenge is not understanding an Elliott wave pattern but understanding yourself.

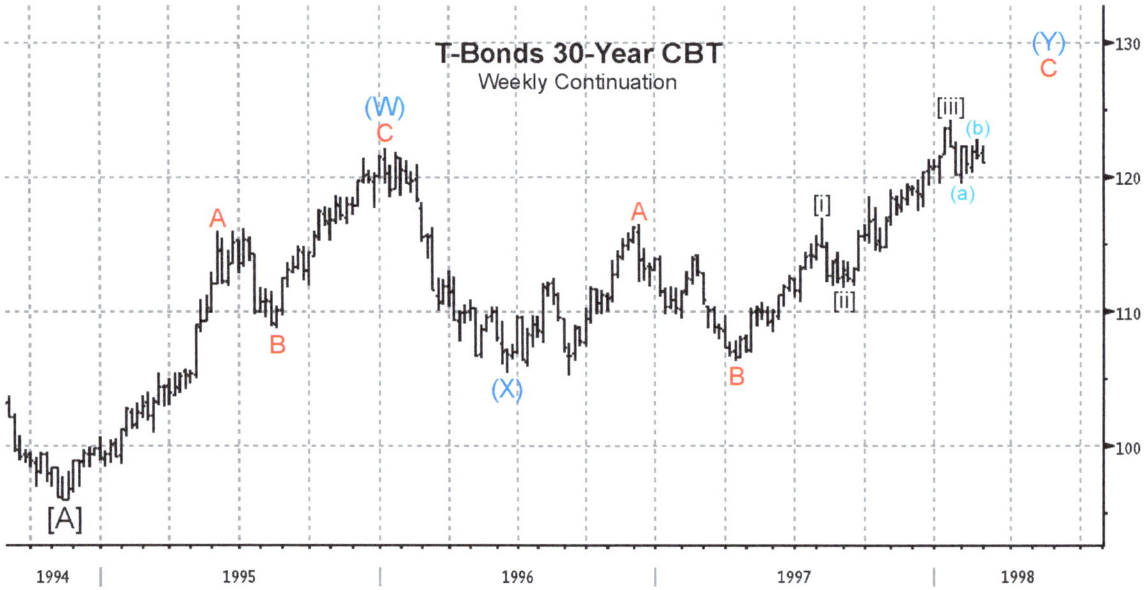

Figure 4.13

Chart reprinted with permission from Bloomberg.

Trading a Third-of-a-Third Impulse Wave

In this next example, I demonstrate how a third-of-a-third impulse wave can be a trader's best friend.

At the time, I followed not only the silver futures and S&P futures but also the U.S. bond futures. In late February 1998, I saw another trading opportunity whereby I could exploit wave C of

Figure 4.14

Chart reprinted with permission from Bloomberg. Copyright 2013 Bloomberg L.P. All rights reserved.

a zigzag. Figure 4.13 shows the later stages of a double three combination in bond futures on the weekly continuation chart through February 23, 1998, where wave (Y) appeared to be a flat pattern.

Within wave (Y), wave C looked to be shaping up as an impulse wave, with its wave [v] appearing to unfold as a zigzag. Using the daily chart (see Figure 4.14), I channeled the impulse wave and then identified waves (a) and (b) of the zigzag in wave [iv].

Wave (a) came close to the lower trendline of the channel at 119^16 and almost achieved an

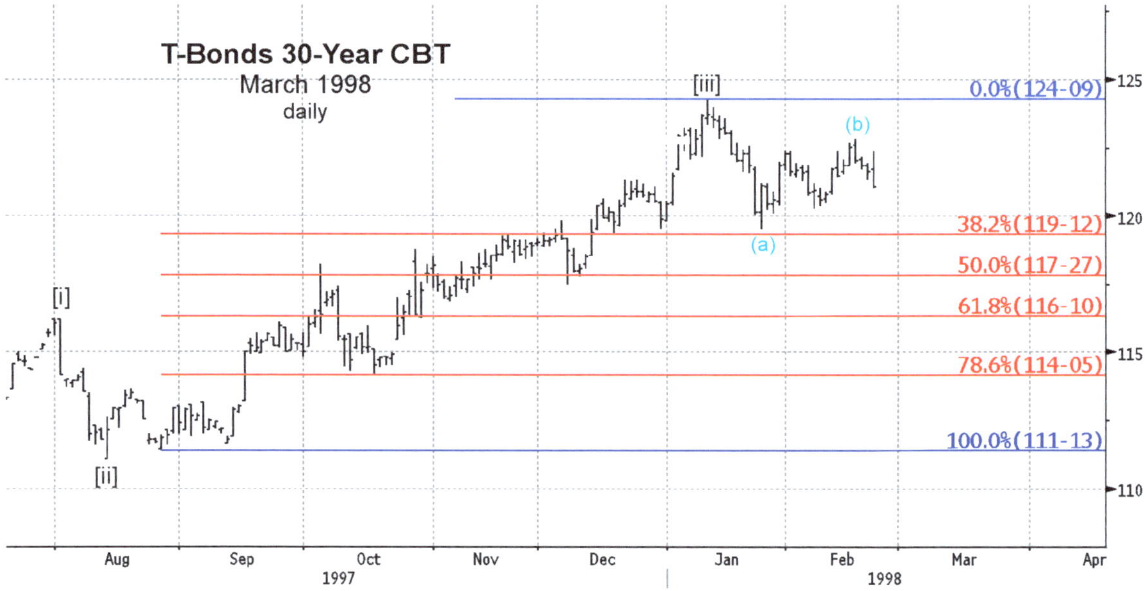

Figure 4.15

Chart reprinted with permission from Bloomberg.

exact .382 retracement of wave [iii]. According to the channel, I would expect a short wave (c), but still long enough to make it worth trading (see Figure 4.15).

KEY POINT

Within a zigzag, waves A and C always consist of five waves.

This initial move down seemed too brief to be the entire correction, and it also had the look of an impulse wave. These two impressions convinced me that the move down was most likely the first leg of a zigzag, labeled wave (a).

Wave (b), then, appeared to be finished at 122^26, since it seemed to have completed a zigzag and achieved more than a .618 retracement

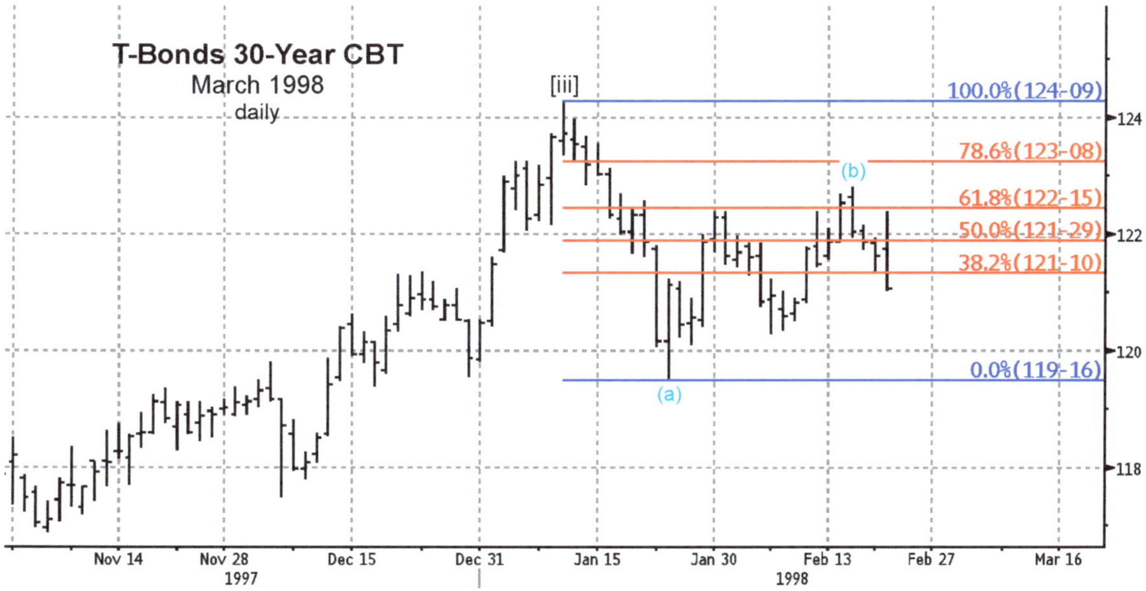

Figure 4.16

Chart reprinted with permission from Bloomberg. Copyright 2013 Bloomberg L.P. All rights reserved.

Figure 4.17

Chart reprinted with permission from Bloomberg.

> **KEY POINT**
>
> **Within a zigzag, the length of wave C commonly equals the length of wave A.**

of wave (a) (see Figure 4.16). Therefore, I decided to short the March 1998 bond futures contract for wave (c) to the downside. My price target was 118^01, because that was where wave (c) equaled wave (a) in the zigzag (see Figure 4.17).

Comparing that price target to the zigzag's trend channel, it seemed reasonable that 118^01 could fall near the lower boundary of the channel.

As I monitored price moves on the morning of February 24 (see Figure 4.18), I could identify a series of 1-2s of an impulse wave in wave (c). That meant that bonds were probably entering the third wave of a third wave. Since a third of a third is the strongest wave of an impulse wave, I immediately sold 25 March 1998 contracts at 121^02.

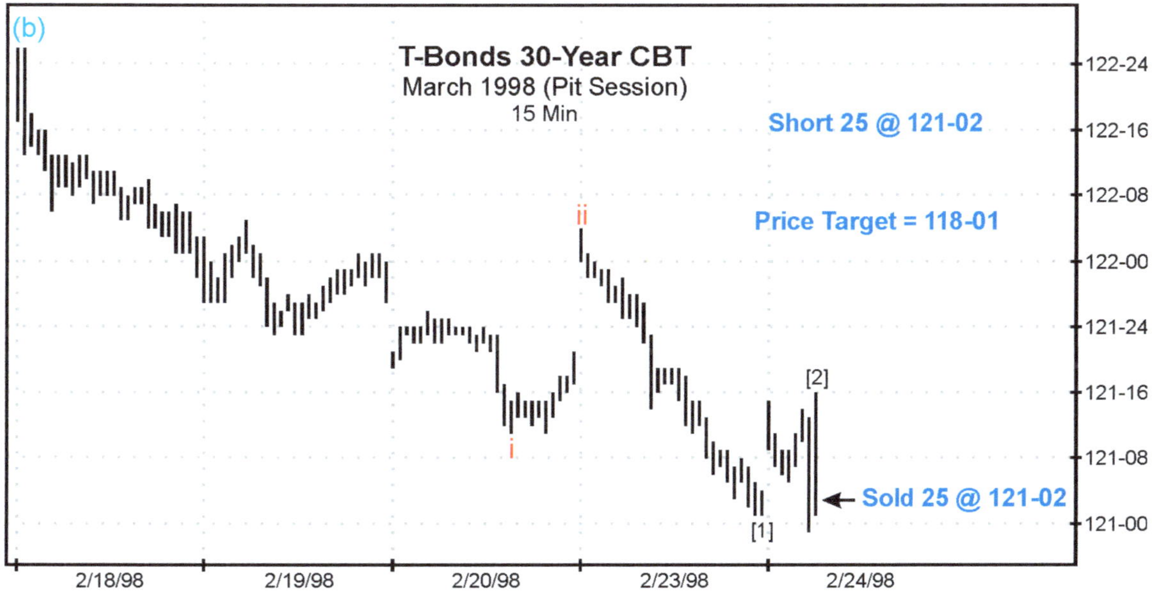

Figure 4.18

Source: Data courtesy TradeNavigator.com.

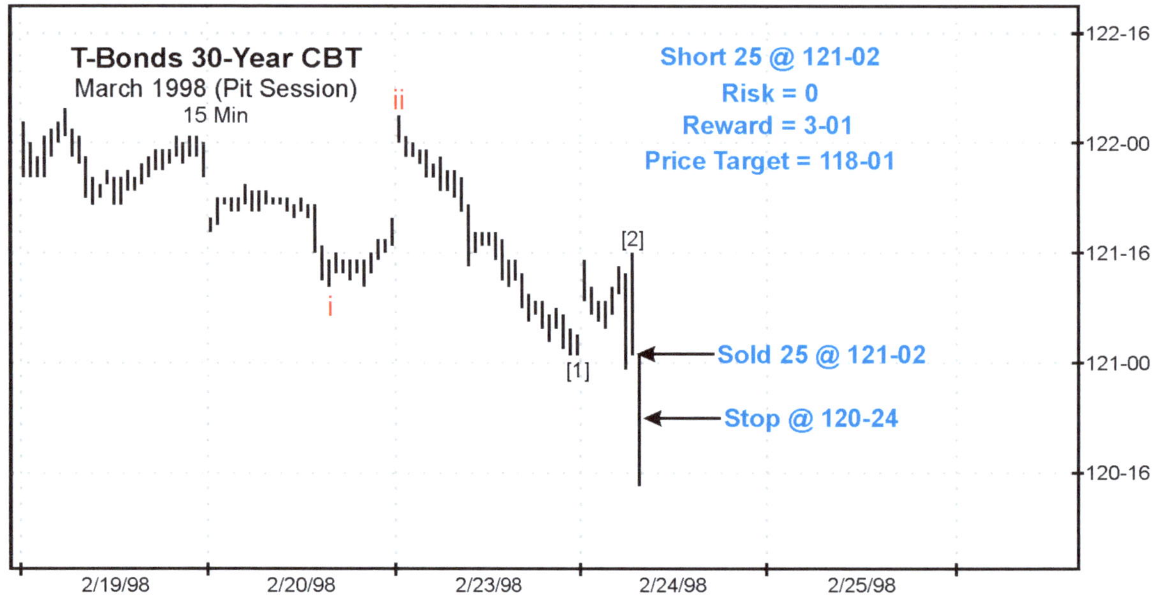

Figure 4.19
Source: Data courtesy TradeNavigator.com.

Smart Investor Tip

An effective trading plan includes a selective entry point, a protective stop, a price target, a favorable risk-reward ratio, and an alternate wave count.

I confess that I was so impatient to act that I did not determine my stop level first. Fortunately, the market dropped half a point over the next 15 minutes (see Figure 4.19). (Got to love those third-of-a-third impulse waves when they let you get away with a hasty decision.)

That gave me some breathing room to set my stop at the 50 percent retracement level of 120^24, which locked in a profit (see Figure 4.20). Actually, I should have set my stop slightly above that level.

Figure 4.21 shows how the market made another new low in the third of the third and then

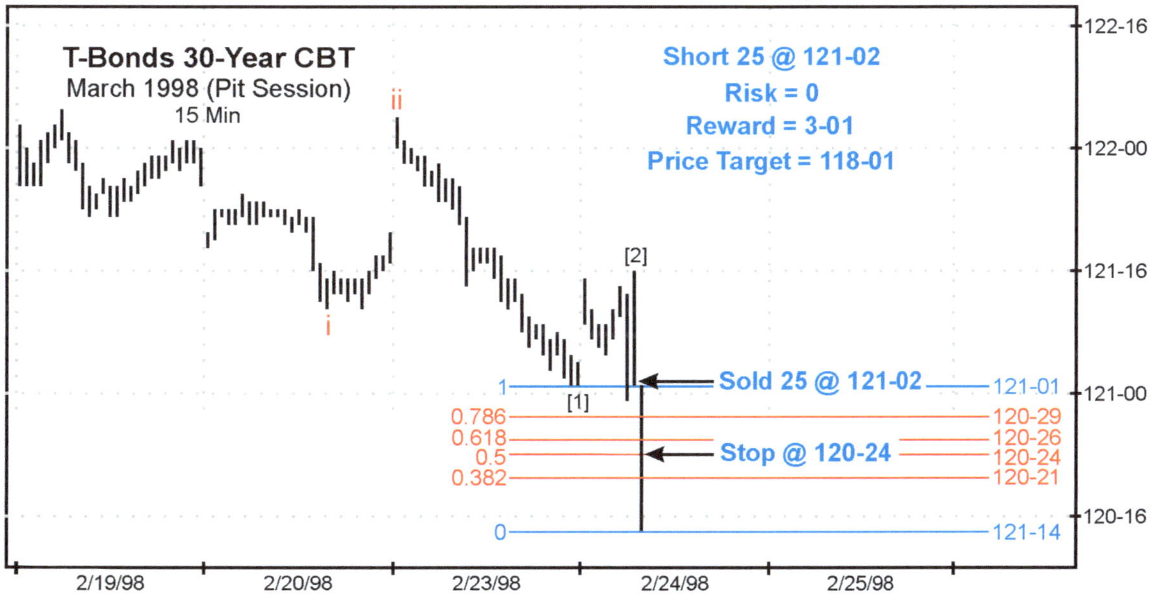

Figure 4.20

Source: Data courtesy TradeNavigator.com.

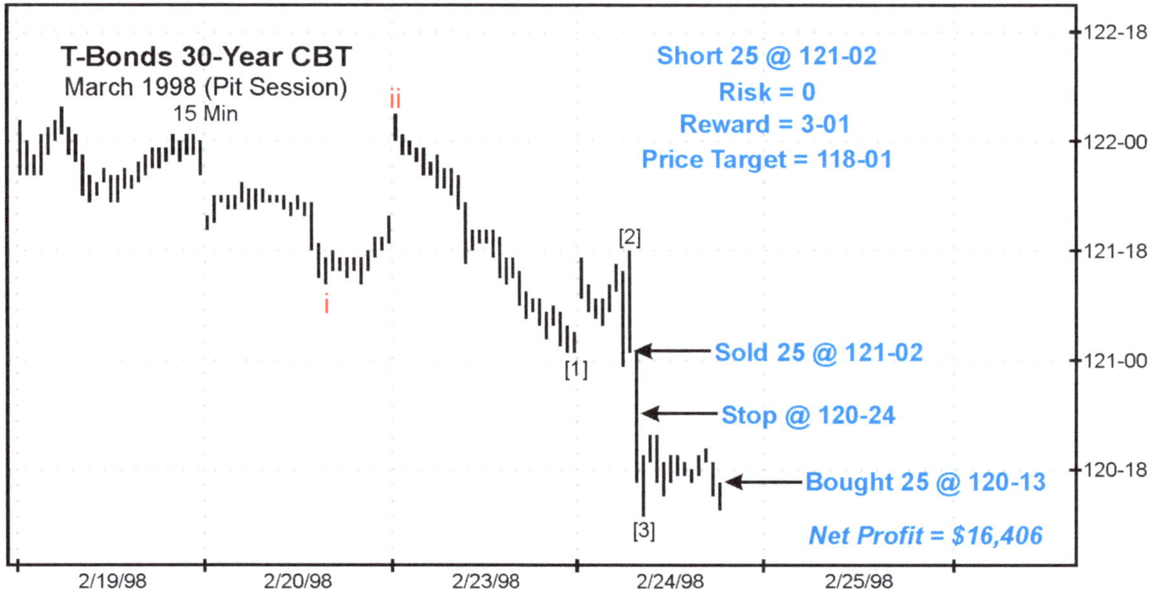

Figure 4.21

Source: Data courtesy TradeNavigator.com.

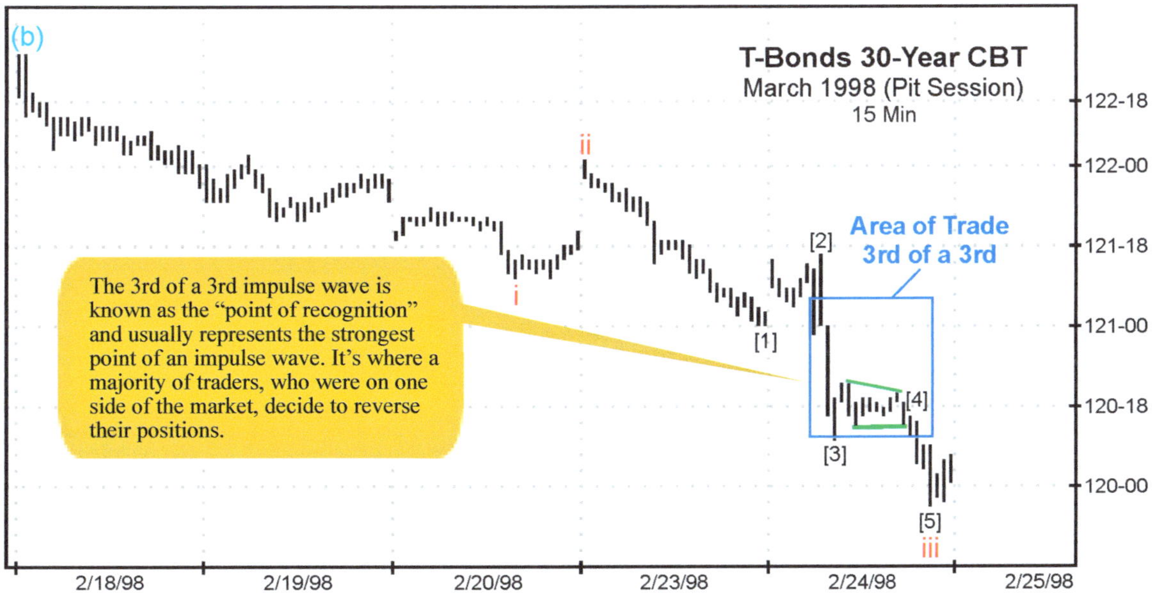

Figure 4.22

Source: Data courtesy TradeNavigator.com.

began a sideways move. Near the end of the day, I decided not to hold the position overnight, so I closed it out by buying 25 contracts at 120^13 for a profit of $16,406.

Here is how the day—and the impulse wave—ended (see Figure 4.22).

Looking back from June of that year (see Figure 4.23), it turned out that I had actually been

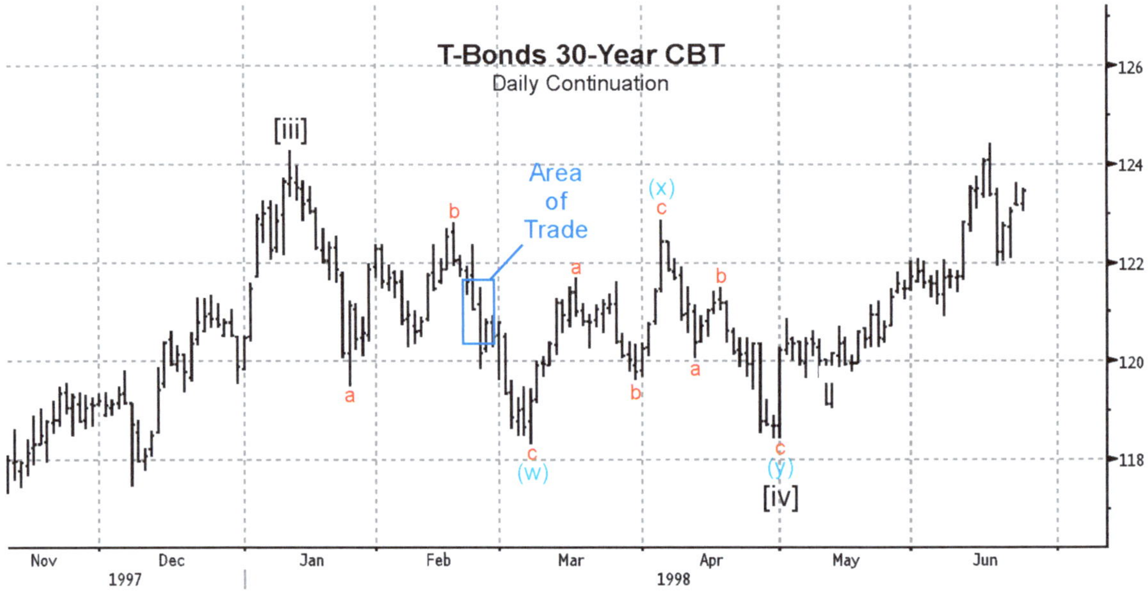

Figure 4.23

Chart reprinted with permission from Bloomberg. Copyright 2013 Bloomberg L.P. All rights reserved.

trading wave c of just the first zigzag of a double zigzag in wave [iv].

Bond futures eventually traded down to 118^23. Notice that the steepest decline occurred in wave (3) of wave [3] (see Figure 4.24). (I adjusted the degree of the wave labels on this chart to take into account the double zigzag.)

Now, to air some dirty laundry: The market turned out to be choppy in wave v, with one-point swings for several days. Since I was spoiled by how easy the previous trade had been—and so as not to be denied achieving my ultimate price target— I stubbornly shorted this market. It turned out to be the middle of wave (1) of [5] and wave (2) of [5], and I got stopped out each time, for a total loss of $10,938. However, I still ended up with a net profit, thanks to the third-of-a-third impulse wave, which turned out to be one of my best trades in bonds that month.

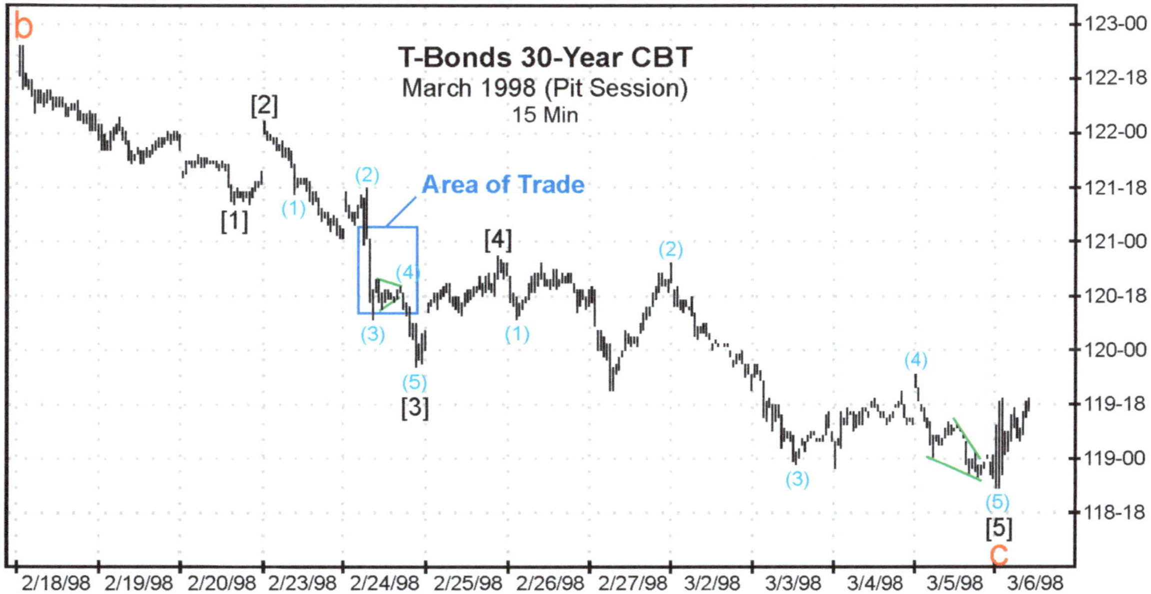

Figure 4.24

Source: Data courtesy TradeNavigator.com.

For More Information

Learn more at your exclusive Reader Resources site. You will find a free online edition of *Elliott Wave Principle* by Frost and Prechter, plus lessons on Elliott wave analysis, how to trade specific patterns, and how to use Fibonacci and other technical indicators to increase your confidence as you apply the Wave Principle in real time. Go to: www.elliottwave.com/wave/ReaderResources.

Test Yourself

1. How important are alternate wave counts?
   (A) Important at first, but less important as you become proficient at reading price charts.
   (B) Very important, because the alternate wave count is usually the correct one.
   (C) They are not really that important or necessary.
   (D) Important, because they provide a contingency plan, in case your top wave count is wrong.
2. True or False: You should not increase the size of your position when the market goes against you in wave C of a zigzag.
3. What is the most common relationship for the length of wave Y of a double zigzag?
   (A) Wave Y equals wave W.
   (B) Wave Y equals .618 times wave W.
   (C) Wave Y equals wave X.
   (D) Wave Y equals 2.618 times wave W.
4. Why is it advantageous to trade C waves of zigzags and flats?
   (A) They always move to the downside, which is a faster move.
   (B) They are extended waves, which offer more profit opportunities.
   (C) They are five-wave structures that move in the direction of the main trend.
   (D) They are always longer than wave A, which is a significant advantage.
5. True or False: In a zigzag, wave C is usually equal to wave A.

Answers: 1. D 2. False 3. A 4. C 5. True

CHAPTER 5

Using Ending Diagonals to Trade Swift and Sharp Reversals

A swift and sharp reversal follows an ending diagonal—and that is what makes it an excellent trade setup.

Trading an Ending Diagonal in the Dow (DJIA)

If there is one Elliott wave pattern to get excited about trading, it's an ending diagonal. This pattern is rare in markets, and novice analysts tend to anticipate diagonals far too often. The pattern allows for tight stop placement, so that errors are not costly. This terminating pattern shows up in the fifth-wave position of impulse waves and in the wave C position of A-B-C formations. Once an ending diagonal terminates, get ready for a swift and sharp reversal in price. That sharp reversal is what makes this wave pattern my favorite. You can see what I mean in these two hourly charts (see Figures 5.1 and 5.2) of the Dow Jones Industrial Average (DJIA) from April 1998.

In Chapter 1, "The Anatomy of Elliott Wave Trading," I described three different ways to trade this pattern, ranging from conservative to extremely aggressive. The extremely aggressive technique is based on each impulse wave of an ending diagonal being smaller than the previous one. To exploit this characteristic, a trader could take a position as wave five develops with a protective stop at the point at which wave five becomes longer than wave three.

KEY POINT

Ending diagonals can form as the fifth wave of impulse waves and as wave C of flat and zigzag corrections.

Figure 5.1
Source: Chart courtesy Elliott Wave International.

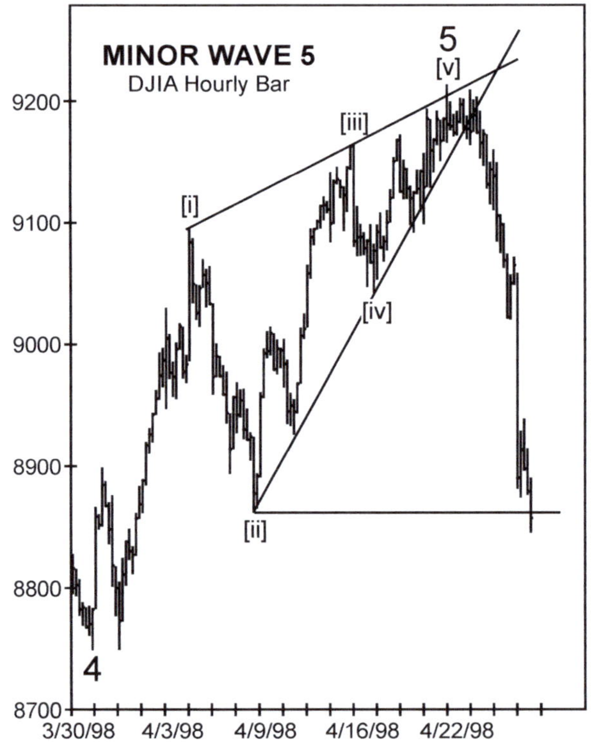

Figure 5.2
Source: Chart courtesy Elliott Wave International.

Smart Investor Tip

The guideline for an ending diagonal provides a good example of how the Wave Principle can let a trader know exactly where his or her analysis is wrong.

If we apply this trading technique to this hourly price chart (see Figure 5.3) of the Dow, a trader would short the market as wave [v] develops from 9041.9 and place a protective stop at 9344.8. That's the point at which wave [v] would become longer than wave [iii], which would negate the labeling of the pattern as an ending diagonal and indicate that a different pattern was forming.

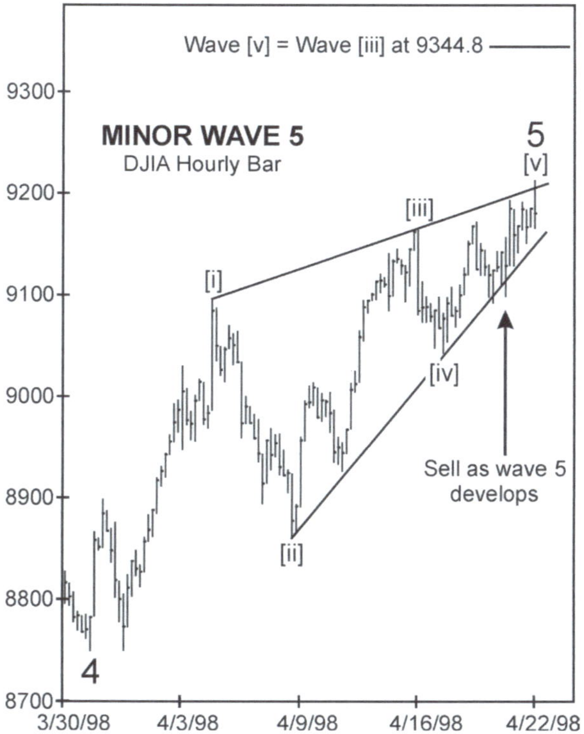

Figure 5.3

Source: Chart courtesy Elliott Wave International.

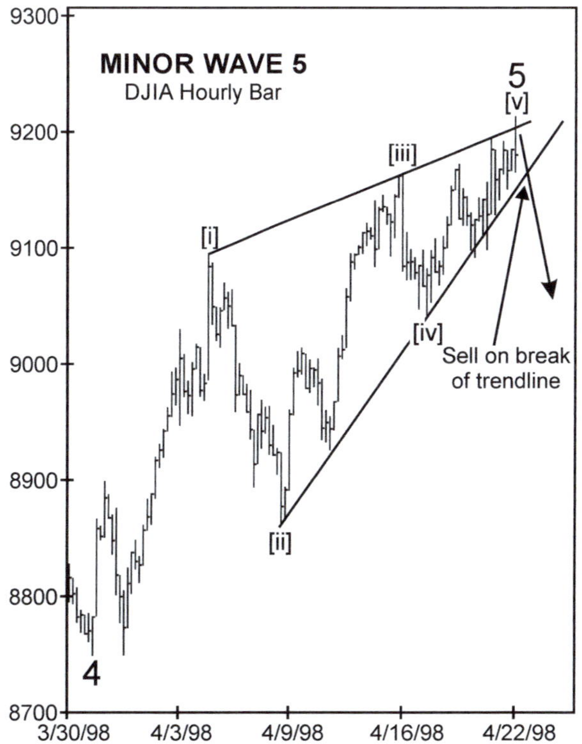

Figure 5.4

Source: Chart courtesy Elliott Wave International.

Notice the Wave Principle's ability to let a trader know exactly where his or her analysis is wrong.

A less aggressive way to trade an ending diagonal would be to wait for a decisive break of the trendline connecting the extremes of waves two and four. On this Dow chart (see Figure 5.4), that event occurred the next day, on April 23.

The most conservative approach for trading ending diagonals is to wait for the extreme of wave four to give way before initiating a trade.

Smart Investor Tip

The conservative approach for trading ending diagonals is to wait for the extreme of wave four to give way before initiating a trade.

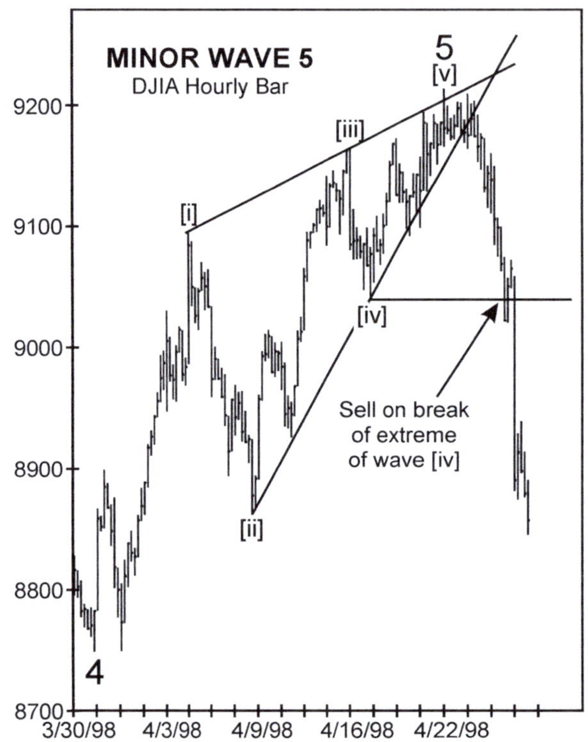

Figure 5.5

Source: Chart courtesy Elliott Wave International.

On this chart (see Figure 5.5), you can see that the Dow moved beyond the extreme of wave [iv] on April 24.

The aggressive approach appeals to some temperaments and has the advantage of allowing for a close stop. The delayed approach benefits traders by preventing them from trying to pick tops and bottoms and by helping them to base their trading decisions more on supportive price action and somewhat less on conjecture.

Regardless of your trading style, ending diagonals are worth looking for because they are easy to identify *and* they offer high-confidence trade setups. In our example, this terminating pattern introduced a 350-point decline. Traded either aggressively or conservatively, this trade setup would have been profitable.

Smart Investor Tip

The slightly aggressive approach for trading ending diagonals is to wait for a break of the trendline that connects the extremes of waves two and four.

Figure 5.6

Trading an Ending Diagonal in Broad Soft (BSFT)

Figure 5.6 illustrates another example of a fifth-wave ending diagonal and its swift and sharp reversal, this time in Broad Soft (BSFT). To trade this ending diagonal aggressively, a trader would have sold shares of BSFT as wave 5 developed (point M on Figure 5.6). The protective stop would have been set at $46.43, the level at which wave 5 would have become longer than wave 3.

Taking a less aggressive approach to trading this pattern, a trader would have waited for a break of the trend-line that connects the extremes of waves 2 and 4 (point N). BSFT moved through this level on May 4, 2012, which means a trader would have entered the trade in the low $41.00 region. The protective stop for this entry guideline is the extreme of the ending diagonal at $45.32.

KEY POINT

Regardless of your trading style—aggressive or conservative—ending diagonals are worth looking for because they are easy to identify *and* they offer high-confidence trade setups.

Figure 5.7

Chart reprinted with permission from Bloomberg. Copyright 2013 Bloomberg L.P. All rights reserved.

Figure 5.7 shows how a conservative entry would not have worked due to a price gap. The low of the day on Friday, May 4, was $40.65, which was 3 cents above the extreme of wave 4 at $40.62. Come Monday morning, the stock gapped down more than 17 percent to open at $33.75. So, opting for the conservative entry technique would have caused a trader to miss out on this trade altogether, because prices never traded at $40.62. Even so, these price charts of BSFT illustrate quite well the swift and sharp reversal that often follows ending diagonals.

Figure 5.8
Chart reprinted with permission from Bloomberg. Copyright 2013 Bloomberg L.P. All rights reserved.

Trading a Wave C Ending Diagonal in Silver Wheaton (SLW)

For the next trading example, based on the price action in a stock named Silver Wheaton (SLW), we will illustrate the trade setup and exploit it using options.

On this 60-minute price chart of SLW (Figure 5.8), let's look primarily at the price move from the $32.43 low on May 12, 2011, to the $37.20 peak on May 31, 2011. It's a slow and choppy move, with many overlapping waves. This is exactly what you would expect to see in a corrective wave pattern. So, this small advance looks like a countertrend rally within a larger downtrend.

Figure 5.9

Chart reprinted with permission from Bloomberg. Copyright 2013 Bloomberg L.P. All rights reserved.

Figure 5.9 shows my Elliott wave interpretation of the price action following the April 8 price peak at $47.60. From that high, I have labeled waves (1)-(2)-(3) as complete at the $32.43 low on May 12. The next move up and sideways subdivides into a flat—three waves up in wave A, three waves down in wave B, followed by an ending diagonal for wave C that contracts slightly.

The Wave Principle provides context for the price action, allowing us to identify the move up from the May low as a fourth-wave correction within a larger unfolding five-wave decline. With

Figure 5.10

Chart reprinted with permission from Bloomberg. Copyright 2013 Bloomberg L.P. All rights reserved.

the idea that we have an ending diagonal in wave C of wave (4), we can forecast another round of selling in wave (5) to below the $32.43 low. Now, what is a good way to take advantage of this trade setup?

One way would be to wait for a few more price bars, and on June 2 buy 10 June 2011 $34.00 puts at 82 cents. When I trade options, I always like buying calls/puts just a little bit out of the money. The cost of the position, not including commissions, would be $820.00 (see Figure 5.10).

In the days that followed, prices adhered to our proposed Elliott wave forecast, pressing

Figure 5.11

Chart reprinted with permission from Bloomberg. Copyright 2013 Bloomberg L.P. All rights reserved.

lower (see Figure 5.11). Moreover, on June 8, prices moved below the low of wave (3) at $32.43. So, we would hang on for the ride for more than a week. Even though the requirements of a completed impulse wave were met, we would conservatively exit the position on June 13 by selling 10 June 2011 $34.00 puts at $2.72. From our entry at 82 cents to an exit at $2.72, we would have made a 230 percent return.

Figure 5.12

Chart reprinted with permission from Bloomberg. Copyright 2013 Bloomberg L.P. All rights reserved.

As it happened, SLW continued down to a final low of $29.79 in the days that followed (see Figure 5.12). Had we held the position for a few more days, it would have been possible to exit with more than a 375 percent return, as the bid for the June 2011 $34.00 put at that time was $3.90. Although some people would be upset about missing that extra gain, when a minimum target is reached, it's usually best to follow the old advice that a bird in the hand is worth two in the bush.

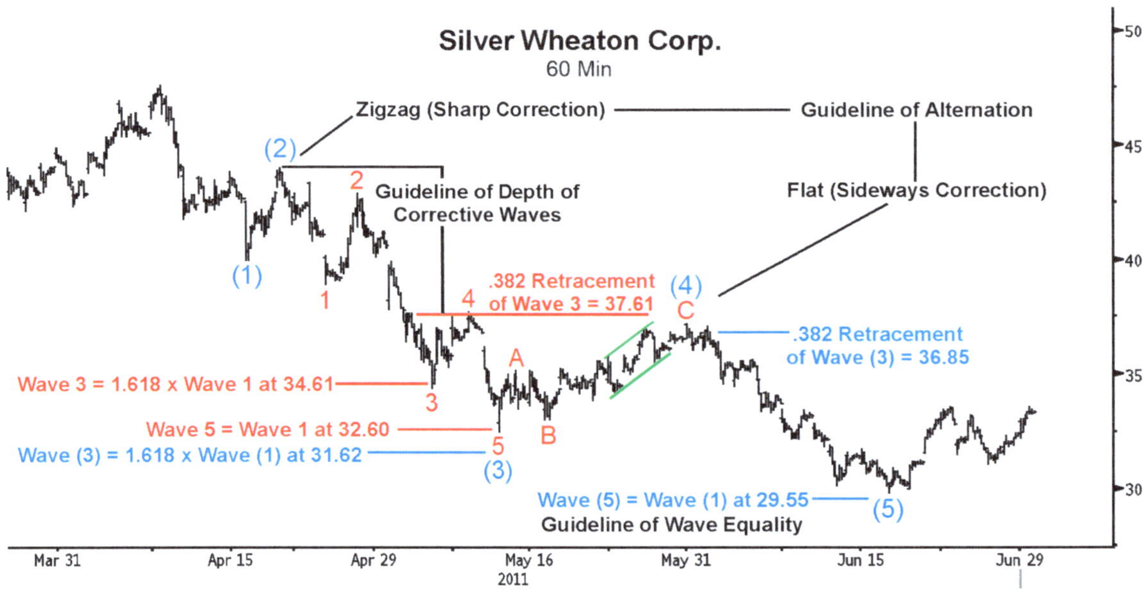

Figure 5.13

Chart reprinted with permission from Bloomberg. Copyright 2013 Bloomberg L.P. All rights reserved.

Let's look at this same SLW price chart (see Figure 5.13) from an analytical perspective rather than a trading perspective. You will see that it adheres to many guidelines of the Wave Principle, one of which is called *alternation*. This guideline applied to corrective waves tells you to look for different forms in waves two and four. For example, if wave two is a sharp correction, expect wave four to be a drawn-out, sideways correction. If wave two is a sideways correction, then expect wave four to be sharp. Zigzags are sharp corrections, while flats and triangles are sideways corrections. What differentiates sharp from sideways corrections is that sharp corrections never include a new price extreme. Notice that in SLW's chart, wave (2) is a zigzag (short and sharp) while wave (4) is a flat correction (sideways and drawn-out). That's alternation.

Another guideline in play in this chart governs the depth of corrective waves: When a five-wave structure is complete, the retracement tends to push prices back into the span of travel of the preceding fourth wave, often ending near its terminus. That is evident here, as wave (4) peaked near the end of wave 4 of (3).

A third guideline is equality: In an impulse wave, waves five and one tend toward equality when wave three extends. The subdivisions within wave (3) follow this guideline. Notice that wave 5, at 32.43 points, equals the distance traveled in wave 1, at 32.60 points, only a 17-cent difference.

There is a corollary to this equality guideline: Within a motive wave, typically one of the motive subwaves will extend. In equities and equity indexes, most often wave three is the one that extends. In commodities, fifth waves are more likely to extend. When wave three extends, waves five and one tend toward equality. Notice that wave (5) in SLW would equal wave (1) at $29.55. The low of $29.79 is less than 1 percent from the level supplied by the guideline of equality.

Next, let's examine some Fibonacci relationships. The most common Fibonacci multiple for a third wave is a 1.618 multiple of wave one. SLW's wave (3) equaled a 1.618 multiple of wave (1) at $31.62. Wave (3) bottomed at $32.43, which is only a few percentage points above the 1.618 target. An even better example of this guideline in action exists within wave (3). Wave 3 of (3) would have been a 1.618 multiple of wave 1 of (3) at $34.61. It terminated at $34.34 less than a percentage point away.

The most common Fibonacci retracement for fourth waves is a .382 multiple of wave three. SLW prices came up to that .382 retracement three times before reversing to the downside in wave (5). The .382 retracement of wave (3) came into play at 36.85, and wave (4) peaked at 37.20.

Ultimately, this trade in SLW would have worked out nicely. It was based on recognizing a basic motive wave, but the guidelines and Fibonacci relationships added confidence to that wave count.

Trading a Wave C Ending Diagonal in Teck Resources Limited (TCK)

Let's turn to one of my actual experiences to illustrate how to trade an ending diagonal in the

KEY POINT

The guideline of alternation applies to corrective waves. For example, if wave two is a sharp correction, expect wave four to be a drawn-out, sideways correction. If wave two is a sideways correction, then expect wave four to be sharp.

KEY POINT

The guideline of equality applies to impulse waves: When wave three extends, waves five and one tend to be equal in length.

Figure 5.14
Chart reprinted with permission from Bloomberg. Copyright 2013 Bloomberg L.P. All rights reserved.

wave C position of an A-B-C formation. The overall wave pattern in Teck Resources Limited (TCK) during March and April 2012 was an expanded flat, with wave (C) taking the shape of an ending diagonal (see Figure 5.14). If I have identified the pattern correctly to this point, then a swift and sharp reversal in price should unfold, following a moderate new high above \$37.97, which is the extreme of wave 3. The reversal should carry prices below the origin of wave (C) at \$33.61.

Figure 5.15

On May 2, 2012, TCK made a moderate new high above the extreme of wave 3 (see Figure 5.15). At that point, the minimum requirements of a completed wave pattern were in place, and the stage was set for a sizable decline in price. In order to take advantage of this trade setup, I decided to employ a modified ending diagonal entry technique.

Rather than selling as wave 5 developed or entering on a break of the 2–4 trendline, I decided to take a small position on a break of the extreme of wave [b] of 5 at $36.94. Doing so was slightly aggressive, but it did still allow me to use confirming price action, because it required a move below a prior swing low. Also, to off set the risk of entering this trade too early, I took only a small position.

Smart Investor Tip

To offset the risk of entering a trade too early, take a small position.

Figure 5.16

When the $36.94 entry was triggered, the initial protective stop was set at the high of the move at $38.09 (see Figure 5.16). If only the minimum objective for this trade had been achieved with a move below $33.61, the risk-reward ratio for this position was a very acceptable 3:1.

At this point, as shown in Figure 5.17, I decided to scale into another 100 shares on a move below $35.13, using the more conservative strategy, discussed in Chapter 1, of selling shares at the extreme of wave 4 of the ending diagonal.

Teck Resources Limited
60 Min
(A)
C
A
B
B
A
C
(B)
1
2
3
4
5
(C)
Short 50 shares at 36.94
Protective Stop = 38.09
35.13
Sell 100 shares at 35.13
39.00
38.00
37.00
36.00
35.00
34.00
33.00
32.00
Mar 15
Mar 30
2012
Apr 16
... May 2

Figure 5.17

Figure 5.18
Chart reprinted with permission from Bloomberg. Copyright 2013 Bloomberg L.P. All rights reserved.

On May 4, this second position was triggered, which made the total position in TCK short 150 shares at an average entry price of $35.73 (see Figure 5.18). Following the first trade, I set the initial protective stop at $38.09. After scaling into the additional 100 shares, I lowered the protective stop to $37.17, the extreme of the most recent second wave.

Figure 5.19

Chart reprinted with permission from Bloomberg. Copyright 2013 Bloomberg L.P. All rights reserved.

Four days later on May 8, TCK fell below $33.61, the origin of the ending diagonal (see Figure 5.19). Since the minimum expectation for this trade had been met, I dramatically lowered the protective stop on the position to $34.00. When lowering the stop, I also considered that it was now possible to count five waves down from $38.09 to $32.67. With a five-wave sell-off apparently in place, I knew that the downside was limited over the short term and that the next significant move would be up.

Figure 5.20

Chart reprinted with permission from Bloomberg.

The next day (see Figure 5.20), I lowered the stop on this trade from $34.00 to $33.00, to lessen my risk and protect my open profits. Later in the day on May 9, TCK traded through $33.00, stopping out the trade. The result was a $2.73 drop in share price, a 7.64 percent decline. Not a bad return for a trade that lasted only six days.

I discuss the ending diagonal often in my *Trader's Classroom* lessons. If you aren't already a member of *Trader's Classroom*, you can get a Visual Guide special offer here: www.elliottwave.com/wave/VGB-TCSpecialOffer.

Trading an Ending Diagonal in the Euro

In April 2008, an interesting situation developed in the euro against the U.S. dollar in the foreign exchange market. After the October 2000 low of .8245, based on the nearest futures contract, the euro rose relentlessly, making one

Figure 5.21

record high after another. Was there any way to know when this market would finally become exhausted? The Elliott wave model had the answer. Ending diagonals in the euro at two different degrees flashed two major sell signals at the record high. But let's start at the beginning.

On this daily continuation chart (see Figure 5.21) of the euro futures contract as of April 22, 2008, we see a decisive move up in waves (i), (ii), and (iii). Within wave (iii), we can count waves i through v as one probable scenario, with wave v peaking at 1.5985. Observe that wave v contains five overlapping waves that contract and form a wedge shape. That is the signature of an ending diagonal, which signals a swift and sharp reversal ahead.

According to Elliott wave guidelines, the reversal will travel at least to where the diagonal began and possibly further. In this case, that level is indicated by the end of wave iv at 1.5273.

KEY POINT

After an ending diagonal is complete, the reversal back to where the diagonal began should take from one-third to one-half the time it took for the diagonal to unfold.

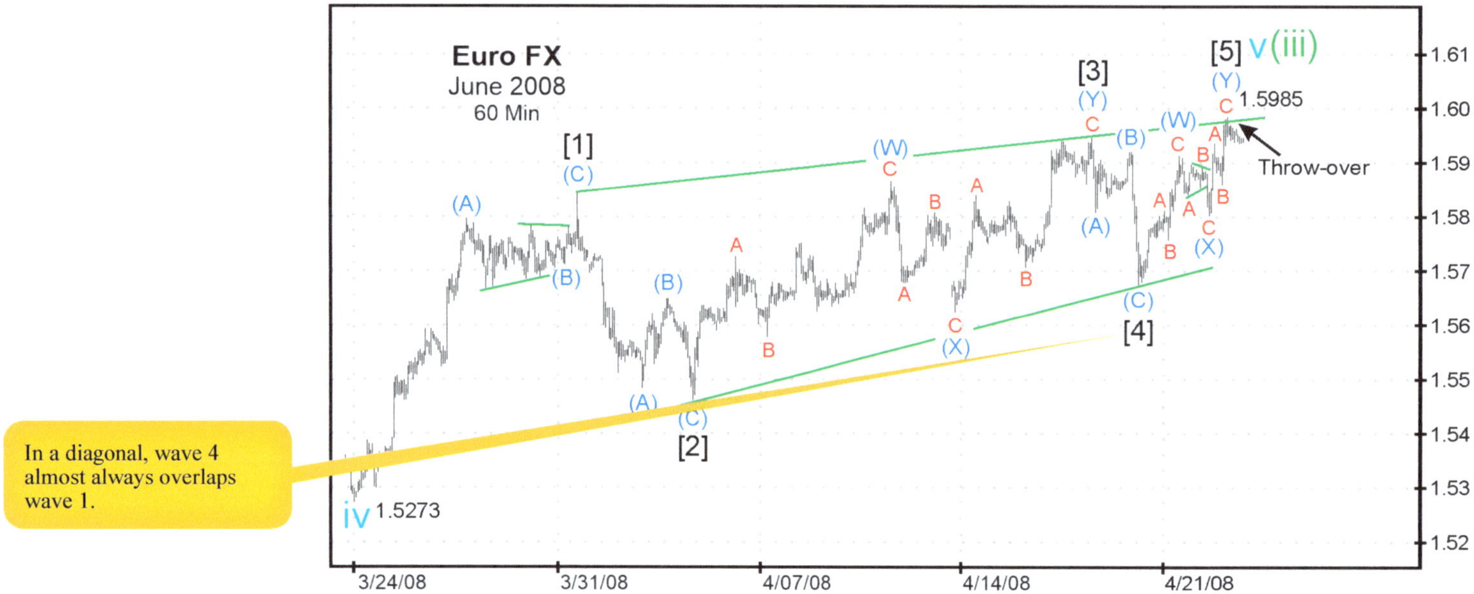

Figure 5.22

Source: Data courtesy TradeNavigator.com.

One key characteristic of ending diagonals is that all the initial subwaves form either single or multiple zigzag patterns. Here is a close-up view of this diagonal on an hourly bar chart (see Figure 5.22) in order to reveal these zigzag patterns.

Waves [1], [2], and [4] appear to be single zigzags, while waves [3] and [5] appear to be double zigzags. Wave [5] makes a throw-over, because it travels slightly beyond the 1-3 trendline. A throw-over often indicates that the diagonal has finished. Once prices move below the 2-4 trendline, we would have strong evidence that the diagonal had terminated at 1.5985. The next event should be a swift move to at least 1.5273 and probably beyond.

Figure 5.23

Chart reprinted with permission from Bloomberg. Copyright 2013 Bloomberg L.P. All rights reserved.

As shown in Figure 5.3, we can establish lower price targets by using Fibonacci retracement levels. In this case, our price target of 1.5273 falls in between the .382 and .500 retracement levels. This target area is consistent with the fact that fourth waves normally make shallow retracements (such as .382) back to the previous fourth wave of one lesser degree.

Based on this knowledge, we would short the euro at this juncture, using the June 2008 futures contract. (All the key price levels on the daily continuation chart involve the June contract.)

Depending on your risk tolerance, you could wait to go short on a break of the 2-4 trendline rather than acting immediately. Personally, I prefer to take action rather than wait for that event,

KEY POINT

Within a contracting ending diagonal, wave three is always shorter than wave one, and wave five is always shorter than wave three.

Figure 5.24

particularly if I have strong evidence that the diagonal has ended.

Let's say that we decided to sell the euro at the closing price on April 22 at 1.5957 (see Figure 5.24). Our price target is 1.5273, where the diagonal began. Our protective stop is 1.6161, the price at which wave [5] would be longer than wave [3], which would make the diagonal invalid. Our potential risk would be 204 points and our potential reward would be 684 points, resulting in a risk-reward ratio of more than 3:1.

Figure 5.25

Source: Data courtesy TradeNavigator.com.

On this hourly bar chart (see Figure 5.25) as of April 24, the euro has broken the 2-4 trendline, strongly suggesting that the diagonal terminated at 1.5985. At this juncture, we could move our stop further down. We would not want to see a significant move back above the 2-4 trendline, so we would place the stop at 1.5839, which is the last significant high before the break of the trendline.

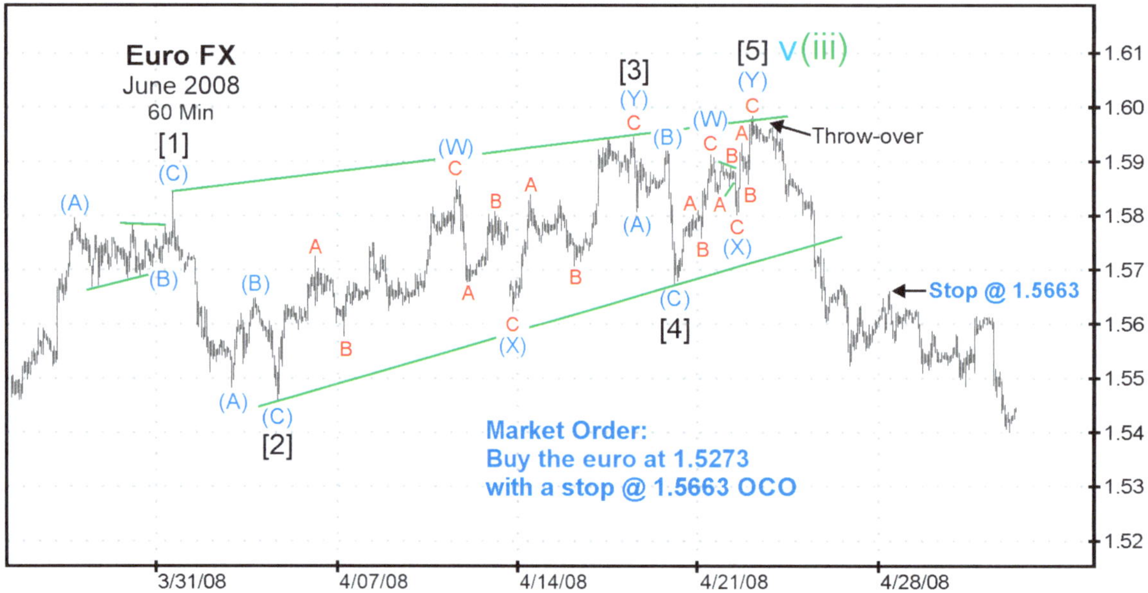

Figure 5.26
Source: Data courtesy TradeNavigator.com.

Here we are a week later (see Figure 5.26), with the euro continuing to decline. This is an opportunity to lower our stop below the 2-4 trendline. One reasonable level to choose would be 1.5663 because it represents the high of a recent correction. We could have also placed a market order to buy the euro at 1.5273 on a stop with a protective stop at 1.5663, OCO (one cancels the other).

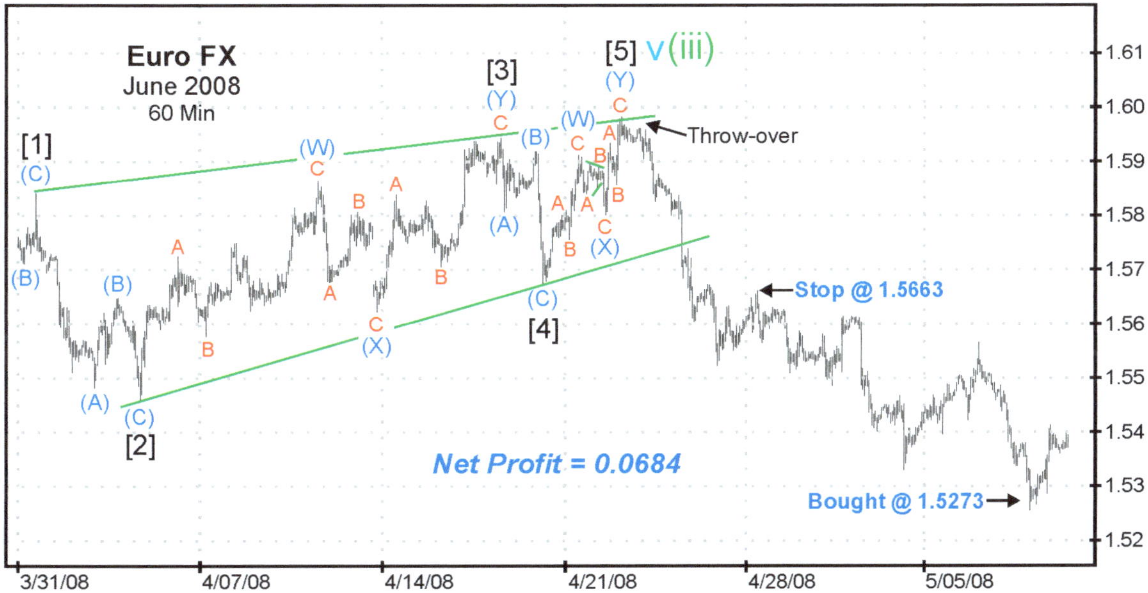

Figure 5.27
Source: Data courtesy TradeNavigator.com.

On May 7, the euro reached a low of 1.5255, and the order would have been filled at 1.5273 for a net profit of 684 points (see Figure 5.27).

This daily chart (see Figure 5.28) shows the euro's further price moves through August 8. Wave (iv) ended at 1.5255. What is interesting is that wave (v) also unfolded as an ending diagonal. It, too, displayed a throw-over and then peaked at 1.5988, only a few ticks beyond the previous all-time high. A swift and sharp reversal followed, and the euro never looked back. Could you have known that the euro would continue to decline past 1.5255, which was the beginning of the diagonal on the daily chart? Yes, but only by analyzing the wave structure of the decline as well as the wave pattern at higher degree. Re-

Figure 5.28

Chart reprinted with permission from Bloomberg. Copyright 2013 Bloomberg L.P. All rights reserved.

gardless, once you had seen the second diagonal, you would have known that a reversal was in the offing and that 1.5255 would have been a good start for the initial price target on your next trade.

Overall, two ending diagonals occurred at different degrees and peaked at about the same price level, signaling exhaustion in the main trend. In the second ending diagonal, the throw-over was greater than the first one and the reversal more violent.

KEY POINT

The greater the throw-over, the more violent the reversal.

For More Information

Learn more at your exclusive Reader Resources site. You will find lessons on recognizing diagonal patterns in your charts and positioning yourself for the market action to come, plus more free resources designed to help you incorporate Fibonacci and technical indicators into your wave analysis. Go to: www.elliottwave.com/wave/ReaderResources.

Test Yourself

1. Where can ending diagonals occur?
   (A) Wave 5 of an ending diagonal
   (B) Wave A of a zigzag or flat
   (C) Wave 5 of an impulse wave and wave C of flats and zigzags
   (D) At the end of a corrective pattern
2. True or False: An ending diagonal is a sign that the main trend will continue for a while.
3. After the termination of an ending diagonal, what can you expect?
   (A) The trend should be sideways.
   (B) The market should reverse sharply to where the diagonal began.
   (C) A triangle should unfold.
   (D) There should be another diagonal in the opposite direction.
4. What do ending diagonals, truncated fifth waves, and fifth-wave extensions have in common?
   (A) They always move to the downside, which is a faster move.
   (B) They are extended waves, which offer more profit opportunities.
   (C) They are all followed by a swift and sharp reversal.
   (D) They are all impulse waves.
5. True or False: In a contracting ending diagonal, wave 3 is shorter than wave 1.

Answers: 1. C 2. False 3. B 4. C 5. True

PART III

Going Beyond Elliott Wave Patterns

CHAPTER 6

Applying Technical Indicators

The study of market action is the essence of technical analysis. The term *technical analysis* includes many different tools technicians use to study market action. The Wave Principle, for example, is a model with which one can practice technical analysis by recognizing wave patterns resulting from shifts in crowd psychology. Other bases for technical analysis are Japanese candlesticks, point and figure, relative strength index, and moving average convergence-divergence.

Which tool is the best? Technicians hotly debate this question, but I see it this way: The best tool is the one that works best for you. For me, that tool is the Wave Principle. Even though I am an Elliottician, I do use other forms of technical analysis to find evidence to support or challenge my analysis, thereby improving my trading.

At times, the Wave Principle and your technical indicators may be at odds. When that happens, the obvious response is to forego the trade and instead keep looking at charts of other markets to find a better trade setup. This situation—when either you have a beautiful wave pattern that is not supported by a technical indicator or you have a flashing technical indicator that does not jibe with the wave pattern—can actually help you manage your risk better. For instance, you could still take a chance on the trade but with reduced risk, using 50 shares rather than the full 100 shares you would normally employ.

Here are three examples showing how I apply technical indicators to my trading.

KEY POINT

The Wave Principle is a model with which one can practice technical analysis by recognizing wave patterns resulting from shifts in crowd psychology.

Figure 6.1
Chart reprinted with permission from Bloomberg. Copyright 2013 Bloomberg L.P. All rights reserved.

Cree (CREE)—Trading a Bearish RSI Divergence

This first example in Figure 6.1 shows how the relative strength index (RSI) helped identify a trade setup in Cree (CREE). Developed by J. Welles Wilder, Jr., RSI is a useful tool for measuring momentum and identifying divergences. Divergence forms when price and an underlying indicator move in opposite directions. In a bullish divergence, prices make new lows while the accompanying indicator does not. In a bearish divergence, they make new highs while the indictor does not.

CREE moved up in five waves from the December 2011 low of $20.25 to the high in May 2012 at $33.45. The Elliott wave guideline on the

Figure 6.2

Chart reprinted with permission from Bloomberg. Copyright 2013 Bloomberg L.P. All rights reserved.

depth of corrective waves suggests that the correction should push prices back into the span of travel of the preceding fourth wave, most often ending near its terminus. In this case, the terminus of wave (4) is $28.81. So a reasonable trade appears to be a short sale, for a drop at least back to $28.81.The trading plan would be to sell 100 shares of CREE on a break of $31.05, the swing low. If filled, then the initial protective stop would be the high at $33.45.

The wave count is not the only evidence that supports taking a short position in CREE. Notice in Figure 6.2 that prices and RSI had been diverging since February—an indication

Figure 6.3

Chart reprinted with permission from Bloomberg. Copyright 2013 Bloomberg L.P. All rights reserved.

of decreasing upside momentum, signaling a weakening uptrend. While CREE made new price highs in March, April, and May, RSI did not. This bearish divergence is often a precursor to a downturn in prices.

So, a bearish Elliott wave pattern combined with a bearish divergence between price and RSI make a stronger case to short this stock than if a trader used only one of these tools.

In the days that followed (see Figure 6.3), CREE fell below $31.05, which triggered the short position. The initial protective stop was set at $32.85, simply because a move above $32.85 would tag the decline from $33.45 as a

Smart Investor Tip

Always manage your risk in every trade by focusing on this trio: Lessen risk, eliminate risk, and protect open profits.

Figure 6.4

Chart reprinted with permission from Bloomberg.

corrective sell-off and argue that the larger uptrend was still intact.

Following our entry on May 15, CREE continued down as expected (see Figure 6.4), so we would lower the protective stop to $31.95. With an entry price of $31.05 a share and a protective stop at $31.95, the risk on this trade would be less than a buck a share.

When initiating a trade, it is prudent to employ an initial protective stop—a level at which your analysis and, therefore, the trade are no longer viable. Then, as the trade progresses,

Figure 6.5

Chart reprinted with permission from Bloomberg. Copyright 2013 Bloomberg L.P. All rights reserved.

> **KEY POINT**
>
> **A successful trade is made up of three ingredients—the psychology of the trader (60 percent), risk management (about 30 percent), and technique (only about 10 percent).**

you incrementally move your stop to lessen risk. Just as the motto of many salespeople is "always be closing," the motto of many professional traders is "always be managing risk." It sounds easy, but a successful trade depends more on the psychology of the trader than on risk management. If I were to break it down, risk management would be about 30 percent of a successful trade, technique only about 10 percent, and psychology 60 percent.

By lowering the protective stop to our entry price at $31.05 (see Figure 6.5), we are able to

Figure 6.6

achieve the second part of our risk management trio—reducing risk to zero. Transaction costs aside, if we were stopped out thereafter, we would lose nothing. This is what I call a free trade.

The next move is to protect open profits by lowering the stop again to $30.05 (see Figure 6.6), which is below our entry price, primarily in response to the gap down that occurred on May 22.

Figure 6.7

Chart reprinted with permission from Bloomberg. Copyright 2013 Bloomberg L.P. All rights reserved.

The next day (see Figure 6.7), we would protect open profits even further by lowering the stop to $27.05. With an entry price of $31.05 a share and a protective stop now set at $27.05, we have successfully locked in a $4.00-per-share profit on this position.

One week later, on May 29, prices hit the $27.05 protective stop (see Figure 6.8). This nine-day trade resulted in a 12.88 percent return, which translated into a $400 profit. As you can see, after being stopped out by mere pennies, CREE fell an additional 15 percent. Does that

Figure 6.8
Chart reprinted with permission from Bloomberg. Copyright 2013 Bloomberg L.P. All rights reserved.

mean the protective stop was set too tight? Possibly, but it's debatable. After all, your goal as a trader is to do one thing—make money. Your goal is not to sell at top tick or buy at bottom tick. Your goal is not to be perfect on every trade or to have the most optimal stop on every trade. In fact, if the $30.05 stop had been hit on May 22, this trade would still have been profitable. Don't berate yourself for imperfection. If you make money, get up from your computer grinning like the Cheshire cat. Remember, the person on the other side of your trade took a loss.

Although you might want to squeeze all the money you can out of each and every trade, that

DEFINITION:
flat correction

A flat consists of three waves, waves A–B–C, wherein each wave subdivides into three smaller waves and wave B ends at or near the origin of wave A.

attitude can lead to some adverse effects, such as getting into a trade prematurely. As a trader, it is wiser to be content with capturing 60 to 80 percent of a trend, rather than competing with the cowboys and ego-traders who try to pick the top or bottom in the market.

Wal-Mart (WMT)—Candlesticks and MACD Support Bullish Wave Count

For our next trading example in Wal-Mart (WMT), shown in Figure 6.9, we will apply Japanese candle-sticks and moving average convergence-divergence (MACD). If you are not familiar with Japanese candle-sticks, I highly recommend Steve Nison's book, Japanese Candlestick Charting Techniques.

Put simply, a candlestick price chart incorporates the same data as an O-H-L-C price chart. The difference lies in how the data are illustrated. Japanese candlestick charts do an excellent job of showing the balance of power between bulls and bears, while also providing early indications of market turns.

MACD is a momentum indicator developed by Gerald Appel in the late 1970s. Although it is a lagging indicator, since it is based on moving averages, MACD is still an excellent timing tool in long-trending markets and for evaluating weakening or strengthening momentum conditions.

On this daily chart of WMT (see Figure 6.9) from March 2011 to May 2012, it is clear that an impulse wave is forming. Within this advance, the first three waves ended at $62.63. In subsequent price action, wave (4) is a **flat correction**, consisting of three waves, A–B–C, wherein each wave subdivides into three smaller waves. The most distinguishing characteristic of this pattern is that wave B ends at or near the origin of wave A. Based on this labeling, we would expect prices to move to new highs in wave (5), above $62.63.

Since I like to rely on more than a single piece of evidence or discipline, let's examine two indicators to see if they agree with our Elliott wave analysis. We will begin with a Japanese candlestick price chart.

A candle, which is a price bar, consists of two shadows, upper and lower, and a real body.

Figure 6.9

Chart reprinted with permission from Bloomberg.

Figure 6.10

Chart reprinted with permission from Bloomberg. Copyright 2013 Bloomberg L.P. All rights reserved.

A bullish candle forms when the close is above the open. It is referred to as the real body. The difference between the high and the close is the upper shadow, while the portion of trading between the open and low is called the lower shadow. Moreover, these candlesticks, both bullish and bearish, form patterns that often coincide with turns in price.

In WMT, the candlestick pattern that formed in late April and early May is called a *bullish engulfing pattern*" (see Figure 6.10). This pattern occurs when prices open below the prior candle's close and close above the prior candle's open. It is a bullish reversal pattern that suggests emerging strength. Combine this candlestick pattern with the equally

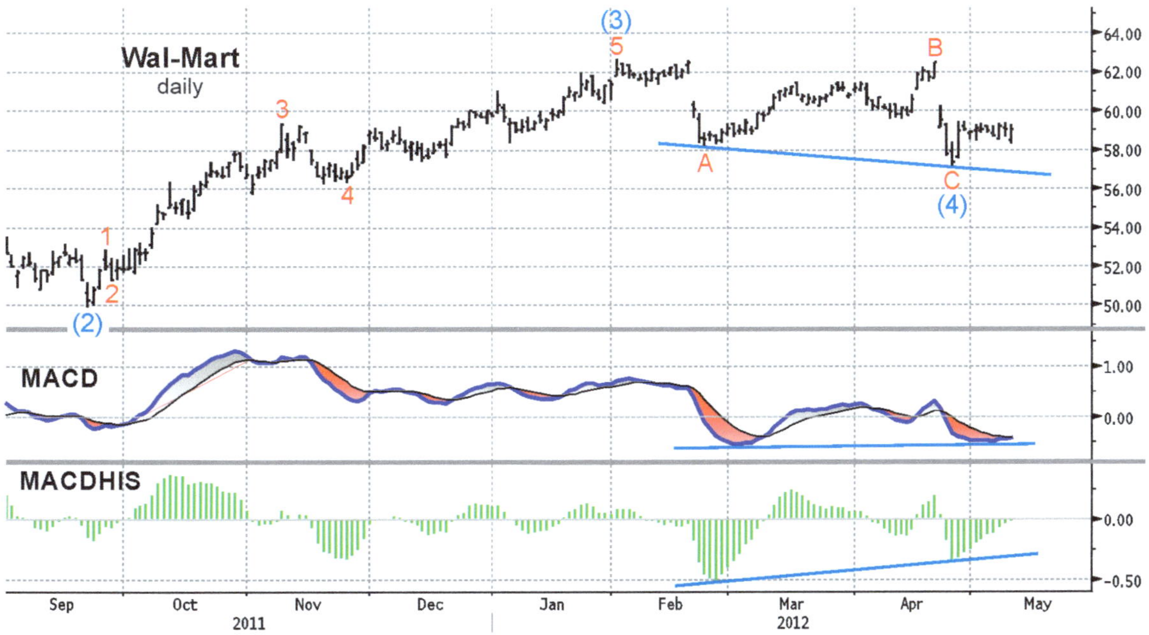

Figure 6.11
Chart reprinted with permission from Bloomberg. Copyright 2013 Bloomberg L.P. All rights reserved.

compelling and bullish wave count, and we have begun to make a solid case for a buy-side trade.

Now, let's add another study. This price chart (see Figure 6.11) includes two indicators: MACD (comprising the MACD line in blue and the MACD signal line in black) and the MACD histogram. The MACD line is the difference between a 12-period and 26-period exponential moving average. The MACD signal line is merely a 9-period exponential moving average of the MACD line. The MACD histogram represents

Figure 6.12

Chart reprinted with permission from Bloomberg. Copyright 2013 Bloomberg L.P. All rights reserved.

the difference between the MACD line and the MACD signal line.

The momentum signature exhibited in both MACD and the MACD histogram is a bullish divergence. Notice that the MACD readings were higher during wave C of our flat fourth wave in WMT than during wave A. This bullish divergence implies that the market is strengthening.

With a bullish wave count, a bullish engulfing pattern on the weekly chart level and bullish divergence present using MACD and MACD histogram, we now have three pieces of corroborating evidence to go long WMT.

In this example (see Figure 6.12), I thought it would be both fun and educational to trade WMT two different ways. First, we will buy 100

Figure 6.13

Chart reprinted with permission from Bloomberg. Copyright 2013 Bloomberg L.P. All rights reserved.

shares of WMT at $59.10 with a protective stop at $58.27. Excluding commissions, the purchase price is $5,910. Second, we will use options and buy 10 September 2012 $60 calls at $1.70 a piece. Excluding commissions, the purchase price for our option position is $1,700.

Figure 6.13 shows that following our purchase, WMT gapped up significantly on May 17. In

Figure 6.14
Chart reprinted with permission from Bloomberg. Copyright 2013 Bloomberg L.P. All rights reserved.

response, we raise our initial protective stop from $58.27 to $59.80, just above our entry price. We also let go of five of our September calls at $3.65 apiece for $1,825, excluding commissions. This allows us to pocket our original $1,700 investment plus $125.00 in profit. Moreover, we still have five September calls that look promising.

After prices gapped up, WMT pushed even higher (see Figure 6.14), so we sold our remaining option position at $4.40 apiece. On our option

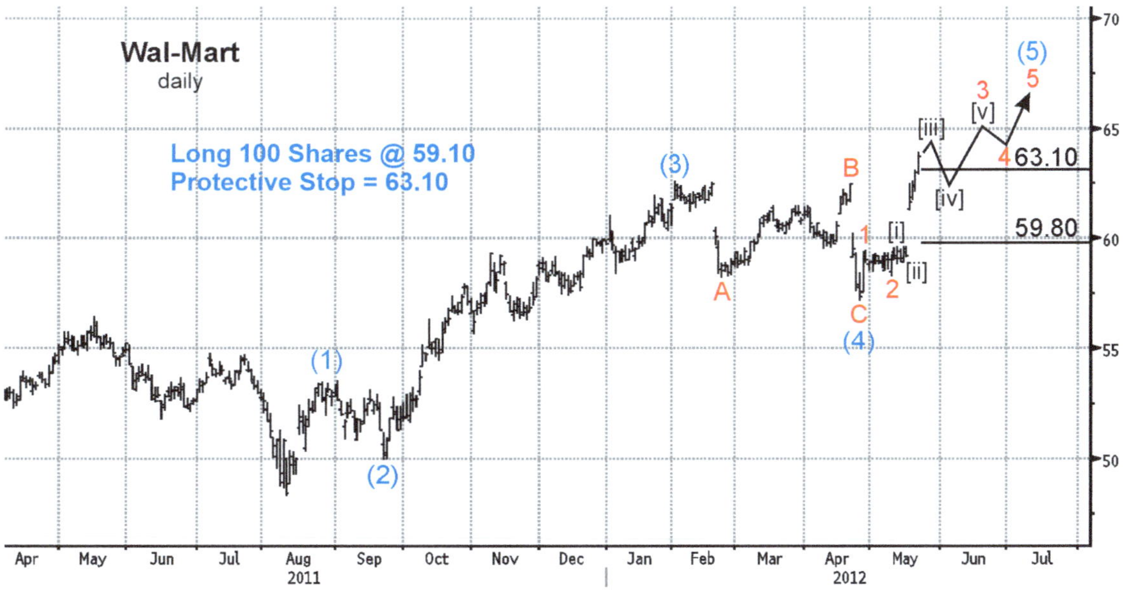

Figure 6.15
Chart reprinted with permission from Bloomberg. Copyright 2013 Bloomberg L.P. All rights reserved.

play, we made back our original sum of $1,700 (excluding commissions), and generated an additional profit of $2,325.

Now back to our open trade. Since risk management should be the number-one priority of every trader, we raise our protective stop to $63.10, locking in a sizable profit.

As shown in Figure 6.15, WMT pushes higher in the days that follow, and as the advance continues, we raise our protective trailing stop from

Figure 6.16

Chart reprinted with permission from Bloomberg. Copyright 2013 Bloomberg L.P. All rights reserved.

$63.10 to $64.10 and then to $65.10, as seen in the next two charts (see Figures 6.16 and 6.17).

At $65.60, our trailing stop is finally hit, and we exit the position for a profit of $650 (or 9.91 percent) (see Figure 6.18).

Video:
To watch a video on how to identify a change in trend, using Elliott and corroborating technical evidence, go to:
www.elliottwave.com/wave/ReaderResources

Figure 6.17

Chart reprinted with permission from Bloomberg. Copyright 2013 Bloomberg L.P. All rights reserved.

Figure 6.18
Chart reprinted with permission from Bloomberg. Copyright 2013 Bloomberg L.P. All rights reserved.

Figure 6.19

Wynn Resorts (WYNN)—Trading with Multiple Technical Indicators

For our third trading example, we will use all three technical indicators—RSI, candlesticks, and MACD—along with wave analysis to trade Wynn Resorts (WYNN).

The advance in Wynn Resorts (WYNN) from \$101.02 in December 2011 to the \$138.28 high in May is a double zigzag, as labeled in Figure 6.19. This Elliott wave interpretation implies that, at some point, the December 2011 advance will be more than fully retraced.

The price action that unfolded in March and April is noteworthy because trading in March took the shape of a contracting triangle, while the wave pattern that evolved in April was an ending diagonal.

A triangle is one of the three Elliott wave corrective patterns. It most often appears as a sideways

Figure 6.20

Chart reprinted with permission from Bloomberg. Copyright 2013 Bloomberg L.P. All rights reserved.

price move within converging trendlines. Labeled A–B–C–D–E, the five waves within the triangle each subdivide into three smaller waves. By itself, a triangle can form only in the wave four, B, or X positions. Most important for a trader, a triangle always precedes the final wave of a sequence.

Ending diagonals are terminating wave patterns that can form only in the fifth-wave position of impulse waves or as wave C of A–B–C formations. While a triangle forewarns that the end is near, an ending diagonal lets you know that the end is at hand.

Both the triangle and the ending diagonal that formed in April are easy to identify.

Having analyzed this chart over the weekend (when I spend much of my time looking for trading opportunities), I devised a trade plan to sell 10 shares of WYNN on Monday, May 7 (see

Figure 6.21

Figure 6.20). I was eager to take this position because WYNN had already traded below the low of wave 4 of the final wave (C) of the double zigzag. If you recall from Chapter 1, a break of the extreme of wave four of a diagonal is the conservative entry technique for trading this pattern. Once filled, the initial protective stop for this trade will be the May high of $138.28.

But beyond the compelling Elliott wave case for taking a short position in WYNN, we can see two pieces of supporting evidence. For example, there is a noticeable bearish RSI divergence on the daily chart level (see Figure 6.21). Although bearish divergence does not always result in a price reversal, it takes on more significance when combined with a bearish Elliott wave labeling.

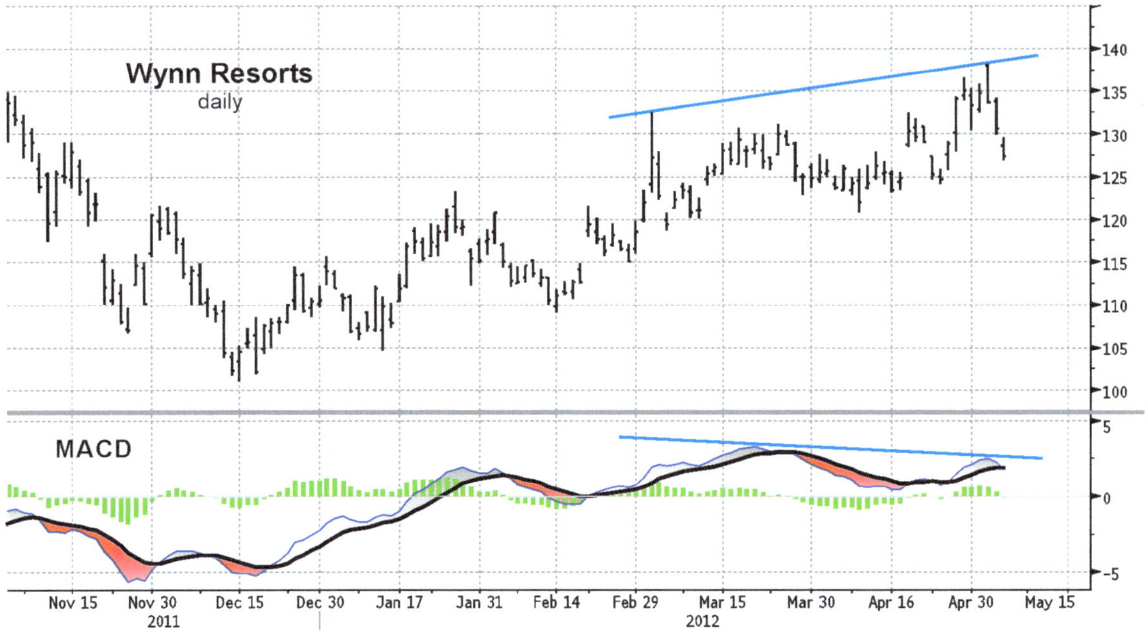

Figure 6.22
Chart reprinted with permission from Bloomberg. Copyright 2013 Bloomberg L.P. All rights reserved.

And we can see a similar bearish divergence using MACD and MACD histogram, as shown in Figure 6.22. Thus, two different measures of momentum support the bearish Elliott wave labeling.

The price charts we have examined thus far have been standard O-H-L-C price charts. Let's see what the Japanese candlestick chart in Figure 6.23 can tell us.

Figure 6.23

Chart reprinted with permission from Bloomberg. Copyright 2013 Bloomberg L.P. All rights reserved.

In early May, a *dark cloud cover* candlestick pattern formed in WYNN. A dark cloud cover is a bearish reversal pattern that forms when a white (or green) candle is followed by a black (or red) candle that opens above the previous candle's high and then closes well into the white (or green) candle's body.

We now have yet another piece of evidence for taking a short position. This is what I call evidence-based analysis and trading. By combining multiple forms of technical analysis to arrive at a trading decision, you increase the odds for a successful outcome. (Even so, it is important to remember that the risks of trading can only be reduced, never eliminated.)

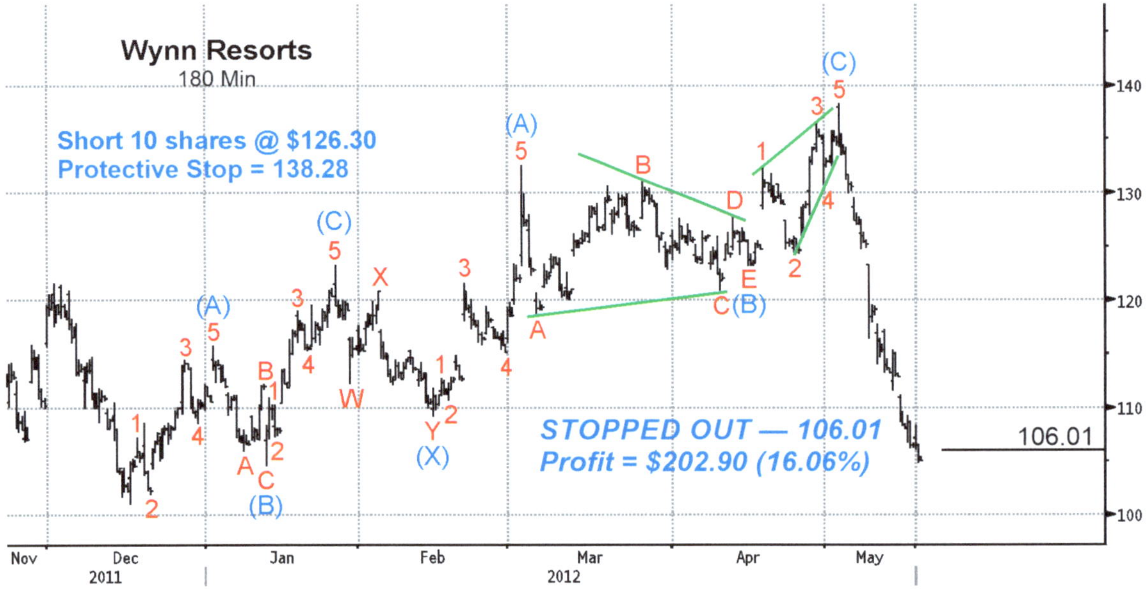

Figure 6.24

Chart reprinted with permission from Bloomberg. Copyright 2013 Bloomberg L.P. All rights reserved.

In the two weeks that followed our initial entry, WYNN fell almost 20 percent, as seen in Figure 6.24. Due to the speed of the decline, it was difficult to manage a trailing stop. In situations like this, I keep things simple by using the previous day's high or low. In WYNN, the previous day's high was exceeded on May 18, when prices traded above $106.01. Thus, this trade was stopped out for a profit of $202.90, or 16.06 percent in just 10 days.

For More Information

Learn more at your exclusive Reader Resources site. You will find video lessons on incorporating candlestick patterns, moving averages, and other technical methods into your wave analysis to increase your confidence as you apply the Wave Principle in real time. Go to: www.elliottwave.com/wave/ReaderResources.

Test Yourself

1. What should you do if your Elliott wave analysis and technical indicators are at odds?
   (A) Don't trade; look for a better setup elsewhere.
   (B) Depend on your wave analysis alone.
   (C) Focus on your favorite technical indicator.
   (D) Change your wave analysis.
2. True or False: When prices have been trending up but RSI (relative strength index) has been trending down, this divergence is often a precursor to an upturn in prices.
3. To manage risk on a trade, focus on this trio:
   (A) Do your analysis, check technical indicators, and set an initial protective stop.
   (B) Set an initial protective stop, get out of the trade before you are stopped out, and collect your profits.
   (C) Lessen risk, eliminate risk, and protect open profits.
   (D) Pick your top wave count, pick your alternate wave count, and compare with your favorite technical indicator.
4. Your goal on each trade is to:
   (A) Be as close to perfect as possible.
   (B) Have the most optimal stop.
   (C) Sell at top tick or buy at bottom tick.
   (D) Make money.
5. True or False: The psychology of a trader is more important than either risk management or technique.
6. 6. What is the main difference between a Japanese candlestick chart and an O-H-L-C price chart?
   (A) How volume data is incorporated
   (B) How the data are illustrated to show the balance of power between bulls and bears
   (C) How divergences show up
   (D) How MACD works better with candle sticks

Answers : 1. A 2. False 3. C 4. D 5. True 6. B

CHAPTER 7

A Basic Options Trade

Elliott wave analysis and options strategies can be a powerful combination. Chapter 7 presents a basic options strategy in comparison to a straight futures trade. Chapter 8 covers more complex options trading strategies.

One of the best reasons to use options on occasion when you trade is that they can turn an anxiety-inducing trade into one with a higher comfort level. While risk-reward ratios are often better when going long or short futures and cash instruments than when using options, the quid pro quo is that options can usually position you for multiple outcomes or generate a better return on capital.

At the end of Chapter 5, we discussed a trading scenario in the euro that involved an ending diagonal. The chart shown in Figure 7.1 shows the wave count as of April 22, 2008, and the details of the trade.

Here is a brief recap: A fifth-wave ending diagonal had either ended or was about to end soon. According to Elliott wave guidelines, there should be a swift and sharp reversal back to at least where the diagonal began, and possibly further. On the close of April 22, we went short the June 2008 euro futures contract at 1.5957 with a price target of 1.5273, which represented the end of wave (iv) and the starting point of the diagonal. The protective stop was 1.6161, which represented the price at which wave [5] would have a greater price range than wave [3], making the diagonal invalid. That stop created a potential risk of 0.0204. Our potential reward was 0.0684, so the risk-reward ratio was 3.4:1.

> **KEY POINT**
> **While risk-reward ratios are often better when going long or short futures and cash instruments than when using options, the quid pro quo is that options can usually position you for multiple outcomes or generate a better return on capital.**

It is not always possible to time a trade exactly the way you want to, which can put you in an uncomfortable spot. Let's assume, for example,

Figure 7.1

Chart reprinted with permission from Bloomberg. Copyright 2013 Bloomberg L.P. All rights reserved.

that you wanted to wait one trading day before putting on this trade, in order to check all your analysis before acting. On the close of April 23, you would have gone short at 1.5854 with the same price target of 1.5273 and the same protective stop of 1.6161. But the potential risk would have been much higher at 0.0307 with the potential reward at 0.0581, creating a risk-reward ratio of 1.89:1. Those are not such great numbers. It is not so much the lower risk-reward ratio and potential reward; it is the higher absolute potential risk.

Suppose you could not stomach the idea of possibly losing more than 3 handles (307 points) on this trade if the forecast turned out to be wrong? What would you do? If you tightened the stop, the trade would become more vulnerable to being stopped out at just the wrong time, and then you would have to scramble to get back in again in time for the move. Remember, this situation portends an imminent swift and sharp move to the downside.

Without proper planning, this trade could be stopped out more than once and end up losing more than the original estimate. Let's also not forget the emotional damage you would experience after being stopped out several times: You might be so shell-shocked that you would not want to pull the trigger again. On the other hand, if you do nothing, you may pass up a great opportunity. Fifth-wave ending diagonals do not come along every day. Let's also assume that your capital is limited and that you were not comfortable with the margin requirement on euro futures contracts. In April 2008, the initial margin requirement was 3,510 U.S. dollars per one euro futures contract on the Chicago Mercantile Exchange.

Fortunately, in this situation, a particular options strategy can help if you are willing to give up some potential reward. It is called the *bear put spread* (see Figure 7.2).

Bear Put Spread

Buy 1 ATM Put

Sell 1 OTM Put

Net Debit

Moderately Bearish
Relatively longer-term strategy, 3–6 months
Maximum risk capped at net debit
Maximum reward capped at strike difference minus net debit

Breakeven: long put strike price minus net debit

Figure 7.2

Here is how the strategy works: You buy an at-the-money (ATM) **put**, which, by definition, has a strike price about equal to the current market price of the underlying asset. This position should take advantage of a downward move in price. You simultaneously sell an out-of-the-money (OTM) put, which, by definition, has a strike price somewhere below the current market price of the underlying asset. You sell the OTM put at a strike price about equal to where you expect the price decline to end within the trading time frame. The OTM put helps to reduce the total

DEFINITION:
put

A put contract represents the right—but not the obligation—to sell the underlying asset. Similarly, a call contract represents the right—but not the obligation—to buy the underlying asset.

risk but also caps the maximum gain at the strike price of the OTM put. Both the long put and the short put have the same expiration date.

This position results in a certain net debit, or cash outflow. Maximum risk is capped at the net debit, and maximum reward is capped at the difference between the ATM and OTM strike prices, less the net debit. The breakeven price at options expiration is the long put strike price less the net debit.

The bear put spread is best suited for short-term countertrend moves, such as waves two or four at relatively low degree. If the forecast is correct about a limited price move, then you can afford to sell the OTM put at a certain price level without sacrificing additional profit potential. A crucial note: Since this strategy results in a net debit, time works against it. Therefore, it is important that you select an options expiration date that allows enough time for the price move to reach its maximum potential.

However, a bear put spread with too much time left to expiration can be a problem, even when the long put reaches its maximum profit potential (in other words, becomes deep in-the-money) and the short put becomes at-the-money. That is because the value of deep in-the-money options is not sensitive to time left to expiration or to changes in implied volatility. The value changes almost one-to-one with changes in the price of the underlying asset and is about equal to the intrinsic value, which is the difference between the strike price and the price of the underlying asset. If there is a lot of time left to expiration and implied volatility goes up, you won't earn much incremental revenue due to those variables, when you have reached your price objective and sell your long put.

In contrast, an at-the-money option's value is most sensitive to the remaining time to expiration and changes in implied volatility. Therefore, if there is a lot of time left to expiration and implied volatility goes up, you will have to pay for that when you have reached your price objective and buy back your short put.

With a bear put spread, the situation that yields maximum benefit is for the expected price move to end on the expiration date and be equal to the strike price of the short put. In that way, there is no need to buy back the short put, which expires worthless.

Let's look at some numbers for a bear put spread on April 23, 2008, using put options on the June 2008 euro futures contract to see if this strategy reduces the potential risk and frees up some cash flow compared with the short futures strategy. Remember, at expiration, an option's value is solely a function of the difference be-

KEY POINT

At expiration, an option's value is solely a function of the difference between the strike price and the closing price of the underlying asset. Prior to expiration, an option's value is a function of several variables, including price of the underlying asset, implied volatility, and time to expiration.

Figure 7.3

tween the strike price and the closing price of the underlying asset. Prior to expiration, an option's value is a function of several variables, including price of the underlying asset, implied volatility, and time to expiration. Figure 7.3 summarizes the details.

In this contract, the price high is 1.5964, the low is 1.5826, and the close is 1.5854. Based on the actual closing option prices, you buy an at-the-money June 2008 put with a strike price of 1.5850 at a cost of .0228, and you sell an out-of-the-money June 2008 put with a strike price

KEY POINT

With a bear put spread, the ideal situation (maximum benefit) would be for the expected price move to end on the expiration date and be equal to the strike price of the short put. In that way, there is no need to buy back the short put, which expires worthless.

of 1.5250 that generates revenue of .0054. That results in a net debit (cash outflow), or maximum risk, that is capped at .0174. Our maximum reward at expiration is capped at .0426.

Since we expect the euro to decline to 1.5273, our potential reward at expiration is .0403, which results in a risk-reward ratio of 2.3:1. Our breakeven price level is 1.5676.

Why did I pick a 1.5250 strike price for the short put? It is the closest strike price to the previously determined price target of 1.5273.

Why did I pick June 2008? To try to make sure that the puts do not expire before the euro reaches 1.5273 and thus to maximize the profit potential.

On the other hand, the further out in the future we push the expiration date, the more costly the puts will be. Our research indicates that the move back to where the diagonal began takes about one-third to one-half the time it took for the diagonal to unfold. This diagonal took 21 trading days or approximately four weeks. Ideally, the puts we want should expire about two weeks from the end of the diagonal. Adding some cushion for error, the date would end up in the middle of May. The May options (on the June contract) expire on May 9, which is ideal, but that leaves little room for error in terms of timing. The June options expire on June 6. That date should supply enough time for the price to get back to where the diagonal began and not be as costly as puts with later expiration dates. Let's see how this options strategy changes the numbers pertaining to the short-futures trade. It lowers the maximum risk from .0307 to .0174. It lowers the maximum potential reward from .0581 to .0403 but improves the risk-reward ratio from 1.89:1 to 2.3:1.

Let's next look at the potential return on investment. In April 2008, a short futures position in the euro required 3,510 U.S. dollars per contract for initial margin. With the bear put spread, the long put requires no margin, because the premium is paid in full. The total net debit is .0174 or 174 points. Each point is worth $12.50 per contract, because a euro futures contract represents 125,000 euros. The total net cash outflow is $2,175. The short put (as part of the spread) requires an initial margin equal to 1 percent of the futures contract margin, which is $35.10. Therefore, the total of cash expense plus cash margin on the options strategy is $2,210.10 versus $3,510 for the futures position. By doing the options, you can free up $1,300 in cash per contract, which you can then use to trade in a different market. Using the options strategy improves the maximum *potential* return on capital.

What is the *actual* return? Time to look at the actual cash flows. In the futures position, it takes $3,510 in margin to earn a potential 581 points, or $7,262.50 per contract. At the end of the trade, we receive back our margin of $3,510. That is a return of 206.9 percent. With the options strategy, it takes $2,210.10 to earn a potential 577 points on the long put, or $7,212.50 per contract. At the

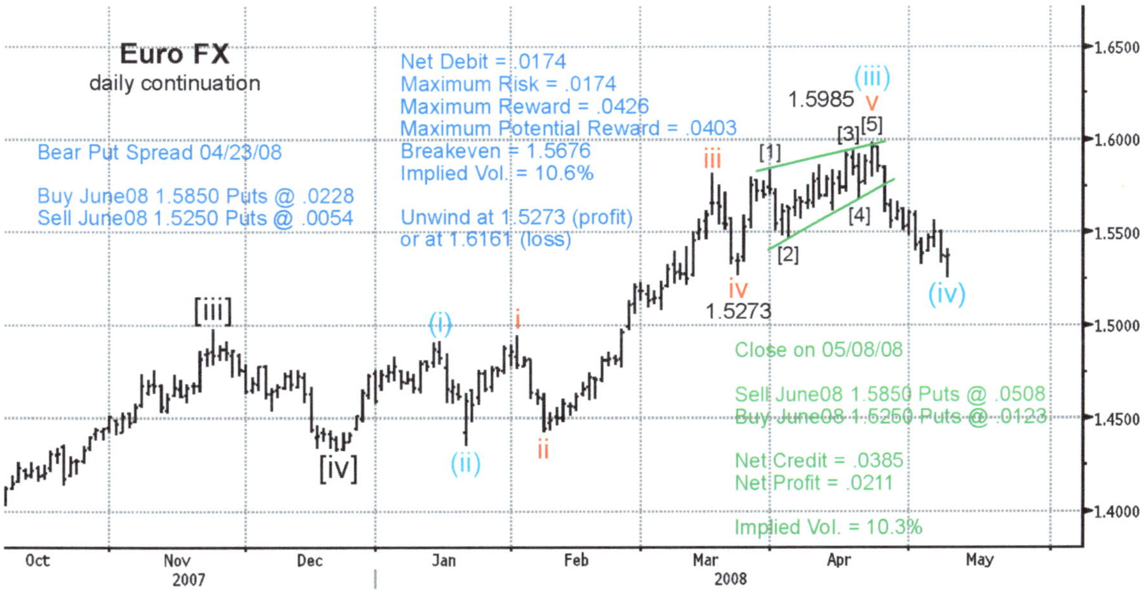

Figure 7.4

end of the trade, we receive back our margin of $35.10. That is a return of 227.9 percent in addition to the freed-up cash of $1,300.

The next part of the strategy is to unwind the options trade when the euro gets to 1.5273, with the hope that it will happen near expiration. If, before reaching 1.5273, the euro rises to 1.6161, the strategy instead is to get out and salvage whatever option premium is left, in order to avoid incurring the maximum loss. Let's see what transpires in the next few days on the next chart (see Figure 7.4).

The fifth-wave ending diagonal does indeed deliver a swift reversal. As you can see, prices reach the target of 1.5273 on May 8. As expected, the retracement took about half the time for the diagonal to unfold. The high that day is 1.5415, and the low is 1.5255. From a risk point of view, there is no reason to stay in this position any longer, so it is time to unwind the options trade.

On the close of May 8, it is possible to sell the June 1.5850 put at .0508 and buy back the 1.5250 put at .0123, which results in a net credit of .0385 and a total net profit of .0211. Why buy back the short put? Once the long put is cashed in, the short put becomes "uncovered." If the forecast turns out to be wrong and the euro declines further, you lose money on the short put and possibly all

A bear put spread at this juncture is too conservative, because of the completion of a fifth wave at high degree. Given the greater downside potential, the preferred options strategy is a put ratio backspread.

Figure 7.5

Chart reprinted with permission from Bloomberg. Copyright 2013 Bloomberg L.P. All rights reserved.

or more of the profit. As shown in Figure 7.5, the euro does rally back to the all-time high.

Having achieved the expected move to 1.5273, why does this trade earn only .0211 and not the maximum potential reward of .0403? Half of that difference is because, on May 8, the euro closes at 1.5366, which is 93 points higher than the target. (We are simulating this trading example based on real closing prices because historical intraday option prices are not readily available.)

In reality, your strategy would be to place an order with your broker to close out your options position when the June euro futures contract trades at 1.5273. That action would result in a profit closer to your maximum potential reward but still not exactly, because the broker execution for this type of order cannot always be perfect in option markets, and prices hit the price target sooner than the ideal time: One month still remains before the expiration date of the puts. With options, that much time can be costly. Because the long put at 1.5850 eventually becomes deep in-the-money, you earn the **intrinsic value** of the put when you sell it but do not make much money in exchange for the remaining days to expiration.

In contrast, because the short put eventually becomes at-the-money, it is necessary to pay more to buy it back, due to its sensitivity to the

DEFINITION:
intrinsic value

Intrinsic value refers to the difference between the strike price and the price of the underlying asset for in-the-money options.

remaining days to expiration. Remember, as I pointed out at the beginning of this discussion: The value of deep in-the-money options is not sensitive to time left to expiration or to changes in implied volatility. The value changes almost one-to-one with changes in the price of the underlying asset and is about equal to the intrinsic value. In contrast, an at-the-money option's value is most sensitive to the remaining time to expiration and changes in implied volatility.

During my trading days at Citibank, whenever someone professed to know which way the market was going, we'd always quip, "Don't tell me what, tell me when!" We were referring, of course, to the importance of knowing *when* the price move would begin, in order to time our entry or exit.

Little did I realize at the time how important that refrain is for option spreads. With certain types of option strategies, it is just as important to know when the price move will end as it is to know when it will begin. So you might say, "One of the Elliott wave guidelines suggests that the move will end from one-third to one-half the time that it took for the diagonal to unfold. Why can't we rely on that estimate to choose a shorter expiration date for our options?" The answer is, you can, but you have to take into account your appetite for stress.

The diagonal took four weeks to unfold. In retrospect, the May options would have been perfect, because they expired on May 9, which is about two weeks from the end of the diagonal. You could have bought back the short put contract on May 8 for almost nothing, since it expired the next day, and you still would have earned almost the same number of points on the long put. So why didn't we use the May options? Only one month left to expiration is risky when time decay is working against you. Just two weeks left to expiration is a nail-biter. This was a case where the amount of time left to expiration posed an undesirable risk, even though it matched an important Elliott wave guideline.

When your Elliott wave analysis signals a turn, it is not always practical to take a position. A lot depends on your own personal risk preferences. This is especially true when setting protective stops. The potential loss might be too much to bear no matter how good the risk-reward ratio. The challenge is to find your own comfort zone between what analysis tells you to do and what you feel comfortable doing.

For More Information

Learn more at your exclusive Reader Resources site. You will find a 12-page eBook covering options strategies for a range-bound market, plus lessons on Elliott wave analysis, how to trade specific patterns, and how to use Fibonacci and other technical indicators to increase your confidence as you apply the Wave Principle in real time. Go to: www.elliottwave.com/wave/ReaderResources.

Test Yourself

1. The bear put spread is best utilized for which of the following: (A) Extended third waves
   (B) Fifth waves
   (C) Ending diagonals
   (D) Short-term countertrend moves
2. True or False: Not all corrections achieve a net retracement.
3. The reason options strategies work well with Elliott wave is because:
   (A) Wave counts can be wrong.
   (B) Options can position you for more than one valid wave count.
   (C) It is too difficult to set protective stops using Elliott wave.
   (D) Elliott wave is an options pricing fore casting model.

Answers: 1. D 2. False 3. B

CHAPTER 8

More Advanced Options Trades

Under the Elliott wave model, there is usually more than one valid wave count at any particular time. Sometimes these wave counts point in opposite directions. If you are trading outright long or short, you are forced to choose the scenario you feel is most likely to occur, or elect to do nothing. Using options, you can create a strategy that can be successful under more than one scenario, even if those scenarios point in opposite directions. You do not have to sit on the sidelines. I will next show two option-strategy examples that demonstrate this point.

Bear Call Ladder in Heating Oil Catches a Big Move

Have you ever taken an outright long or short trading position not because you were confident about the direction of the next move in the market but because you were afraid you would miss "the big one" that was going to happen at any moment? Then you were stopped out for a loss—or even stopped out more than once. So you decided that the next time that situation arose, you would not do anything. And then you *did* miss the big one! Elliott wave analysis does not always fully mitigate such uncertainties.

Figure 8.1

Chart reprinted with permission from Bloomberg. Copyright 2013 Bloomberg L.P. All rights reserved.

Fortunately, an options strategy can help in this scenario. Let's look at a situation in heating oil futures from 2008.

Figure 8.1 shows a weekly continuation chart of heating oil futures as of April 11, 2008.

From the 2007 low, we can count waves 1, 2, 3, and possibly 4. Within wave 3, we can count waves [i], [ii], [iii], [iv], and [v]. Although wave 3 appears to be extended, we know that, in larger degrees in commodities, the fifth wave is usually the extended wave. A double extension would be rare.

In our example, there could be a big opportunity to go long heating oil for wave 5. The main question is whether wave 4 has ended. Maybe

Figure 8.2

Chart reprinted with permission from Bloomberg. Copyright 2013 Bloomberg L.P. All rights reserved.

the small rise from the end of wave 4 is part of an expanded flat, and oil will come back down. Or, maybe it is going to skyrocket up in wave 5. We need to quantify the opportunities to the downside as well as the upside before making a decision. Let's first look at the retracement made by wave 4.

Remember that all corrections must achieve some net retracement of the wave they correct. In Figure 8.2, we see that wave 4 has made only a Fibonacci .236 retracement of wave 3, to 284.89. That is an acceptable correction, albeit shallow.

A .382 retracement of wave three is far more common to fourth waves. A bigger concern is that wave 4 has not yet reached the price territory of the previous fourth wave at one lesser degree, which is wave (iv) of wave 3. That is a common

KEY POINT:

All corrections must achieve some net retracement of the wave they are correcting.

Figure 8.3

Chart reprinted with permission from Bloomberg. Copyright 2013 Bloomberg L.P. All rights reserved.

stopping area for fourth-wave corrections. Both facts argue for further downside potential within wave 4.

Let's examine the upside potential.

For Figure 8.3, I have calculated two common Fibonacci projection points for the end of wave 5. When I multiply .382 times the net distance traveled of waves 1 through 3 and add that distance to the end of wave 4, I get an estimate of 352.47. When I multiply .618 times the net distance traveled in waves 1 through 3 and add that distance to the end of wave 4, I get an estimate of 394.21.

The high on April 11 is 332.04, so there is the potential for further upside in the range of 6 to 19 percent.

Figure 8.4
Chart reprinted with permission from Bloomberg. Copyright 2013 Bloomberg L.P. All rights reserved.

In Figure 8.4, I show how to use Fibonacci dividers to estimate the end of wave 5. The end (or beginning) of wave four often divides the entire impulse wave into either the Golden Section (.618/.382) or two equal parts. This chart identifies those two areas based on the end of wave 4. To create a Golden Section, wave 5 would end at 371.16, which falls between the two Fibonacci multiple projections. If wave 4 were to divide the entire price range into two equal parts, wave 5 would end at 424.48, which is beyond the higher projection based on Fibonacci multiples. Although there is no Fibonacci cluster to rely on (yet), there is a range of potentially higher prices for wave 5.

To make a trade using options, which are time sensitive, we need to identify a time target for wave 5.

Figure 8.5

Chart reprinted with permission from Bloomberg. Copyright 2013 Bloomberg L.P. All rights reserved.

> KEY POINT:
>
> **As a guideline, the time duration of wave five may equal the time duration of waves one through three multiplied by .382, .5, or .618.**

Figure 8.5 shows the Fibonacci time multiples I would use to estimate the termination point of wave 5. As a guideline, the duration of wave five may equal the duration of waves one through three, multiplied by .382, .5, or .618. You can see where these time multiples occur in the future on the weekly bar chart. The estimates are September 12, October 31, and December 19, 2008.

The dilemma is that wave 4 could continue down-ward in the form of an expanded flat, or it could travel sideways in the form of a triangle. On the other hand, it is possible that wave 4 has ended, and the market is now moving up in wave 5. If you attempt to go long, you could be stopped out at a loss in the expanded flat scenario or chopped up for a loss in the triangle scenario. If you do nothing for fear of losing money, you could miss a significant opportunity to the upside. How do you resolve this quandary? You can use the options strategy that fits this situation like a glove; it is called the *bear call ladder* . It is also known as the *short call ladder*. Figure 8.6

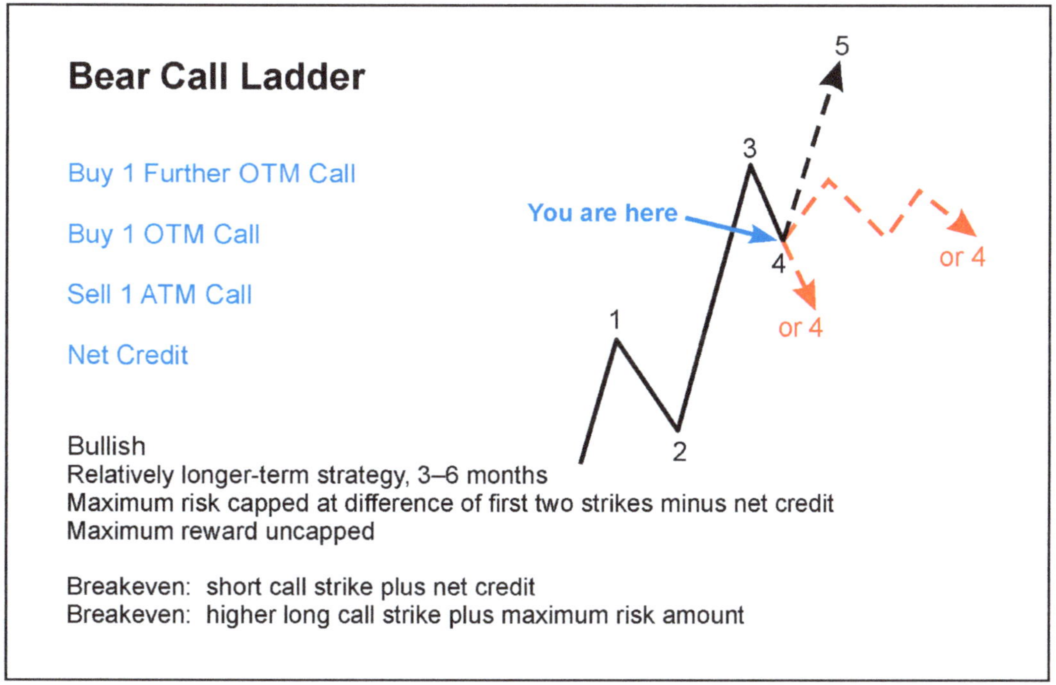

Figure 8.6

illustrates both the various Elliott-wave scenarios and shows the structure of this options strategy.

In options literature, people categorize the bear call ladder as somewhat ambiguous and confusing. Are you bullish? Are you bearish? You are selling an at-the-money (ATM) call, but you are also buying two different out-of-the-money (OTM) calls. What's going on? The irony is that from an Elliott wave perspective, it is not ambiguous at all. It helps to protect against the possibility that an alternate wave count may occur. Let's see why this strategy helps in this situation.

The bear call ladder is basically bullish. It is a relatively longer-term strategy, applicable for trades lasting three to six months. You structure it by selling one in-the-money or ATM call and using that revenue to buy one OTM call and one further OTM call. You should try to generate a total net credit or net cash inflow in order to maximize the effectiveness of this strategy. Your maximum risk is capped; it is the difference between the first two strikes minus the net credit. The maximum reward is uncapped. The strategy provides two breakeven price levels: the short call strike plus the net credit, and the higher long call strike plus the maximum risk amount (in the area beyond the further OTM call). If the market goes down or goes sideways (at the level that you sold your calls) between now and options expiration, you keep your net credit and walk away. If the market rallies strongly between now and options expiration, your further OTM calls will increase in value. If the market only goes higher marginally, you will lose money.

In a nutshell, you are betting on a big move up. Your bias is in the direction of the main trend. Either way, though, you have some protection if prices move down or sideways. You get hurt only if prices go in the direction of the main trend for only a small move. In other words, you sacrifice a small up move in exchange for a big up move, a sideways move, or a down move. This strategy comes in handy when you are bullish but equally nervous about the prospects of the market going down or sideways. (In bear markets, its counterpart is called the "bull put ladder" and is constructed in the same way, but using puts.)

Let's apply this strategy to a situation in heating oil.

Figure 8.7 displays a close-up view of wave 4 in heating oil futures on the daily continuation

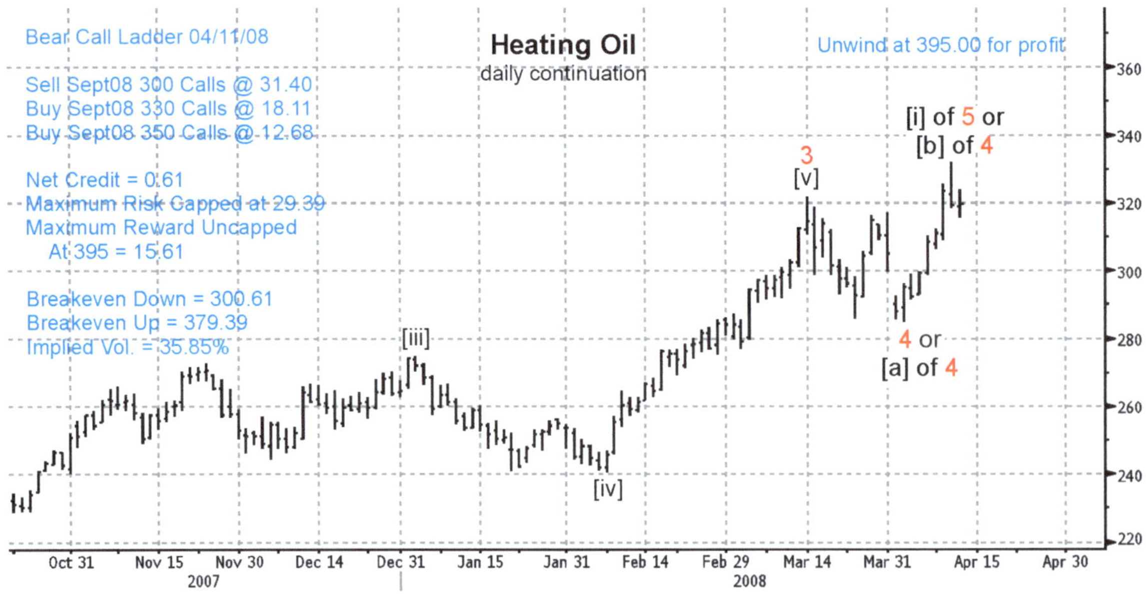

Figure 8.7

Chart reprinted with permission from Bloomberg. Copyright 2013 Bloomberg L.P. All rights reserved.

chart. The decline from the end of wave 3 could be wave [a] of 4, and the subsequent rise could be wave [b]. That would lead to a drop for wave [c]. Wave 4 could also go sideways as a triangle, flat, or combination, or prices could skyrocket in wave 5.

Given this setup, it is time to do a bear call ladder. On April 11, I sell the September 300 calls at 31.40. The September options are based on the September futures contract. On April 11, the high for the September futures contract was 316.05, and the low was 311.60. On the daily continuation chart, the front contract is the May futures contract, which registered a high of 323.76 and a low 315.57. Therefore, at that time, the September futures were trading at a slight discount to May futures. Although I am trading the September contract, I am doing my Elliott wave analysis on the continuation chart, because the historical data affords me a better picture of the wave patterns. The September options expire on August 26, 2008, close to the .382 time relationship (see Figure 8.5). That gives us about five months, a suitable time period, since this is not a short-term strategy. Remember, we are looking for a big move at a relatively high degree. The 300 calls were slightly in-the-money. The September futures were trading around 312 to 316. I buy the OTM September 330 calls at 18.11. If there is just a small up move, I will give up 30 points, but I know I have to sacrifice a small move to implement this strategy.

Then I buy further OTM September 350 calls at 12.68. Why 350? As you may recall, if wave 5 were .382 times waves 1 through 3, then it would go up to 352.47 (see Figure 8.3). I look for wave 5 to go at least to 352, with the potential to go much higher. Net credit is 0.61. The maximum risk is capped at 29.39. The maximum reward is technically uncapped, but 394.21 is a good price target, as derived previously (see Figure 8.3). Rounding up to 395, this trade would make 15.61 points.

At minimum, the market should get up to 352. The lower breakeven is 300.61. The higher breakeven is 379.39. The implied volatility is 35.85 percent. If prices collapse, I have the net credit.

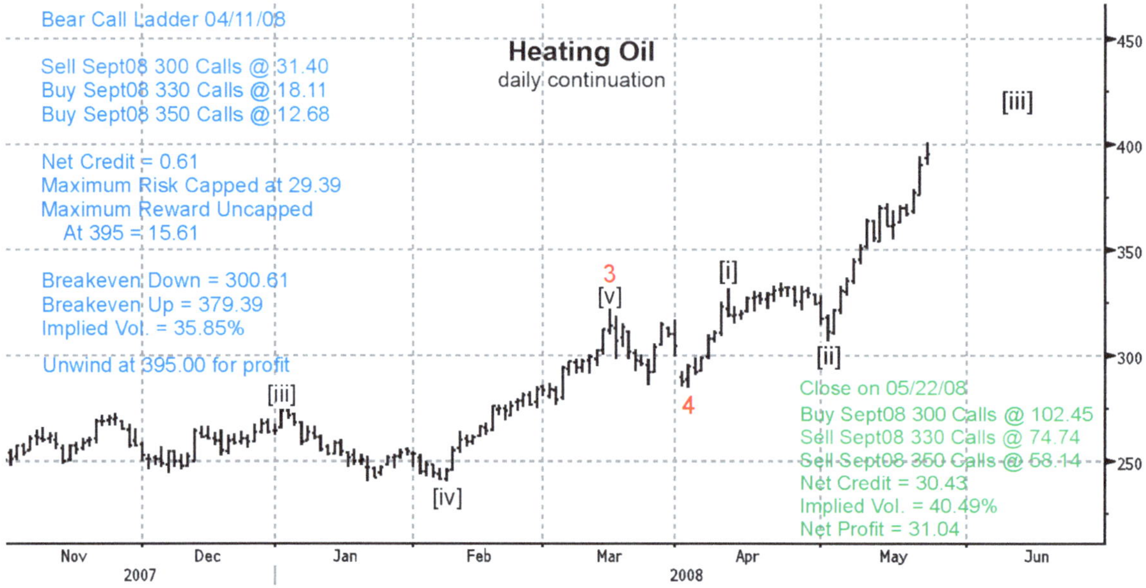

Figure 8.8

Chart reprinted with permission from Bloomberg. Copyright 2013 Bloomberg L.P. All rights reserved.

KEY POINT:

Breakeven prices correspond to option values at expiration. Prior to expiration, breakeven prices provide a general estimate and fluctuate according to remaining time to expiration and changes in implied volatility.

Figure 8.8 shows the result. Yes, heating oil has sky-rocketed. The last bar on this chart is for May 22 and represents the June futures contract. It registered a high at 401.53 and a low at 390.80, so prices did get to (and past) that 394 level. The September futures contract recorded a high of 406.65 and a low of 397.53, and therefore began trading at a premium to the front contract.

It is time to unwind the position. I buy back the September 300 calls at 102.45, sell the 330 calls at 74.74, and sell the 350 calls at 58.14. The trade earns a net credit of 30.43 points, in addition to the net credit of .61 at the beginning of the trade. The implied volatility on the at-the-money options was 40.49 percent. However, that is a bit misleading. That number pertains

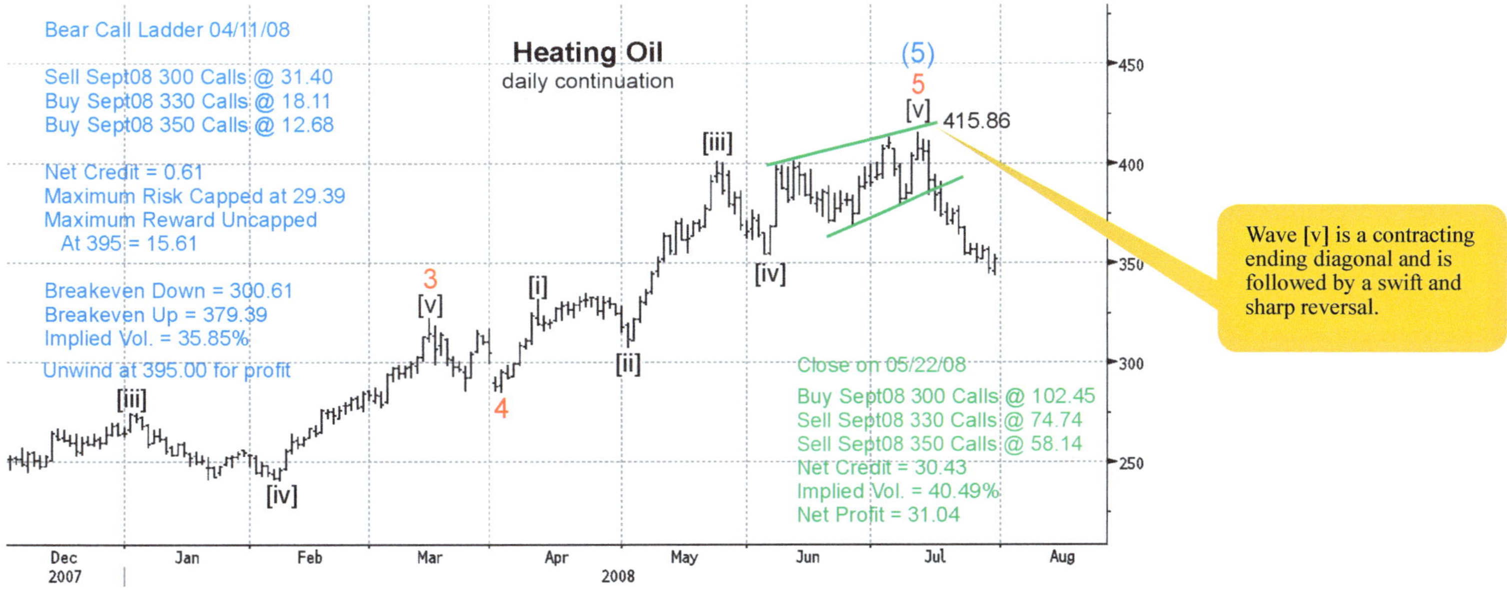

Figure 8.9

Chart reprinted with permission from Bloomberg. Copyright 2013 Bloomberg L.P. All rights reserved.

to the June contract, which had only about two weeks to run. Volatility on the September contract, which was active during the entire trade, was around 34 percent—so no major change there. Finally, this trade produced a net profit of 31.04 points.

As shown in Figure 8.9, wave 5 ended at 415.86, which is close to the 424.48 level marked in Figure 8.4 . At 424.48, the end of wave 4 divides the entire price range into two equal parts, fulfilling one of our target calculations.

In retrospect, it is easy to say I could have gone long and made more. But would you have gone long? Where would you have put your stop? At the low of wave 4? That is a big risk. In situations where doing nothing makes you just as nervous as taking an outright long or short position, this options strategy provides a useful alternative. The key is being able to generate a net credit at the outset, which is not always possible. The ability to achieve that goal will change according to market conditions at the time.

Figure 8.10
Chart reprinted with permission from Bloomberg. Copyright 2013 Bloomberg L.P. All rights reserved.

Long Straddle in Soybeans Harvests a Wave 5 Blow-Off Top

What would you do in the previous example if the stakes were much higher? In other words, what if your Elliott wave analysis told you that there was an equal chance of the market moving up or down by 10 to 15 percent over a relatively short period of time? Would you stay on the sidelines? This next example deals with how to solve this dilemma.

Figure 8.10 is a daily chart of the May 2008 soybeans futures contract for all sessions combined as of February 6, 2008. Soybean futures are quoted in U.S. cents per bushel, and the smallest increment of price change is one quarter of a

Figure 8.11
Chart reprinted with permission from Bloomberg. Copyright 2013 Bloomberg L.P. All rights reserved.

cent, expressed in eighths. For example, 1436^6 means 1436 and 6/8, or ¾, of a cent. One cent equals one point, which is worth $50 a contract.

From the August 16, 2007, low, we can count five waves up to a high of 1392^0, forming an impulse wave. But the questions are: Is wave [5] over or at least close to being over? If so, will there be a major decline? If it is not over, will there be a major advance? Using Elliott wave analysis, I will examine both scenarios, starting with trying to build a case for an imminent and major decline.

In Figure 8.11, I have drawn a trend channel for the five-wave impulse. Wave [5] is approaching

Figure 8.12

Chart reprinted with permission from Bloomberg. Copyright 2013 Bloomberg L.P. All rights reserved.

the top of the channel, which argues for an imminent completion of this wave and a reversal to the down-side. Let's see if there is a Fibonacci cluster near the top of the channel in the 1400 to 1450 area, which is where the upper channel line sits over the next month. If so, it would support the case for an imminent reversal.

As shown in Figure 8.12, if wave [5] ends at 1435^6, the end of wave [4] will have divided the entire impulse wave into the Golden Section.

Figure 8.13

Chart reprinted with permission from Bloomberg. Copyright 2013 Bloomberg L.P. All rights reserved.

Figure 8.13 shows that if wave [5] ends at 1407^0, it will equal .382 times the net distance traveled of waves [1] through [3]. We now have two estimates for the end of wave [5] that are close to each other and slightly beyond the current high of 1392^0. If wave [5] does end near these levels, let's see how far down this market could go.

To begin conservatively, let's look at how far a shallow retracement would travel (see Figure

Figure 8.14

Chart reprinted with permission from Bloomberg.

8.14). If wave [5] were to peak at 1435^6, a .382 correction of waves [1] through [5] would occur at 1207^0, which also represents the upper portion of the Golden Section. That level coincides with the previous wave [4] low of 1207^0. To reach it, the market would undergo approximately a 16 percent decline. If wave [5] were to peak at the current high of 1392^0, the .382 retracement would travel to 1180, achieving about a 15 percent decline. Let's look at the bigger picture to see if there is potential for even greater declines.

Figure 8.15

Chart reprinted with permission from Bloomberg.

Figure 8.15 displays the weekly continuation chart for soybean futures for all sessions combined as of February 6, 2008.

Our impulse wave that began at the August 2007 low appears to be forming an extended fifth wave within a larger impulse that began at the September 2006 low at 526^2. If wave [5] of V ends at 1435^6, the .382 retracement of waves I through V would carry prices to 1088^2, resulting in a 24 percent decline. After completion of a fifth-wave extension, the correction will often travel to the area of the second wave of the extension. In this case, such a move would result in a decline to about the 900 level. Since we're looking at this weekly continuation chart, let me add that if wave [5] of V ends at 1418^0, wave V will equal 1.618 times the net distance traveled of waves I through III, which is a common Fibonacci relationship for an extended fifth wave. Therefore, in terms of being close to a top, we

Figure 8.16

Chart reprinted with permission from Bloomberg. Copyright 2013 Bloomberg L.P. All rights reserved.

> DEFINITION:
> **blow-off**
>
> **A blow-off top is a steep and rapid rise in prices that is often characterized as panic buying. It is followed by an equally steep and rapid decline in prices.**

have a Fibonacci cluster in the low 1400s area and the potential for an imminent and major correction to the downside.

Let's explore the upside potential. In commodities, it is common for the fifth wave to extend and end with a nearly vertical move called a blow-off . Within the wave V extension, it is also possible that wave [5] will extend and thereby record much higher prices than we have estimated so far.

Let's see what price levels our Fibonacci guidelines can give us regarding the upside. On the long-term chart shown in Figure 8.16, if wave V ends at 1544^0, the beginning of wave IV will have divided the entire impulse that began at the Septem-

Figure 8.17

ber 2006 low into the Golden Section. At this price level, wave V would appear to be fully extended. Notice that its subwaves would be as long as or longer than the nonextended impulse waves preceding it. That much further advance from the current high would result in approximately an 11 percent gain.

Per the daily chart of the May 2008 contract shown in Figure 8.17, if wave [5] ends at 1577^0, the end of wave [4] will have divided the entire impulse wave into two equal parts. Such an advance from the current high would result in approximately a 13 percent gain.

Figure 8.18

Chart reprinted with permission from Bloomberg. Copyright 2013 Bloomberg L.P. All rights reserved.

As shown in Figure 8.18, if wave [5] ends at 1530^4, it will equal .618 times the net distance traveled of waves [1] through [3]. That would be about a 10 percent gain. Therefore, we have a Fibonacci cluster in the mid-1500s toward which prices may gravitate before the impulse wave is complete.

Figure 8.19 illustrates our forecasts as well as our dilemma if we were constrained to trade only outright long or short. What do you do if a market can plausibly take off in either direction? The options strategy fitting this situation is called the *long straddle*.

Figure 8.19

Chart reprinted with permission from Bloomberg. Copyright 2013 Bloomberg L.P. All rights reserved.

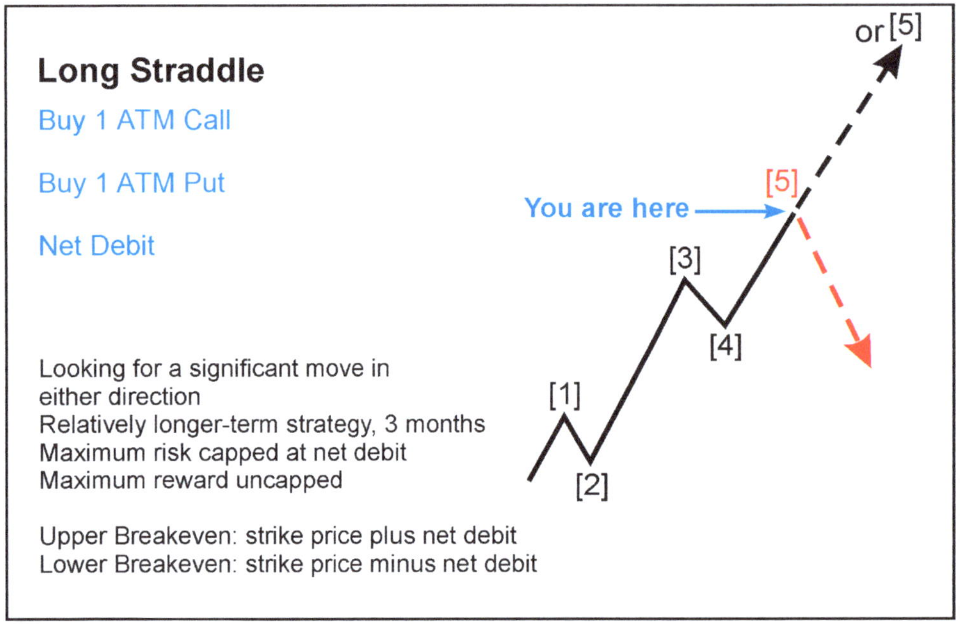

Figure 8.20

Figure 8.20 illustrates, from an Elliott wave perspective, the ideal scenario for doing a long straddle and outlines its structure.

To create a long straddle, you purchase an at-the-money (ATM) call and an ATM put. In this manner, you are positioned for a significant up or down move. This results in a net debit or cash outflow. Both options have the same strike price and expiration date. The expiration date is usually about three months from the trade date. The economics of the trade are straightforward. Given the total cost of the options, you need to determine if the market can move far enough up or down before expiration to allow you to recover your cost plus make a profit.

Using Elliott wave analysis, we have already determined the upside and downside potential. Now we have to compare these forecasts to the cost of buying the options and then calculate the breakeven price level for an up move and a down move. If the market moves sideways, you lose money.

As in the previous example, a key component of the cost of buying the options is the implied

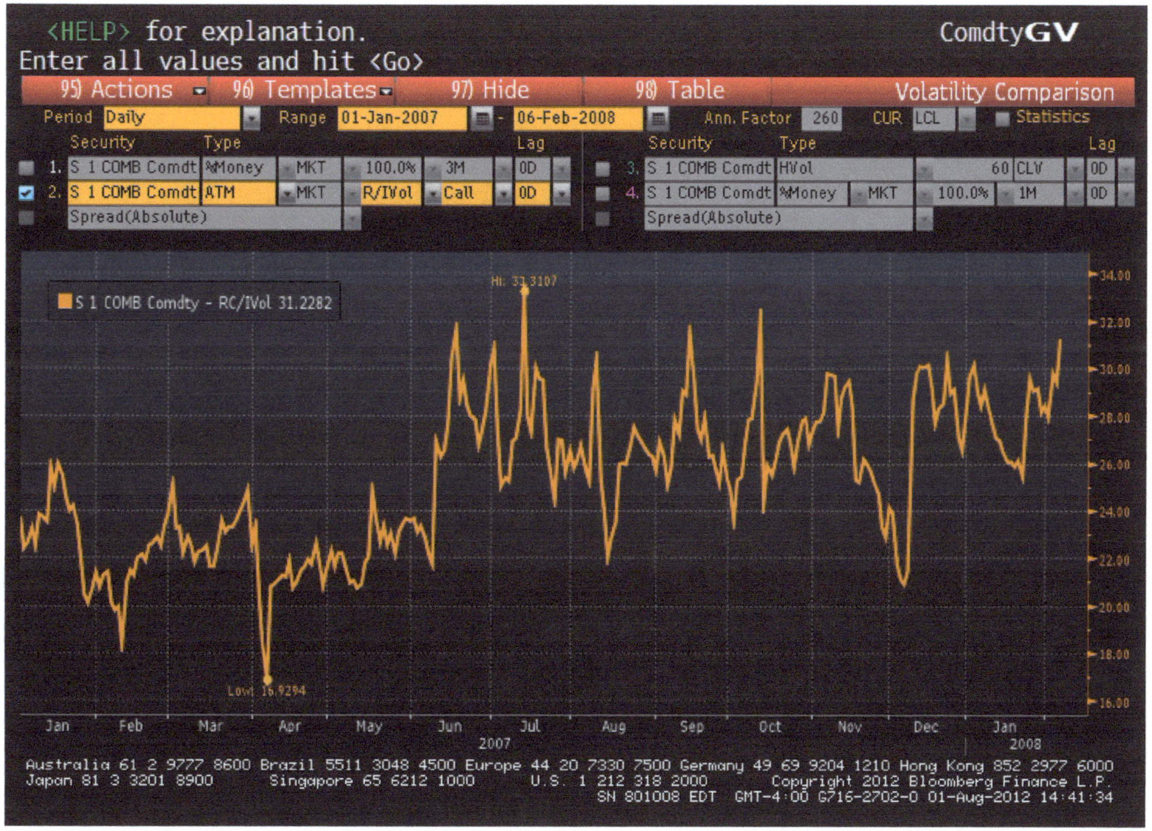

Figure 8.21

Chart reprinted with permission from Bloomberg. Copyright 2013 Bloomberg L.P. All rights reserved.

volatility for the ATM options. Figure 8.21 shows the level of implied volatility for ATM soybean options for the nearest active contract over the past year.

Therein lies the bad news: If you transact now, you would be paying near the highest volatility premium this market has seen over the last 12 months. Still, if the breakeven prices fall within the forecast, you can do the trade. Another way to reduce cost is to shorten the time to expiration as much as possible yet still leave enough time for the wave pattern to unfold.

Let's see if the trade can work.

If you buy options with an expiration date three months out, which is May, it is just too expensive. If you buy the April 2008 options, which expire on March 20, you have a chance. That would give you slightly less than two months for the wave pattern to unfold one way or another. The underlying futures contract for the April options is the May 2008 futures contract.

Using Fibonacci time analysis, the entire impulse wave (waves [1] through [5]) will have lasted a Fibonacci 144 days if wave [5] ends on March 13. Next, the duration of wave [5] would be equal to .382 times the net duration of waves [1] through [3] if wave [5] ends on March 19. Finally, on the long-term chart, the duration of wave V would equal .618 times the net duration of waves I through III if wave V ends on February 22. So we have a fairly tight Fibonacci time range for a turning point—February 22 through March 19. The good news is that it ends one day before the options expire.

Does all of th1is point to enough time? Quick answer: Yes, maybe.

In Figure 8.22, I have constructed the straddle. On February 6, the May 2008 futures

Smart Investor Tip

Another strategy for reducing cost is to use a *long strangle*. In the long strangle, you would purchase a put and a call that are slightly out-of-the-money. You would then need to calculate your breakeven price, up and down, to see if they are consistent with your forecast.

Figure 8.22

Chart reprinted with permission from Bloomberg. Copyright 2013 Bloomberg L.P. All rights reserved.

Figure 8.23

Chart reprinted with permission from Bloomberg. Copyright 2013 Bloomberg L.P. All rights reserved.

contract was trading between 1392 and 1332 and approached 1339 toward the close. I bought the April 2008 1340 calls at 60 and the 1340 puts at 61. That is a total net debit or cost of 121 points. The breakeven price to the upside is 1461, and the breakeven price to the downside is 1219. Both these levels are within the potential market moves based on the forecasted price levels that we discussed to compute potential reward. Okay, let's see what happened.

In Figure 8.23, it is March 3, and the market has catapulted to a high of 1586^2! Prices reached our upside objective of 1577 during the day of March 3. Notice the throw-over in wave [5]. With only two weeks left to expiration, there's no great advantage to holding the call position any longer, so I sold the calls on March 3 for 222¼ points (May 2008 futures closed at 1559^4), which results in a net profit of 101¼ points. The puts have little value right now, since they are so far out-of-the-money. It would be best just to hold the puts. If this is a blow-off top, there should be a violent reversal, and perhaps—with a bit of luck—it might be possible to squeeze out some money from those puts.

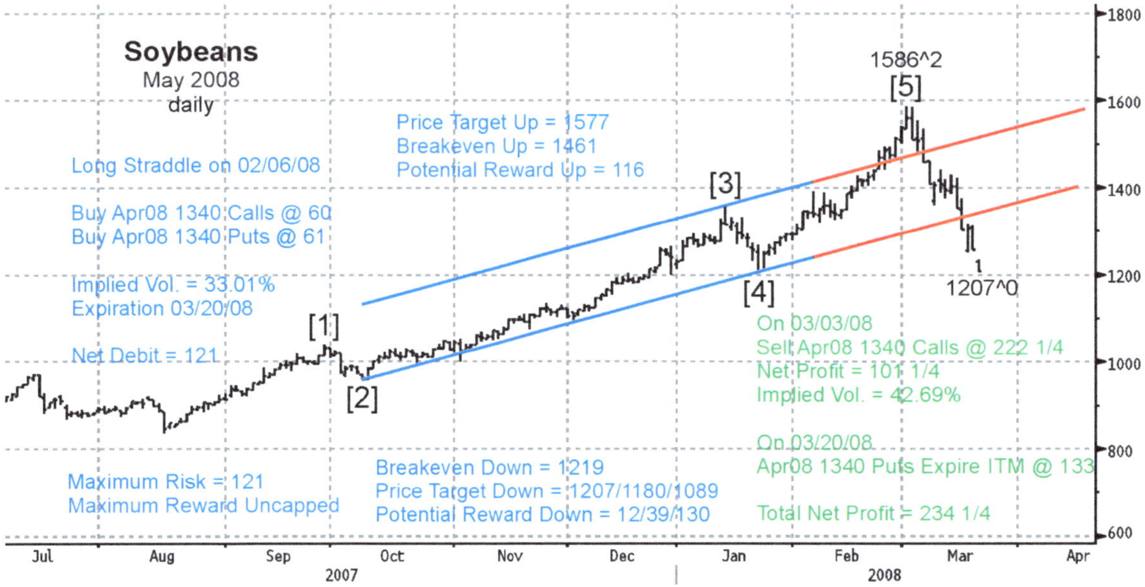

Figure 8.24

Chart reprinted with permission from Bloomberg. Copyright 2013 Bloomberg L.P. All rights reserved.

In any case, at this juncture, the trade has been a success. Let's move forward to March 20, which is the expiration date of the puts (see Figure 8.24).

Soybeans collapsed and traded all the way down to—you guessed it—1207 and closed at that same level. The puts expired in-the-money by 133 points. The total net profit on the straddle was 234¼ points.

Figure 8.25 shows the aftermath. Soybeans traded down to a low of 1106^4 and then rebounded from there. Notice how the lower boundary of the trend channel served as stiff resistance for any rally, a common occurrence. That trendline was not breached significantly until June 16, 2008, and even then, the rally did not last long.

In this example, our Elliott wave analysis led us to a crossroads. I could have managed the situation by choosing one route or the other along with a protective stop. But I might have lost significant money. The chosen options strategy gave me a viable alternative that fit well with the wave

Figure 8.25

Chart reprinted with permission from Bloomberg.

count and, as it turned out, opened up a whole new world of profit.

With options in mind, the great advantage of using Elliott wave is not solely to determine which way the market is going and how far, but also to inform us whether the market is likely to go sideways anytime soon. In this Soybeans market, the wave pattern provided strong evidence that a blow-off top was on the horizon, so it predicted substantial volatility, one's best friend when employing the long straddle.

For More Information

Learn more at your exclusive Reader Resources site. You will find a 12-page eBook covering options strategies for a range-bound market, plus lessons on Elliott wave analysis, how to trade specific patterns, and how to use Fibonacci and other technical indicators to increase your confidence as you apply the Wave Principle in real time. Go to: www.elliottwave.com/wave/ReaderResources.

Test Yourself

1. Which of the following is true about extended waves?
   (A) Wave 1 is usually extended.
   (B) Wave 4 is usually extended in commodities.
   (C) A double extension normally refers to an extremely long impulse wave.
   (D) Wave 5 is often extended in commodities.
2. The best time to use the bear call ladder is when:
   (A) You are totally confused about the wave count.
   (B) You expect the market to go sideways in wave 4 or decline.
   (C) Your bias is to the upside, but the market could go sideways or down.
   (D) You expect the market to make a swift move in wave 5 or wave C.
3. Which of the following often leads to being whipsawed?
   (A) Extended third wave
   (B) Zigzag
   (C) Expanded flat and Triangle
   (D) Truncated fifth wave
4. How long would you expect an extended fifth wave to be?
   (A) 1.618 times the net distance traveled of waves 1 through 3
   (B) Equal to the length of wave 1 plus wave 2
   (C) .618 times the length of wave 3
   (D) Two times the length of wave 1

Answers 1. D 2. C 3. C 4. A

CHAPTER 9

Parting Thoughts

Parting thoughts from Jeffrey Kennedy...

What does it take to become a consistently successful trader? It takes having a clearly defined trading methodology and the discipline to follow it, money management rules, patience, and realistic expectations. Lacking even one of these elements will not only make it impossible to succeed at trading, but it will also hurt your bottom line.

Let me give one example to show why discipline is important. By discipline, I mean the ability to stay with your trading plan rather than to follow the crowd, which loses money by buying at high prices and selling at low prices. At the end of 2009, the *Wall Street Journal* did the research to find out which stock fund had been the most successful from 2000 through 2009. The article noted that the best performing mutual fund of the decade was CGM Focus fund, which rose 18.2 percent annually ("Best Stock Fund of the Decade: CGM Focus" by Eleanor Laise, December 31, 2009).

With this remarkable return, an investor could have seen $100,000 grow to more than $500,000 over the 10-year period. Unfortunately, the average CGM Focus investor *lost* 11 percent annually, according to MorningStar, Inc. In other words, an initial $100,000 investment dwindled on average to just over $30,000.

How could the average investor in the best performing mutual fund of the decade lose money? Chalk it up to the herding impulse of investors, wrote Robert Prechter in the April 2011 issue of *The Elliott Wave Theorist*. Each time the fund's returns surged, investors would dump money into the CGM Focus fund hand over fist. But when the fund's returns sank, investors could not take their money out fast enough. Astounding as it may seem for investors to lose money in a bull market, it is the all-too-familiar reality of trading.

That is why it is wise to follow basic risk management rules. Many successful individual traders limit their risk on each position to 1 to 3 percent of their portfolio. If we apply this rule to a $5,000 trading account, then the risk on any given trade is limited to between $50 and $150. The guideline that we recommend for risk is to keep your risk-reward ratio at a minimum of 3:1. That is, if your risk on a given trading opportunity is $500, then the profit objective for that trade should equal $1,500 or more. (Remember, even though it is called a risk-reward ratio, the ratio is conventionally stated with the reward figure first. This explains why a 3:1 risk-reward ratio is desirable. It is actually a reward-risk ratio.)

Even with a methodology, discipline, and money management techniques, impatience can destroy your trades. How do you overcome the tendency to be impatient? By understanding the two triggers that cause it: *fear and boredom*. The first step in overcoming impatience is to consciously define the minimum requirements of an acceptable trade setup and vow to accept nothing less. Next, feel comfortable in knowing that the markets will be around tomorrow, next week, next year, and many years after, so there is plenty of time to wait for the ideal opportunity. Remember, trading is not a race, and overtrading does little to improve your bottom line.

If there is one practice that will improve your trading skills, it is patience. Be patient, and focus on trading textbook wave patterns and high-confidence trade setups like the ones we have described in this book. When it comes to being a consistently successful trader, it's all about quality—not quantity.

Consistently successful trading is not easy; it's hard work. If anyone suggests otherwise to you, then run the other way—and fast. That hard work, though, can be rewarding. Above-average returns, the sense of satisfaction, and the feeling you get after hitting one out of the park is priceless. But you must be realistic about it. Remember what I wrote at the beginning of this book: An excellent example of a realistic expectation for a trader in his or her first year should be *to avoid losing money*. If you shoot for a 0 percent return and achieve it, then you are ahead of the crowd and well on your way to becoming a consistently successful trader. In year two, try simply for a 5 or 10 percent return.

Trading is personal. It's all about you and how much anxiety (on bad days) or satisfaction and elation (on good days) you can handle. Knowing who you are as a trader, understanding your role in the trading equation, and learning how to control your emotions will ultimately determine your success or failure as a trader. Using Elliott wave analysis can help provide the structural template that may help keep your head clear once you have initiated a trade and the market is moving fast; however, it cannot protect you from your emotions. They will become powerful adversaries when your own money is involved. Just reread some of the trading examples in this book to understand what I mean.

To learn more about the importance of methodology, discipline, money management, patience, and realistic expectations, I highly recommend *The Disciplined Trader* by Mark Douglas and *Super Trader* by Van K. Tharp, PhD.

Parting thoughts from Wayne Gorman...

Each trader has a trading style. For instance, I like to take a somewhat risky posture. I prefer to use Elliott wave patterns to set up my trades as early as possible in anticipation of a trend change rather than waiting for further confirmation. In other words, I look for the best level and the tightest protective stop possible in lieu of waiting for evidence that the trend has indeed changed.

In anticipating where the market is headed, I am willing to take the risk that sometimes I will be wrong. If I were going short, I would rather go short at a high level with my stop just above the recent high, even if I were not certain that the trend had actually turned down. I do not like waiting for confirmation and then going short at a lower level with a stop that incurs greater risk, even though I might be more certain that the trend has turned.

This approach depends on accumulating enough evidence to support the case for an imminent trend change. Others who have a different trading style will argue that it is best to wait for an impulse wave in the opposite direction that decisively breaks a trend channel or major trendline of the previous pattern. That is a valid strategy, too. In deciding between these two approaches, is it simply a matter of personal risk tolerance, or can one make an analytical determination which to use? The answer is "Yes" to both questions. Let's look at an example.

In Figure 9.1, we have identified a Fibonacci cluster that satisfies three key Fibonacci relationships at the market's current level. In this type of situation, I would go short with a stop one tick beyond the beginning of wave (1). Why does this seem risky despite the evidence? To use courtroom jargon, the evidence is only circumstantial. No smoking gun suggests that the trend has changed, although some strong evidence suggests that it will.

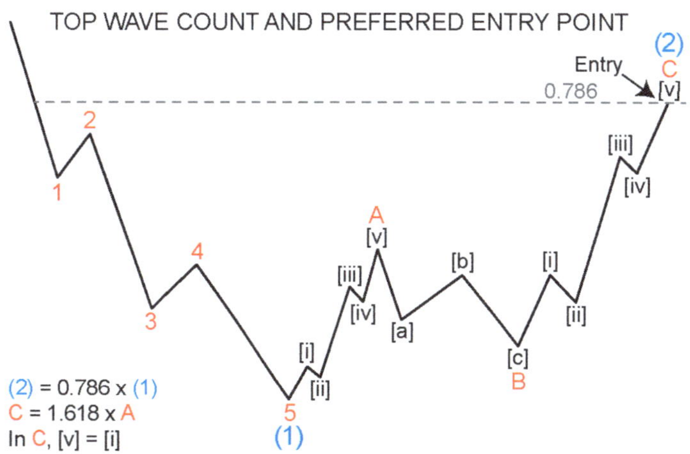

Figure 9.1

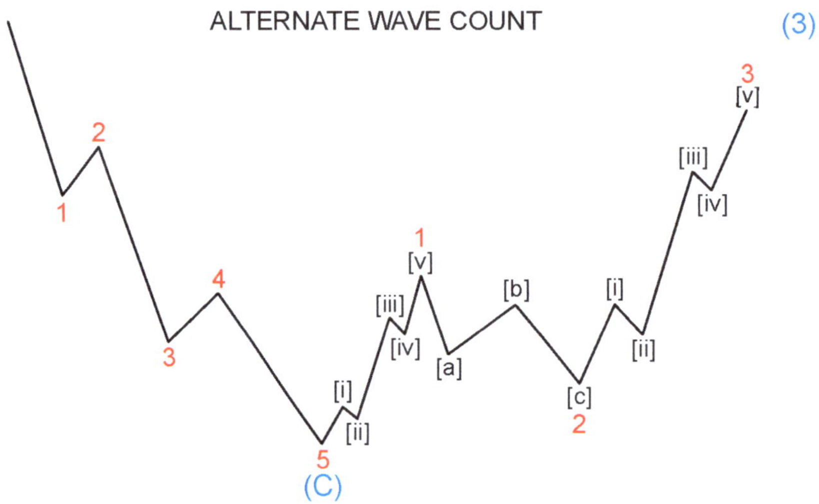

Figure 9.2

I could have made a mistake. If the trend has not changed, what might be the correct wave count? It is possible that the low on the chart (see Figure 9.2) completed wave (C) of an expanded flat, so the market is trending to the upside in wave 3 of wave (3). I have seen this scenario play out a number of times. For those who are somewhat risk-averse, Figure 9.3 offers an alternate strategy.

You could wait for an impulse wave to the down-side that breaks the lower line of the trend channel formed by the wave (2) zigzag. Then go short in wave [i] of wave 3 of wave (3), when it breaks the trend channel formed by wave 2. Without strong evidence that a turning point is near, it would be prudent to wait for further confirmation, as illustrated in Figure 9.3. Using this same logic, you would wait for a break of the B-D trendline of a triangle and wait for a break of the 2-4 trendline of an ending diagonal.

When I traded for a living with my own capital, people used to ask me, "What tools do you

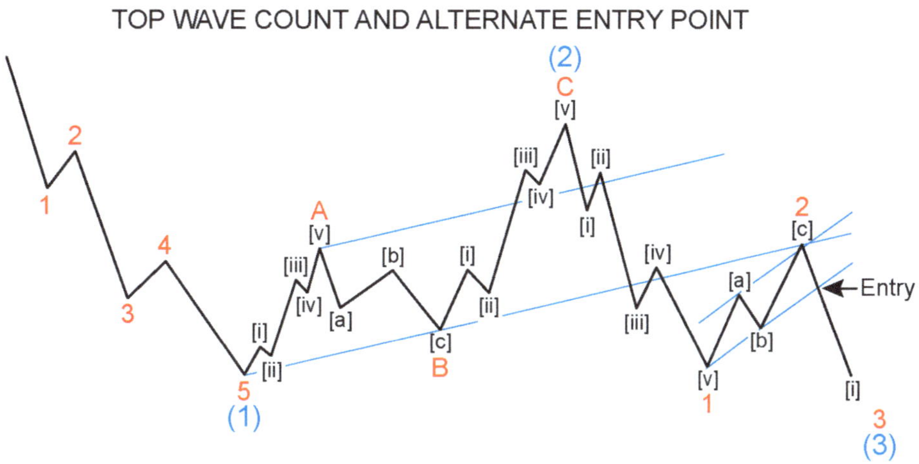

Figure 9.3

use besides Elliott wave?" I always replied, "I use anything I can get my hands on, if it makes sense."

Using other technical indicators can help reinforce your Elliott wave analysis or warn you that something is wrong with it (see Chapter 6). Technical indicators fall into three categories: sentiment (measures of investor psychology), momentum (changes in price, breadth, and volume), and patterns outside of Elliott wave (such as time cycles and head-and-shoulders formations). Just keep it simple and use what works best for you. Using a large array of indicators can be more of a hindrance than a help.

Finally, keep in mind that our knowledge about Elliott wave analysis is still growing. What we know about wave patterns is fascinating and useful, but there will always be more to discover. You do not have to wait for someone else to make a discovery. As you analyze and trade, see if you can add to our body of knowledge.

Appendix A: Introduction to the Wave Principle

In the 1930s, R. N. Elliott discovered that market price movements adhere to a certain pattern composed of what he called *waves* . He called the pattern's characteristics the Wave Principle. Every wave has a starting point and ending point in price and time. The pattern is continuous in that the end of one wave marks the beginning of the next wave. The basic pattern consists of five individual waves that are linked together and achieve progress as market prices move up or down (see Figure A.1).

This five-wave sequence, labeled with numbers 1 through 5, is called a *motive wave*, because it propels the market in the direction of the main trend. Subwaves 1, 3, and 5 are also motive waves. Subwaves 2 and 4 are called *corrective waves*, because they interrupt the main trend and travel in the opposite direction.

Two Elliott wave rules govern motive waves: Wave 2 always retraces less than 100 percent of

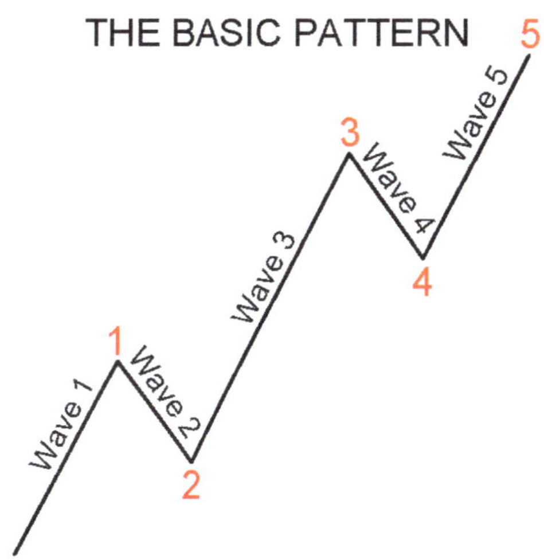

Figure A.1
Source: Adapted from Elliott Wave Principle.

wave 1, and wave 3 can never be the shortest motive subwave (although it does not have to be the longest).

After a five-wave sequence is complete, the corrective wave begins. The corrective wave partially retraces the progress made by the motive wave. It follows a three-wave sequence or a specific combination of three-wave structures. Its waves are labeled using letters, for example A, B, and C (see Figure A.2).

All waves are part of other waves at larger degree. They are also divisible into waves at lower degree, as shown in Figure A.3. Motive and corrective waves can move up or down.

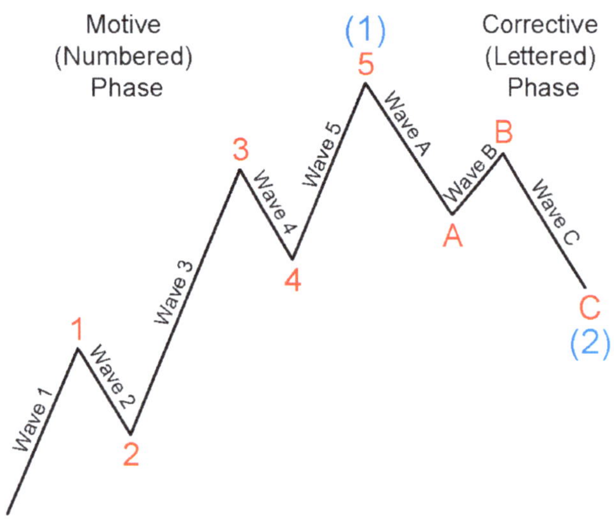

Figure A.2
Source: Adapted from Elliott Wave Principle.

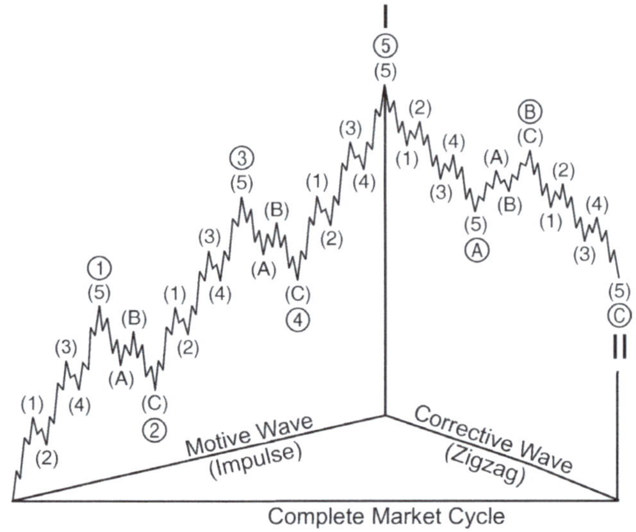

Figure A.3
Source: Adapted from Elliott Wave Principle.

A number of rules and guidelines apply to wave formations. Guidelines differ from hard-and-fast rules in that they describe what is most likely to occur, even though it may not always occur.

Motive Waves

The two types of motive waves are *impulse* and *diagonal*.

Impulse

The impulse wave, which is the strongest form of motive wave, follows these three rules:

1. Wave 2 never moves beyond the start of wave 1. In other words, it always retraces less than 100 percent of wave 1.

2. Wave 3 is never the shortest motive subwave, but it does not have to be the longest.
3. Wave 4 never enters the price territory of wave 1.

Add to these rules one strong guideline: Wave 4 should not enter the price territory of wave 2.

Rules are crucial to real-time application. In Figure A.4, the first wave count is incorrect, because the end of wave 4 enters the price territory of wave 1. The second wave count is incorrect, because wave 3 is the shortest motive wave. The third wave count correctly displays the first three subdivisions of wave 3. The next wave count is correct because, even though wave 3 is not the longest motive wave, it is also not the shortest one. The last wave count is incorrect, because wave 2 here retraces more than 100 percent of wave 1.

In an impulse wave, waves 1 and 5 are always motive waves (that is, either impulse or diagonal), while wave 3 is always an impulse wave. Waves 2 and 4 are always corrective waves. Therefore, we call an impulse wave a 5-3-5-3-5 structure.

Extension

In an impulse wave, often one of the motive waves, usually wave 3 or wave 5, is extended. An *extended wave* is an elongated impulse wave whose motive subwaves at next lower degree are as large as or larger than the non-extended motive wave(s) of the same impulse wave.

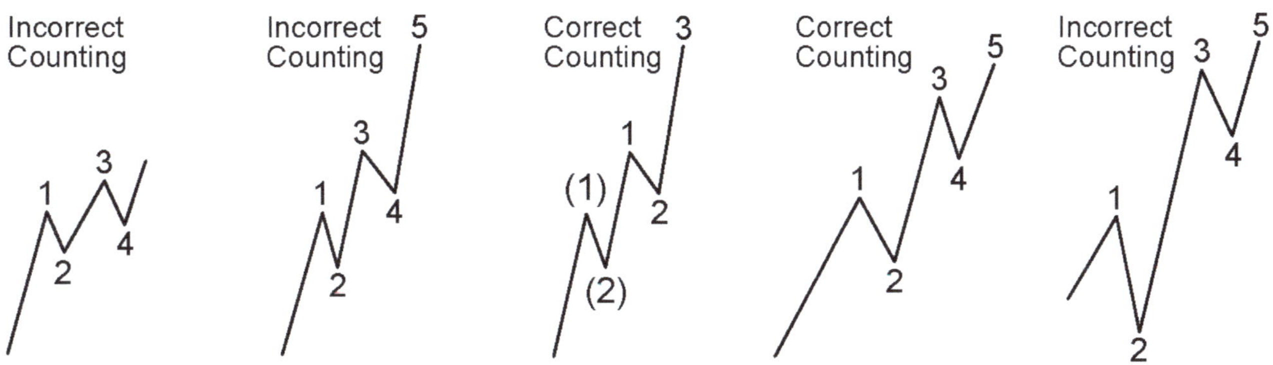

Figure A.4
Source: Adapted from Elliott Wave Principle.

Figure A.5 shows diagrams of extensions for waves 1, 3, and 5. Sometimes the initial subwaves of an impulse wave are all about the same length, and therefore it is difficult to determine which motive wave is extended. This aspect is displayed in the diagram at the bottom, where the extended wave could be 1, 3, or 5. For all practical purposes, it does not matter which one is extended, as long as there is a total of nine waves. Third-wave extensions are often seen in the stock market, while fifth-wave extensions are often seen in commodity markets.

If wave 1 is extended, expect waves 3 and 5 to be about equal in length. If wave 3 is extended, expect wave 5 to be about equal to wave 1. If waves 1 and 3 are about equal, expect wave 5 to be extended. After a fifth-wave extension terminates, expect a swift and sharp reversal back to the second subwave of the extension. Rarely do two motive waves extend, but if that does happen, it is usually waves 3 and 5. We call that structure a *double extension.*

When an extension occurs within an extended wave, it is common for the extension at lower degree to be in the same wave position as the

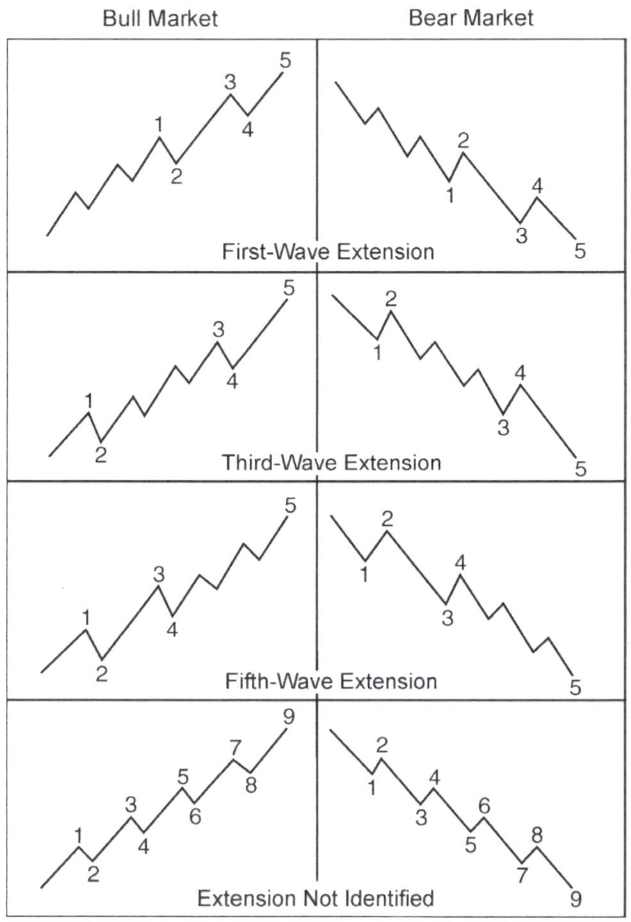

Figure A.5
Source: Elliott Wave Principle.

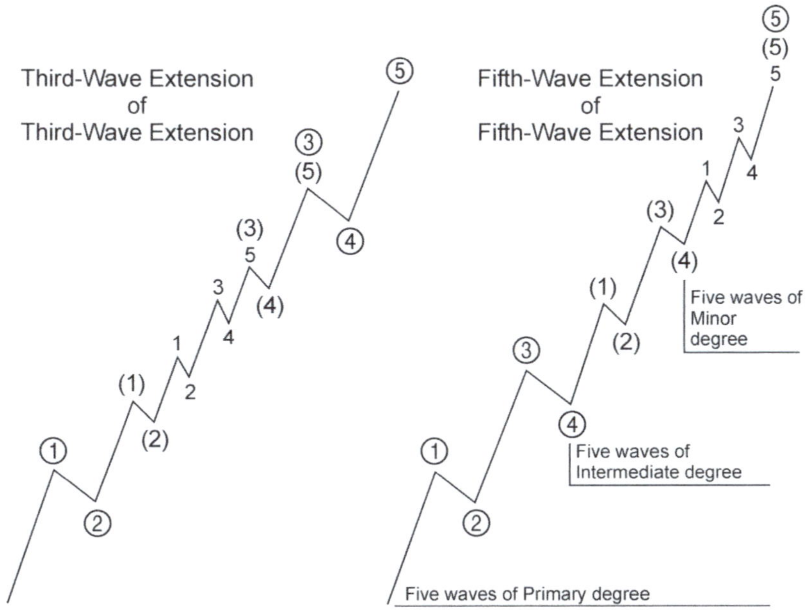

Figure A.6
Source: Elliott Wave Principle.

extension of which it is a part. For example, in a wave 3 extension, subwave 3 is often extended (see Figure A.6).

Truncation

In an impulse wave, a *truncation* occurs when wave 5 fails to terminate beyond the end of wave 3. A truncated fifth wave still unfolds as a five-wave structure (see Figure A.7). A truncated fifth wave, which is a sign of exhaustion in the main trend at next higher degree, is often preceded by

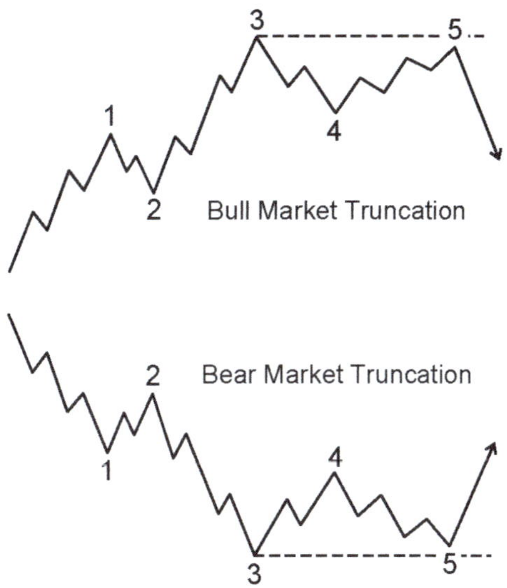

Figure A.7
Source: Elliott Wave Principle.

an exceptionally strong third wave of the same degree. A truncated fifth wave is often followed by a swift and sharp reversal.

Diagonal

Although diagonal and impulse waves are both motive waves, diagonals differ significantly from impulse waves in that they follow the first two rules but not the third rule about wave 4 never entering in the price territory of wave 1. In a diagonal, in fact, wave 4 almost always enters in the price territory of wave 1.

A diagonal is typically contracting but, in rare occasions, expanding. In the contracting variety, wave 3 is shorter than wave 1, wave 5 is shorter than wave 3, and wave 4 is shorter than wave 2. In the expanding variety, wave 3 is longer than wave 1, wave 5 is longer than wave 3, and wave 4 is longer than wave 2. Since expanding diagonals are so infrequent, we will confine the rest of our discussion to the contracting variety.

The two types of diagonals are leading diagonal and ending diagonal, with the ending diagonal being more common. Within an ending diagonal, subwaves 1, 2, 3, 4, and 5 always take corrective-wave form, specifically either a single or multiple zigzag. Ending diagonals can form only as fifth waves of impulse waves and C waves of zigzags and flats. (We will cover zigzags and flats in the section on corrective waves.)

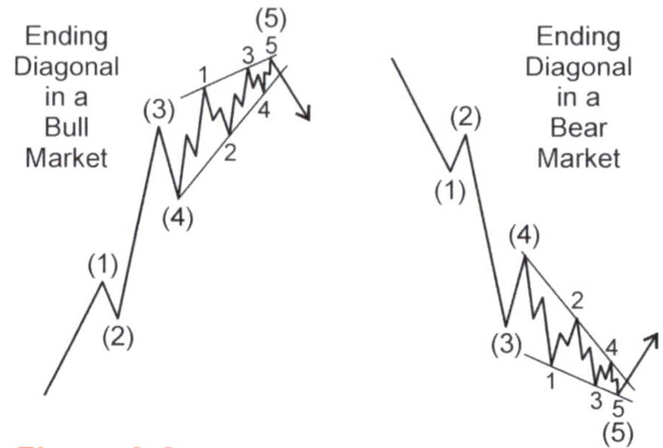

Figure A.8

Source: Adapted from Elliott Wave Principle.

In Figure A.8, wave (5) is a contracting ending diagonal. It is bounded by two converging trendlines, which gives the diagonal a wedge shape. One trendline connects the termination points of waves 1 and 3, and the other trendline connects the termination points of waves 2 and 4. Wave 5 can end either on or slightly above or below the 1-3 trendline. If wave 5 moves beyond that trendline, it is called a throw-over. A swift and sharp reversal usually brings prices at least back to where the diagonal began and usually far further. The reversal usually takes anywhere from one-third to one-half the time that it took the diagonal to form.

In a leading diagonal, waves 1, 3, and 5 are all impulse waves or all corrective waves in the form of zigzags. Waves 2 and 4 are always zigzag patterns. A leading diagonal can form wave 1 of an impulse wave and the first wave of a zigzag, which we call wave A. This formation is exceptionally rare.

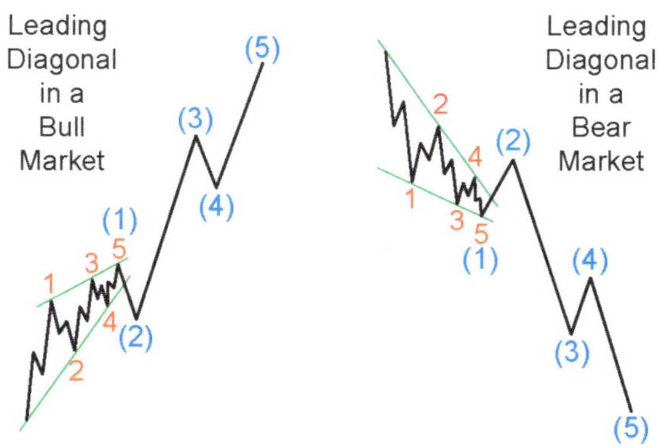

Figure A.9
Source: Adapted from Elliott Wave Principle.

In Figure A.9, wave (1) is a contracting leading diagonal and has the same structural characteristics as the contracting ending diagonal. After a wave 1 leading diagonal terminates, expect wave 2 to retrace a significant portion of wave 1.

Corrective Waves

In markets, we have all heard the old adage, "nothing moves in a straight line." The Elliott wave model incorporates this observation. Market trends invariably encounter interruptions. In Elliott wave terms, we refer to these interruptions as corrective waves.

Corrective waves are either *sharp* or *sideways*. A sharp corrective wave usually has a relatively steep angle, never registering a new price extreme beyond the previous wave that it is retracing. A sideways correction's boundaries are closer to horizontal and, before terminating, it usually records a new price extreme beyond the previous wave that it is retracing. All corrective waves achieve some partial retracement of the preceding wave of the same degree. Because corrective waves come in many variations, it is a challenge to identify them in real time and to know when they are complete.

The three basic types of corrective wave patterns are *zigzag*, *flat*, and *triangle*. Elliotticians often use the word "three" as a noun, meaning a corrective pattern. When two or more of these patterns link together to form a sideways correction, they are called a *combination*.

Zigzag

A zigzag is a sharp, three-wave corrective pattern, labeled A-B-C. Wave A is always an impulse or leading diagonal, and wave C is always

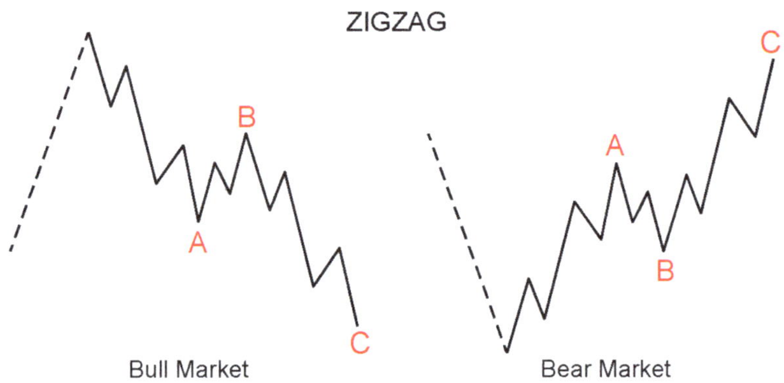

Figure A.10
Source: Adapted from Elliott Wave Principle.

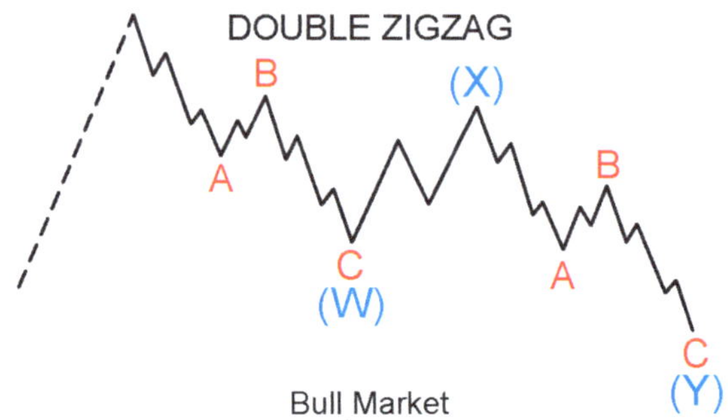

Figure A.11
Source: Adapted from Elliott Wave Principle.

an impulse or ending diagonal. Wave B is always a corrective wave, that is zigzag, flat, triangle or combination. Therefore, we call the zigzag a 5-3-5 structure (see Figure A.10).

In a zigzag, wave B can never go beyond the start of wave A, and wave C almost always goes beyond the end of wave A. If wave C does not go beyond the end of wave A, it is called a truncated wave C.

Zigzag corrections can take the form of one, two, or three zigzags. Three zigzags appear to be the limit. Whenever there is more than one zigzag, another corrective wave forms in order to link one zigzag to the other. In a double zigzag, the first zigzag is labeled W, the second zigzag is labeled Y, and the corrective wave that links the two zigzags together is labeled X. In a triple zigzag, the third zigzag is labeled Z. Wave X can form any corrective structure but is usually a zigzag. It always moves in the opposite direction of wave W (see Figure A.11).

Flat

A flat is a sideways, three-wave corrective pattern, also labeled A-B-C. Waves A and B are always corrective waves, and wave C is always a motive wave. Therefore, we call the flat a 3-3-5 structure. In flats, waves A and B are never triangles and rarely flats. Wave B usually retraces at least 90 percent of wave A. There are three types of flats: regular, expanded, and running. The most common type of flat is the expanded flat. Running flats are rare.

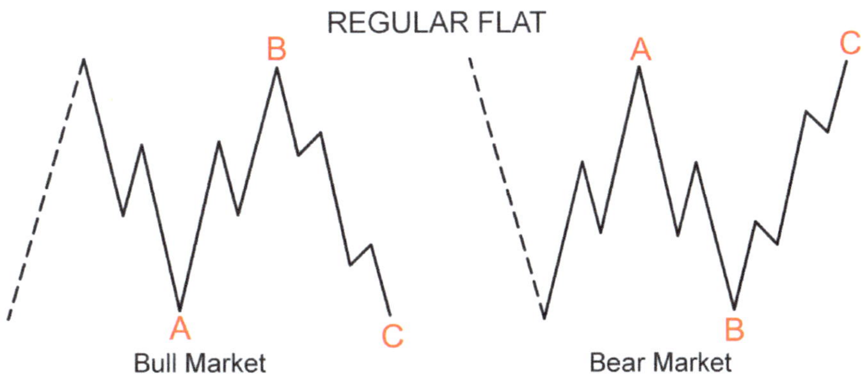

Figure A.12
Source: Adapted from Elliott Wave Principle.

In a regular flat, wave B ends at about the same level as the beginning of wave A, and wave C ends slightly past the end of wave A (see Figure A.12).

In an expanded flat, wave B ends beyond the start of wave A, and wave C ends substantially beyond the end of wave A (see Figure A.13).

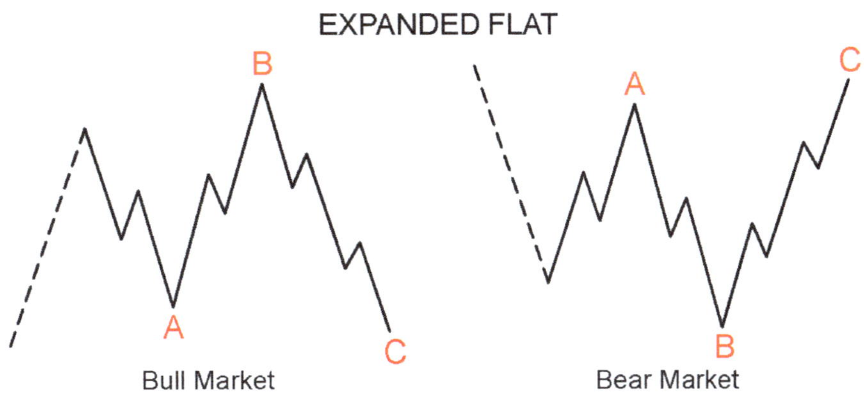

Figure A.13
Source: Adapted from Elliott Wave Principle.

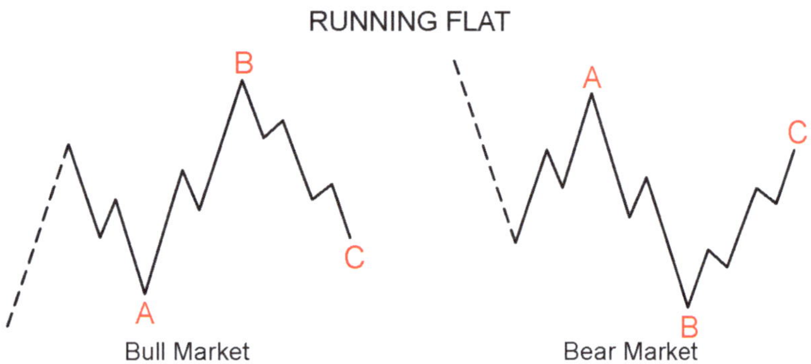

Figure A.14
Source: Adapted from Elliott Wave Principle.

In a running flat, wave B ends beyond the start of wave A, and wave C fails to reach the end of wave A (see Figure A.14).

Triangle

A triangle is a sideways corrective wave with sub-waves labeled A-B-C-D-E. In most cases, all the sub-waves of a triangle are zigzags or multiple zigzag patterns. Therefore, we call the triangle a 3-3-3-3-3 structure. On occasion, one of these subwaves takes the form of another triangle, and that subwave is usually wave E. Only one of these subwaves can be complex, meaning strung out over time, and that subwave is normally wave C, D, or E. Figure A.15 shows the three types of triangles: contracting, barrier, and expanding.

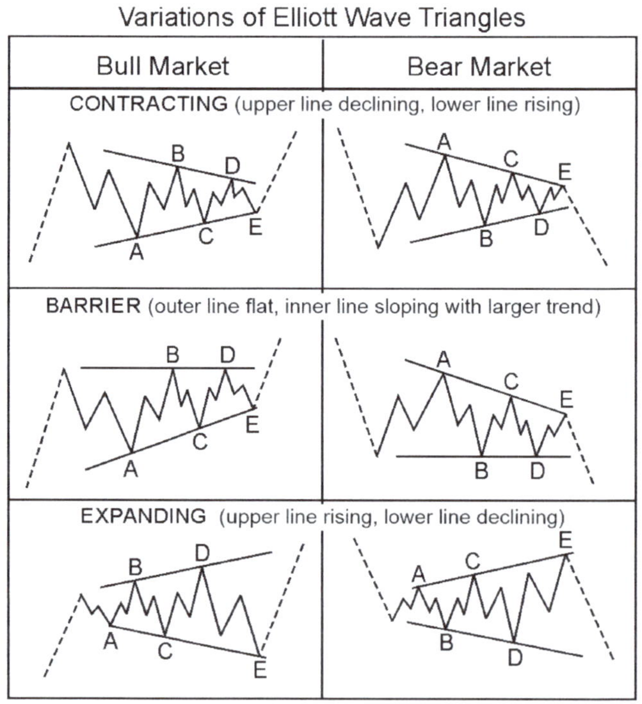

Figure A.15
Source: Elliott Wave Principle.

In a triangle, the line that connects the termination points of waves A and C is called the A-C trendline, and the line that connects the termination points of waves B and D is called the B-D trendline. Wave E may terminate at, short of, or beyond the A-C trendline.

In contracting and barrier triangles, the A-C and B-D trendlines converge. In barrier triangles, the B-D trendline is horizontal, and the A-C trendline points in the direction of the main trend at next higher degree. In expanding triangles, the A-C and B-D trendlines diverge. In a contracting triangle, wave C never moves beyond the end of wave A, wave D never moves beyond the end of wave B, and wave E never moves beyond the end of wave C. Wave B may or may not move beyond the start of wave A. As shown in Figure A.16, if wave B moves beyond the start of wave A, the triangle is called a running contracting triangle. Running triangles are common.

A barrier triangle has the same characteristics as a contracting triangle, with the following exception:

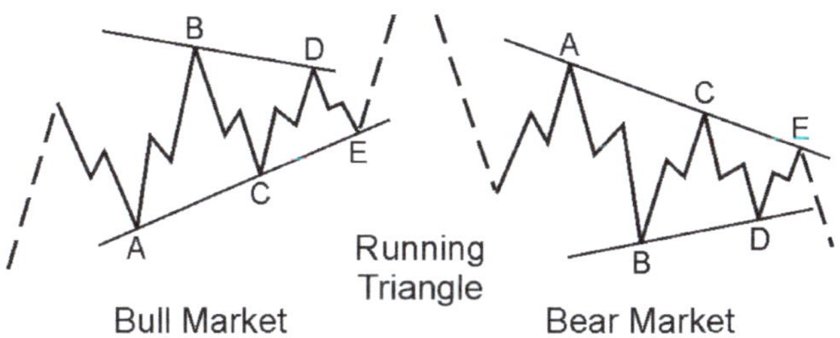

Figure A.16
Source: Elliott Wave Principle.

POST-TRIANGLE THRUST MEASUREMENT

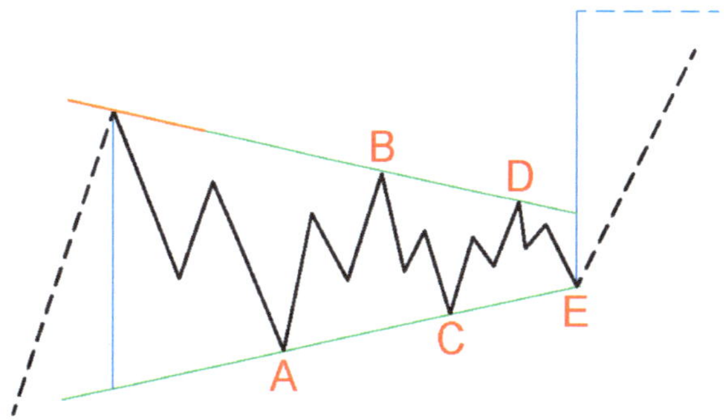

Figure A.17
Source: Elliott Wave Principle.

In a barrier triangle, wave D ends at about the same level as wave B. In an expanding triangle, after completion of wave A, each new subwave moves beyond the starting point of the previous subwave.

A triangle always precedes the final motive wave in the direction of the main trend at next higher degree. That final motive wave normally makes a swift and sharp move, which is called the *post-triangle thrust* (see Figure A.17).

For a contracting or barrier triangle, we can estimate the minimum termination point of the thrust by extending the A-C and B-D trendlines back to the start of wave A and then drawing a vertical line that connects those two trendlines. That vertical distance defines the "width" of the triangle. We then apply the width of the triangle to the end of wave E to give us an estimate for the next move in the direction of the main trend at next higher degree.

Within an impulse wave, a post-triangle thrust measurement estimates the minimum length for wave 5. If wave 5 goes beyond the estimated termination point, expect a prolonged fifth wave.

Combination

A combination is a sideways corrective pattern that includes two or more corrective structures. Three corrective structures appear to be the limit. Each corrective structure is linked by an X wave, which has three characteristics: It can be any corrective pattern; it always moves in the opposite direction of the previous corrective pattern; and it is usually a zigzag. There never appears to be more than one triangle in a combination, and, when one appears, it always seems to be the final corrective structure in the combination. The two types of combinations are double three and triple three.

A double three combination includes two corrective patterns—the first labeled W and the second labeled Y—that are linked by an X wave. Figure A.18 represents one of many variations of a double three correction. A triple three combination includes three corrective patterns, labeled W, Y, and Z, each linked by X waves. Triple threes are rare. Within double and triple threes, X waves are usually zigzags and never triangles.

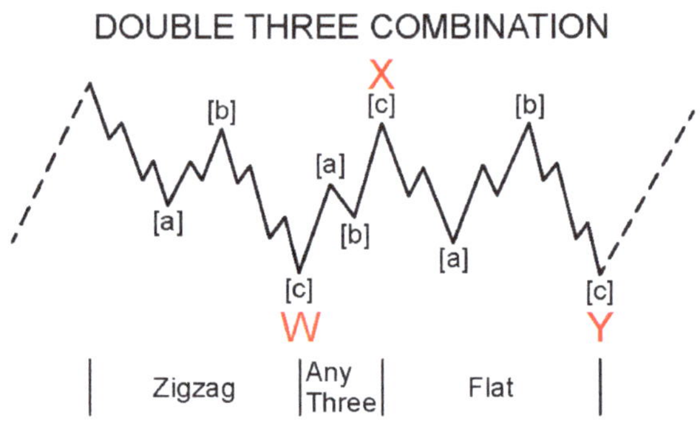

Figure A.18
Source: Elliott Wave Principle.

Fibonacci Relationships

Price and time aspects of wave patterns often reflect *Fibonacci ratios*. In wave formations, the key Fibonacci ratio is .618, which is known as the Golden Ratio or Golden Mean. It is represented by the Greek letter *phi* (ϕ), pronounced "fie." Its inverse is 1.618. *Phi* is the only number which, when added to one, is also equal to its inverse. If we square *phi* or subtract *phi* from 1, the result is .382, which is another Fibonacci ratio.

Figure A.19 displays a number of Fibonacci ratios.

Each ratio can be expressed as *phi*—either .618 or its inverse 1.618—raised to a power. Other important Fibonacci numbers related to

Fibonacci Ratios and Multiples		
Ratio	Inverse	Φ^N
.618	1.618	$(1.618)^1$
.382	2.618	$(1.618)^2$
.236	4.236	$(1.618)^3$
.146	6.854	$(1.618)^4$
.090	11.089	$(1.618)^5$

Figure A.19

wave formation are 0.5 (1/2), .786 (square root of .618), 1.0 (1/1), and 2.0 (2/1).

In Elliott wave patterns, the key types of Fibonacci relationships are *retracements*, *multiples*, and *dividers*. Although these relationships are more commonly used to estimate the length of certain waves with respect to price, they can also be used to estimate the length of waves with respect to time.

Retracements

In impulse waves, second waves usually make deep retracements near .618 times the length of wave one. Fourth waves usually make shallow retracements that are often close to .382 times the length of wave three (see Figure A.20).

In a zigzag, the retracement of wave A by wave B will depend on the structure of wave B. For example, in Figure A.21, if wave B is a zigzag, it should retrace 0.5 to .786 of wave A. If wave B is a triangle, it should retrace .382 to 0.50 of wave A.

FIBONACCI RETRACEMENTS

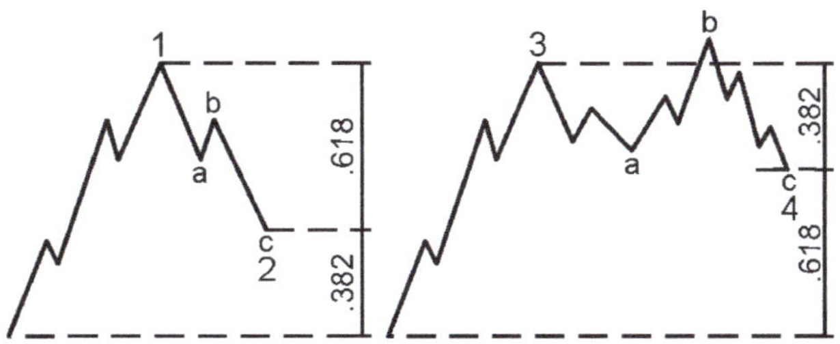

Figure A.20
Source: Elliott Wave Principle.

Guidelines for Typical Retracements of Wave A by Wave B in Zigzags

Wave B	Net Retracement (%)
Zigzag	50–79
Triangle	38–50
Running Triangle	10–40
Flat	38–79
Combination	38–50

Figure A.21

Multiples

In an impulse wave, wave 5 will often equal .618 or .382 times the net distance traveled of waves 1 through 3 (see Figure A.22).

When wave 3 is extended, expect wave 5 to be related to wave 1 by equality or .618. When wave 5 is extended, expect wave 5, in price terms, to travel 1.618 times the net distance traveled of waves 1 through 3. If that length is exceeded,

FIBONACCI MULTIPLES IN IMPULSE WAVES

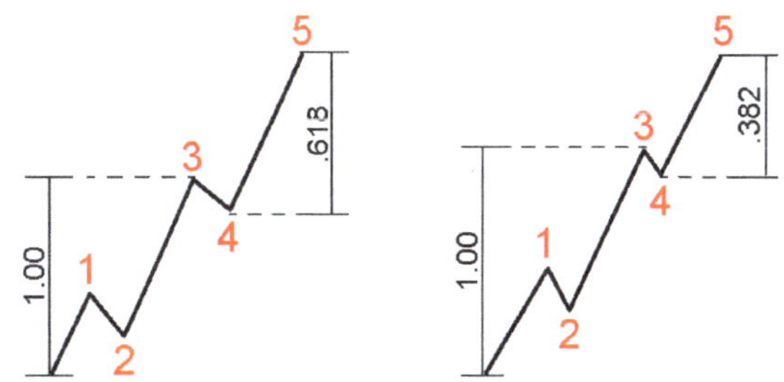

Figure A.22
Source: Elliott Wave Principle.

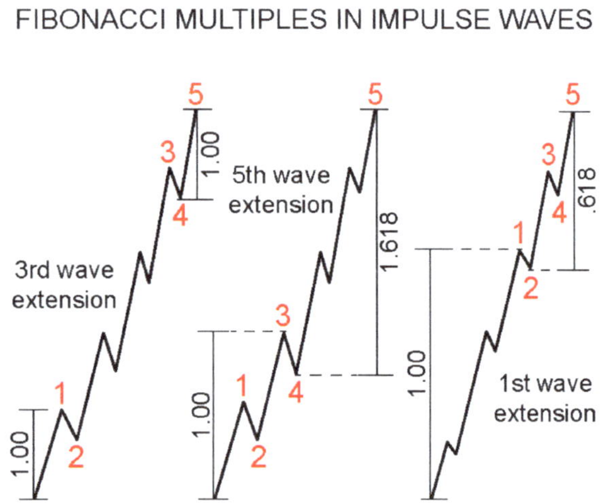

Figure A.23

Source: Adapted from Elliott Wave Principle.

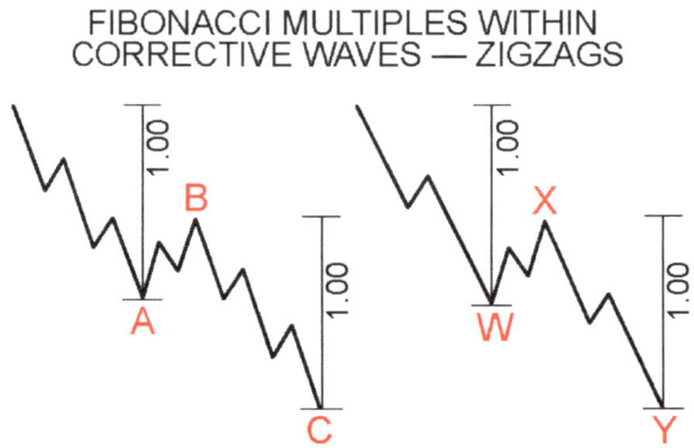

Figure A.24

Source: Adapted from Elliott Wave Principle.

look for larger multiples as shown in Figure A.22. When wave 1 is extended, expect the net distance traveled of waves 3 through 5 to equal .618 times the length of wave 1 (see Figure A.23).

The most common Fibonacci relationship in single zigzags and multiple zigzag structures is *equality*—for example, C = A in the single zigzag, and Y = W in the double zigzag (see Figure A.24).

When equality is not present, look for the other Fibonacci relationships, as shown in Figure A.25.

The relationships for multiple zigzags are analogous to those for a single zigzag.

Fibonacci Relationships
Single Zigzag
Wave C = Wave A
Wave C = .618 Wave A
Wave C = 1.618 Wave A
Wave C = .618 Wave A past Wave A
Double Zigzag
Wave Y = Wave W
Wave Y = .618 Wave W
Wave Y = 1.618 Wave W
Wave Y = .618 Wave W past Wave W
Triple Zigzag
Equality for W, Y, and Z
Ratio of .618, i.e., Wave Z = .618 Wave Y

Figure A.25

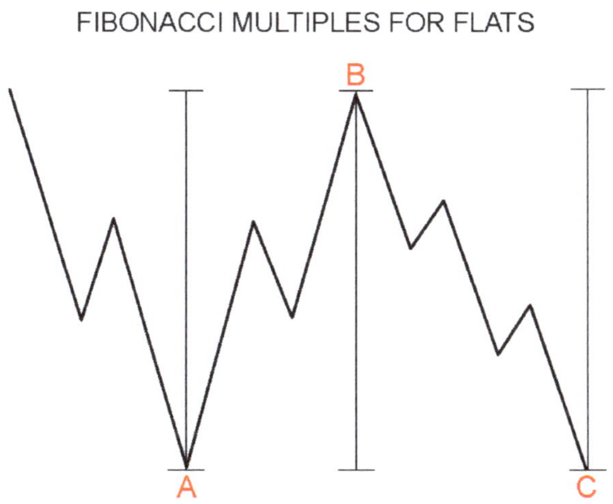

Figure A.26
Source: Adapted from Elliott Wave Principle.

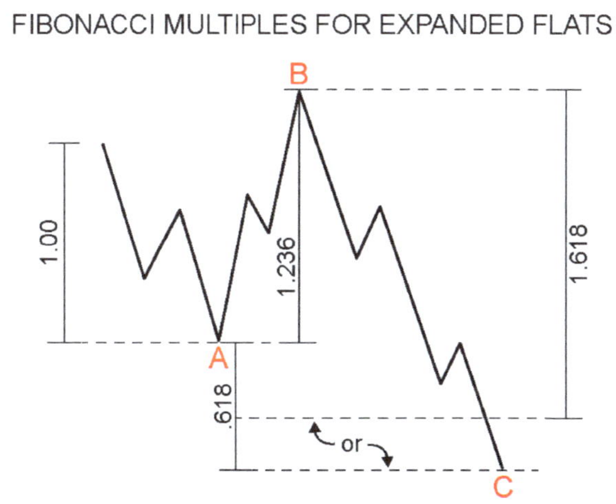

Figure A.27
Source: Adapted from Elliott Wave Principle.

In a regular flat, waves A, B, and C are generally equal to each other (see Figure A.26).

In an expanded flat, expect wave C either to equal 1.618 times the length of wave A or to terminate at a price equal to .618 times the length of wave A past wave A. Expect wave B to equal 1.236 or 1.382 times the length of wave A (see Figure A.27).

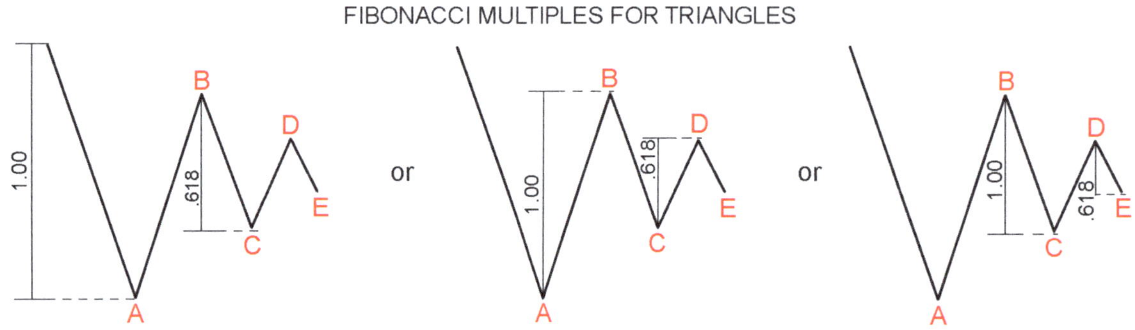

Figure A.28
Source: Adapted from Elliott Wave Principle.

The alternate waves of a contracting triangle are often related to each other by the Fibonacci ratio of .618 (see Figure A.28).

For expanding triangles, that ratio is 1.618.

Dividers

If we divide any length in such a way that the ratio of the smaller part to the larger part is equal to the ratio of the larger part to the whole, that ratio will always be .618 (see Figure A.29).

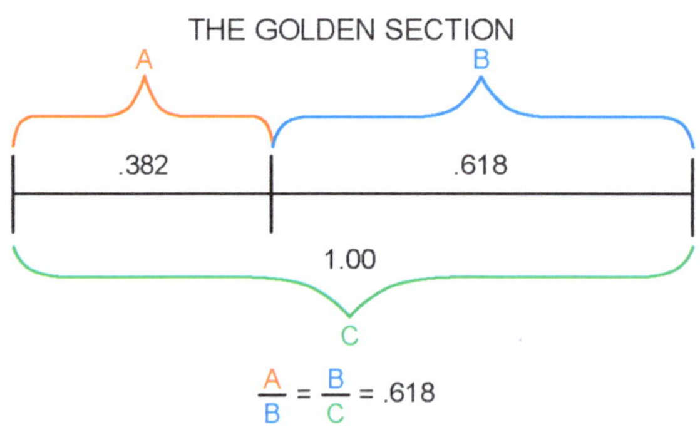

Figure A.29
Source: Adapted from Elliott Wave Principle.

This is called the *Golden Section*, which results in a .382/.618 split. Certain wave termination points will often divide wave patterns into the Golden Section or sometimes a .50/.50 split.

In an impulse wave, wave 4 (usually its origin or termination point) will often divide the entire wave into the Golden Section or into two equal parts (see Figure A.30).

Clusters

Whenever possible, we prefer not to rely on just one Fibonacci relationship in forecasting market movements. The most powerful application of Fibonacci analysis is the identification of *Fibonacci clusters*. A Fibonacci price cluster occurs when two or more Fibonacci price relationships project to approximately the same price level. (A Fibonacci time cluster occurs when two or more Fibonacci time relationships project to approximately the same time.) Since wave patterns unfold at all time frames simultaneously, there is often an opportunity to spot a Fibonacci cluster. The diagram in Figure A.31 illustrates a Fibonacci price cluster.

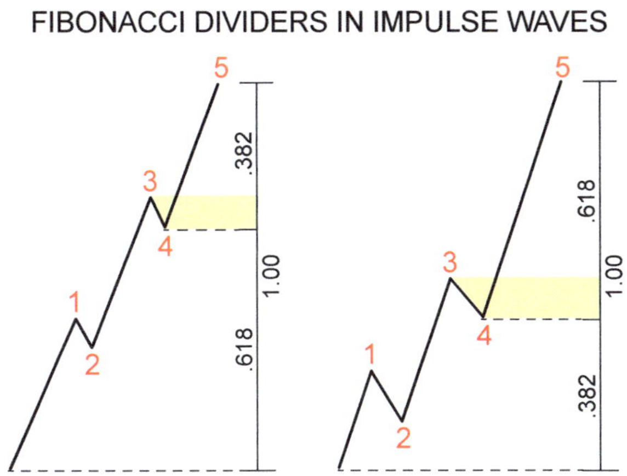

Figure A.30
Source: Adapted from Elliott Wave Principle.

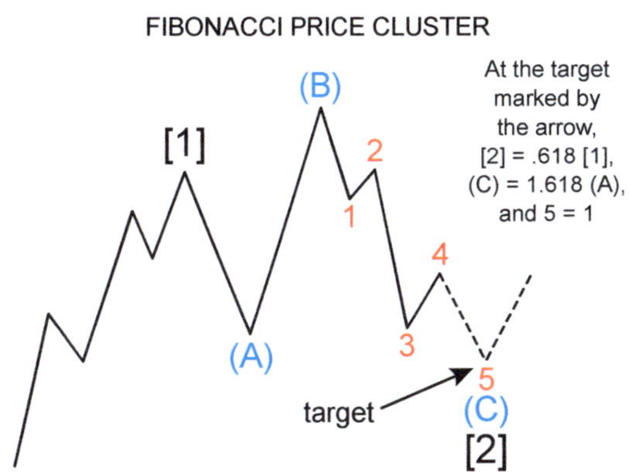

Figure A.31
Source: Adapted from Elliott Wave Principle.

Figure A-31 identifies, at the same general price level, the following three Fibonacci relationships:

1. Primary wave [2] retraces .618 of Primary wave [1].
2. In the expanded flat, Intermediate wave (C) equals 1.618 times the length of Intermediate wave (A).
3. Within the Intermediate wave (C) impulse wave, Minor wave 5 equals Minor wave 1.

For More Information

Learn more at your exclusive Reader Resources site. You will find a free online edition of *Elliott Wave Principle* by Frost and Prechter, plus lessons on Elliott wave analysis, how to trade specific patterns, and how to use Fibonacci and other technical indicators to increase your confidence as you apply the Wave Principle in real time. Go to: www.elliottwave.com/wave/ReaderResources.

Glossary of Elliott Wave Terms

alternation (guideline) In an impulse wave, if wave two is a sharp correction, wave four will usually be a sideways correction, and vice versa.

apex Intersection of the two boundary lines of a contracting triangle or contracting diagonal.

barrier triangle A triangle pattern where the B-D trendline is horizontal and the A-C trendline points in the direction of the main trend at next higher degree.

channeling (guideline) Impulse waves, zigzags, and multiple zigzag patterns will often travel within a trend channel, whose boundaries are defined by parallel upper and lower price trendlines.

combination A sideways pattern composed of two or three corrective patterns linked by intervening X waves.

contracting triangle A triangle pattern whose A-C and B-D trendlines converge.

corrective wave A three-wave pattern or combination of three-wave patterns.

depth of corrective waves (guideline) Within impulse waves, often the corrective waves—especially fourth waves—end in the price territory of the previous fourth wave of one lesser degree and usually at that fourth wave's termination point.

diagonal A motive wave that almost never travels within a parallel trend channel, and whose wave four almost always ends in the price territory of wave one. The four kinds of diagonal waves arc:

> **ending contracting:** A diagonal whose boundary lines form a wedge-shaped pattern. It can occur only as the fifth wave of an

impulse wave and as wave C of flats and zigzags. Subdivides into 3-3-3-3-3, where each wave is a zigzag or multiple zigzag pattern.

leading contracting: A diagonal whose boundary lines form a wedge-shaped pattern. It can occur only as the first wave of an impulse wave and as wave A of zigzag. Subdivides into 3-3-3-3-3, where each wave is a zigzag or multiple zigzag pattern, or 5-3-5-3-5.

ending expanding: An ending diagonal whose boundary lines diverge (quite rare).

leading expanding: A leading diagonal whose boundary lines diverge (quite rare).

double three Combination that comprises two corrective wave patterns, labeled W and Y, linked by a corrective wave pattern labeled X.

double zigzag Sharp wave pattern that comprises two zigzags, labeled W and Y, linked by a corrective wave pattern labeled X.

equality (guideline) In an impulse wave, two of the actionary waves will tend to be equal in terms of time and magnitude.

expanded flat **A version of a flat wave pattern where** wave B goes beyond the start of wave A, and wave C goes beyond the end of wave A.

expanding triangle A triangle wave pattern whose A-C and B-D trendlines diverge.

extension Elongated impulse wave whose subwaves, especially the actionary waves, are usually as long or longer than the waves at next higher degree.

failure (see truncation)

flat Sideways corrective wave pattern, labeled A-B-C, that subdivides 3-3-5.

Fibonacci relationships These describe how the length of waves with respect to price and time are mathematically related to each other by the Fibonacci ratio of .618, as well as other Fibonacci numbers.

Golden Section The beginning or end of wave 4 will often divide an impulse wave into the Golden Section (.618 and .382) or two equal parts. This relationship is called a Fibonacci price divider.

guidelines Characteristics of wave formation that usually—but don't always—occur.

impulse wave A motive wave pattern that subdivides 5-3-5-3-5. It usually travels within a parallel trend channel, and its wave four never ends in the price territory of wave one.

irregular flat (see expanded flat)

motive wave A five-wave pattern that makes progress in the direction of the main trend, where wave two always retraces less than 100 percent of wave one, and wave three can never be the shortest wave. The two kinds of motive wave are impulse and diagonal.

orthodox top (or bottom) Price level that represents the end of the wave pattern.

post-triangle thrust measurement After a triangle ends, the next wave, which is usually sharp and fast, is called a thrust. The post-triangle thrust measurement, which is calculated by applying the width of the triangle to the end of wave E, estimates the expected minimum distance traveled of that thrust.

regular flat A flat wave pattern where wave B terminates at about the start of wave A, and wave C ends just slightly past the end of wave A.

right look When wave patterns conform to certain shapes, proportions, and trendlines, they are said to have the "right look."

rules Characteristics of wave formation that always occur.

running flat A flat wave pattern where wave B terminates well beyond the start of wave A, and wave C ends prior to the end of wave A.

running triangle A contracting triangle where wave B terminates beyond the start of wave A.

sharp corrective wave A corrective wave pattern that usually forms a relatively steep angle and never registers a new price extreme beyond the previous wave that it is retracing.

sideways corrective wave A corrective wave pattern that is usually relatively horizontal in shape, and, before terminating, usually records a new price extreme beyond the previous wave that it is retracing.

third-of-a-third impulse wave Normally the most powerful segment of an impulse wave, because it is the third wave of five waves that make up the third wave of the impulse.

three Often used as a synonym for a corrective wave, because almost all corrective waves consist of three waves.

throw-over When wave five of an impulse wave terminates beyond the corresponding trendline of a parallel trend channel, or when wave five of a contracting diagonal terminates beyond the wave one-three trendline.

triangle A sideways corrective pattern, labeled A-B-C-D-E, that subdivides 3-3-3-3-3, where the initial subwaves are all zigzags or multiple zigzag patterns.

triple three Combination pattern that comprises three corrective wave patterns, labeled W, Y, and Z, linked by corrective wave patterns labeled X (quite rare).

triple zigzag Sharp wave pattern that comprises three zigzags, labeled W, Y, and Z, linked by corrective wave patterns labeled X.

truncation When wave five of a motive wave fails to exceed the end of wave three, or when wave C of a zigzag fails to go beyond the end of wave A.

width of a contracting or barrier triangle Equals the length of a vertical line that connects the A-C and B-D trendlines at the origin of wave A of the triangle.

width of an expanding triangle Equals the length of a vertical line that connects the A-C and B-D trendlines at the end of wave E of the triangle.

zigzag Sharp corrective wave pattern, labeled A-B-C, that subdivides 5-3-5.

Educational Resources

Books

Elliott Wave Principle: Key to Market Behavior, by Robert R. Prechter & A. J. Frost

Prechter's Perspective, by Robert R. Prechter

Beautiful Pictures from the Gallery of Phinance, by Robert R. Prechter

For more information, please visit: www.elliottwave.com/books.

eBooks

How to Use the Elliott Wave Principle to Improve Your Options Trading Strategies—Vol. 1: Vertical Spreads, by Wayne Gorman

How to Use the Elliott Wave Principle to Improve Your *Options Trading Strategies—Vol. 2: Range Bound Strategies*, by Wayne Gorman

How You Can Identify Turning Points Using Fibonacci, by Wayne Gorman

Trading the Line—How to Use Trendlines to Spot Reversals and Ride Trends, by Jeffrey Kennedy

Introduction to Spotting Elliott Wave Trading Opportunities, by Jeffrey Kennedy

How to Use the Wave Principle to Boost Your Forex Trading, by Jim Martens

For more information, please visit: www.elliottwave.com/On-Demand-Courses.

Online Courses

The Basics of the Wave Principle—Wayne Gorman

The Wave Principle Applied—How to Spot a Pattern You Recognize and Put Your Trading Plan into Action—Jeffrey Kennedy

3 Technical Indicators to Help You Ride the Elliott Wave Trend—Chris Carolan

5 Options Strategies Every Elliott Wave Trader Should Know—Wayne Gorman

How to Use the Elliott Wave Principle to Improve Your Options Trading Strategies—Course 1: Vertical Spreads—Wayne Gorman

How to Use the Elliott Wave Principle to Improve Your Options Trading Strategies—Course 2: Range Bound Strategies—Wayne Gorman

How to Use the Elliott Wave Principle to Improve Your Options Trading Strategies—Course 3: Volatility Strategies—Wayne Gorman

How to Use the Wave Principle to Boost Your Forex Trading—Jim Martens

How You Can Identify Turning Points Using Fibonacci—Wayne Gorman

Trading the Line—How to Use Trendlines to Spot Reversals and Ride Trends—Jeffrey Kennedy

How to Trade Choppy, Sideways Markets—Wayne Gorman

How to Trade When the Market Zigzags—Wayne Gorman

How to Trade the Bull/Bear Opportunities in Expanded Flats—Wayne Gorman

How to Catch and Ride Extended Waves—Wayne Gorman

How to Trade Triangles and the Thrust that Follows—Wayne Gorman

How to Trade Diagonal Triangles— Jeffrey Kennedy

Introduction to Spotting Elliott Wave Trading Opportunities—Jeffrey Kennedy

How to Spot Tops and Bottoms with Confidence—Jeffrey Kennedy

How to Actively Manage and Close a Trade Using Simple Elliott Wave Analysis— Jeffrey Kennedy

Which Elliott Wave Scenario Is the Right One—Jeffrey Kennedy

How to Capitalize on Volatile Markets—Jeffrey Kennedy

3 Steps to Spotting High-Confidence Setups in Your Charts—Jeffrey Kennedy

How to Formulate a Solid Trade Plan and Know When to Pull the Trigger—Jeffrey Kennedy

Where to Start Your Elliott Wave Count on a Chart—Jeffrey Kennedy

For more information, please visit: www.elliottwave.com/On-Demand-Courses.

DVDs

Implication of the Wave Principle for Technical Analysis—Robert Prechter

Trading the Elliott Waves—Winning Strategies for Timing Entry & Exit Moves—Robert Prechter

5 Basic Elliott Wave Patterns + Technical Tools = Trading Success—Jeffrey Kennedy

Elliott Wave Trading: Principle and Trading Strategies—Jeffrey Kennedy

For more information, please visit: www.elliottwave.com/videos.

Live Classes or Events

Elliott Wave Educational Series

4 Critical Elements of High-Confidence Trading—Jeffrey Kennedy

Trade Small, Win Often: The Dick Diamond Method of Trading for a Living—Vadim Pokhlebkin

For more information, please visit: www.elliottwave.com/Live-Classes-Events.

About the Authors

Jeffrey Kennedy, MSTA, CFTe, CMT, CEWA-M, is Chief Commodity Analyst at Elliott Wave International (EWI), with 25-plus years of experience as an analyst, trader and teacher. He writes *Commodity Junctures*, EWI's premier commodity forecasting package. He also produces *Trader's Classroom*, an educational service that shows how to spot trading opportunities with wave analysis and supporting technical methods. Jeffrey has taught thousands of students around the world how to trade using the Wave Principle, and he served as an instructor in the Quantitative and Computational Finance Program at Georgia Tech, where he taught technical analysis. In 2014, Jeffrey achieved the title of a Chartered Market Technician, certifying his proficiency in multiple technical analysis tools. He is a Certified Elliott Wave Analyst - Master, having received the highest Elliott wave certification available.

Wayne Gorman, headed Elliott Wave International's (EWI) Educational Resources. He has taught thousands of people how to forecast and trade with Elliott wave analysis through seminars and online courses. With more than thirty years of experience as a risk manager and trader, Gorman began his career at Citibank where he managed trading positions in money markets and derivatives. He traded full time with his own capital for more than four years before joining EWI.

Index

U

W

Z

www.ingramcontent.com/pod-product-compliance
Lightning Source LLC
LaVergne TN
LVHW070818210926
848482LV00004B/285